Great Desserts

Great Desserts
from
Ceil Dyer

McGraw-Hill Book Company
New York • St. Louis • San Francisco
Toronto • Hamburg • Mexico

1 2 3 4 5 6 7 8 9 DOCDOC 8 7 6 5

ISBN 0-07-018545-X {H.C.}

ISBN 0-07-018544-1 {PBK.}

LIBRARY OF CONGRESS CATALOGING IN PUBLICATION DATA

Dyer, Ceil.
  Great desserts from Ceil Dyer.

  1. Desserts. I. Title.
TX773.D84   1986   641.8'6   85-11647

        ISBN 0-07-018545-X
        ISBN 0-07-018544-1 (pbk.)

Book design by Barbara M. Marks

Contents

Introduction

When you want to serve a particularly splendid, forget-the-calories-and-indulge-your-passions dessert, where do you begin? It's easy, really. Just take a leaf from a professional pastry chef's book: start with something very basic: a classic cake batter, a perfect pastry, a silky smooth custard, fresh fruit, a dense, rich ice cream. Add a touch of inspiration, and a bit of wit, and there you have it! A totally new recipe, an original masterpiece—and a glorious way to end any meal luxuriously.

This, then, is not a dictionary of sweets from A to Z but a handful of basic recipes plus the numerous ways I have used them over the years to create literally hundreds of delicious desserts for formal and informal parties, picnics, and festive gatherings of all kinds, both large and small.

Unlike free-wheeling stews, sautéed dishes, and stir-fry recipes that can be added to, changed, and seasoned to taste as they cook, great desserts must start with a precisely measured base put together with care. Still, these recipes are not difficult—and once you have made any one of them, you can construct an incredible variety of inspired creations that are totally your own. In dessert cookery, you are limited only by available ingredients and the range of your imagination.

All the recipes in this book—both the basics and the variations—have been precisely tested, and then tasted by many very willing but nonetheless critical friends, so I can assure you the results will always be delicious. I hope, however, that once you have prepared any one of them as written, you will then want to prepare it again—but this time in a slightly different way and to suit your own taste. This, you see, was my paramount thought as I put each chapter together: not only to give you a great collection of recipes but also to start you on your way to a new and adventurous approach to dessert cookery.

A Glossary of Techniques for the Dessert Cook

To Stir: Mix with a wooden spoon or a spatula, scraping from the bottom and around the sides of the bowl or pan until the ingredients are blended.

To Beat: Whip with a whisk, electric mixer, beater, or spoon, to create a smooth, even, lumpless mixture—or to incorporate air. Sufficient air is beaten into egg whites or heavy cream to lift them to snowy white peaks. Egg yolks *may* be beaten. Batters for cakes, puddings, custards, mousses, and such usually are.

To Fold: Incorporate ingredients while minimizing the release of air. For example, you fold beaten egg whites or heavy cream into a cake batter or vice versa. You also often fold in dry ingredients. Add beaten or dry ingredients about a third at a time; then, using a rubber spatula or similar tool, reach to the bottom of the mixing bowl and bring the bottom batter up and over the ingredients to be incorporated. Repeat this procedure, scraping the sides of the bowl and turning it, only until all of the ingredients are evenly mixed. Be quick and efficient, but use a light hand.

To Sift: You sift to lighten, eliminate lumps, and "aerate" flour, confectioners' sugar, and such. A sifter can also be used to distribute a number of different dry ingredients evenly. Use a hand or electric sifter, or place the ingredients in the work bowl of a food processor and process briefly, turning the motor on and off.

To Separate Eggs: Don't take chances. Before separating two or more eggs, have ready a small bowl, a medium bowl or container for the yolks, and a larger bowl for the whites. Taking one egg at a time, sharply tap the shell against a blunt edge to break it approximately in half across the width. Working over the small bowl, transfer the yolk from one half of the shell to the other while allowing the whites to fall into the bowl. Place the yolk in the bowl or container. Transfer the white to the larger bowl. Repeat with the remaining egg or eggs. You can allow a little of the white to stick to the yolk, but even a smidgen of yolk in the whites will keep them from being beaten successfully.

To Beat Egg Whites: The only trick to beating egg whites successfully is to start with a clean, dry, fat-free bowl and beater. It takes less time to beat them when they are at room temperature, but they can attain full volume even if cold. Beat egg whites without sugar until they are stiff but not dry, or until they will mound softly but will not form stiff peaks. Beat whites with sugar until they are very shiny and stiff peaks will form when the beater is lifted from the bowl. If both the egg whites and yolks are to be beaten separately, beat the whites first, then slide them onto a piece of waxed paper. You can then beat the yolks in the same bowl and with the same beaters, without washing.

To Beat Egg Yolks: Beat yolks, with or without sugar, until they are very pale yellow in color, so thick that the beater will leave marks when lifted from the bowl, and at least tripled in volume.

To Whip Cream: Place the whipping bowl, beaters, and cream in the freezer for 10 to 15 minutes before you begin. Whip chilled cream only until soft peaks form; do not overwhip, or the cream will lose its delicate texture. To sweeten and flavor whipped cream, fold in confectioners' sugar to taste and, if you like, a teaspoon of liqueur.

To Chop Nuts: Use a chef's knife or cleaver. A blender or food processor will grind nuts too finely.

To Grind Nuts: Use a hand-operated grinder, an electric blender, or a food processor. If the nuts have been stored in the freezer or refrigerator where they may have absorbed moisture, first spread them out on a baking sheet and place them in a 350°F. oven until very warm to the touch. If you are using a food processor or electric blender, you can keep the nuts from turning into nut butter by first lightly coating them with sugar or flour (and subtracting the amount of sugar or flour used from the amount specified in the recipe).

To Cook Until "the Mixture Coats the Spoon": When a custard or cream is cooked to exactly the right point, it will completely cover a spoon with a film that does not run off when the spoon is lifted from the pan.

To Measure Flour: Place a metal measuring cup on paper, then lightly spoon in flour until it overflows. Do not shake the cup or pack the flour down. Scrape overflow off of the top so the flour is level with the cup.

To Measure Cocoa and Cornstarch: Sift these ingredients immediately before they are to be measured. If they are not sifted, or are sifted long before they are used, they will pack down from their own weight, giving you more than is called for in the recipe. Sift onto paper, sifting a bit more than you will need, then follow the method for measuring flour, above.

To Measure Sugar: Follow the method for measuring flour, above. If granulated or brown sugar is lumpy, first either smooth out the lumps with the back of a wooden spoon or press the sugar through a fine sieve. (Hard lumps in brown sugar won't disappear in mixing or baking.)

To Measure Liquid Ingredients: Use a glass or plastic measuring cup with the measurements marked on the side. With the cup at eye level, fill carefully to exactly the line indicated.

To Measure Small Quantities: Use standard measuring spoons that come in sets of 4: 1/4 teaspoon, 1/2 teaspoon, 1 teaspoon, and 1 tablespoon. When measuring dry ingredients, fill the spoon until it overflows, then scrape off the excess with the flat edge of a knife.

To Add Dry Ingredients Alternately with Liquid: Begin and end with dry ingredients. Start by adding about a third of the dry; then add half of the liquid, a second third of the dry, the rest of the liquid, and the rest of the dry.

Equivalents

1 pound = 16 ounces
3/4 pound = 12 ounces

1/2 pound = 8 ounces
1/4 pound = 4 ounces

1 1/2 teaspoons
   = 1/2 tablespoon
3 teaspoons = 1 tablespoon
4 tablespoons = 1/4 cup
5 tablespoons
   + 1 teaspoon = 1/3 cup

8 tablespoons = 1/2 cup
10 tablespoons
   + 2 teaspoons = 2/3 cup
12 tablespoons = 3/4 cup
16 tablespoons = 1 cup

1 cup = 8 ounces = 1/2 pint
1 pint = 16 ounces

2 pints = 1 quart = 32 ounces
4 quarts = 1 gallon

Note: Throughout, an asterisk (*) will indicate a recipe that appears elsewhere in this book. Please see the Index for page numbers.

A Repertoire
of
Romantic Cakes

From delicate and simple to simply exquisite.
Cakes that live up to the occasion.

The idea that an elegant and festive cake must take hours to prepare and requires special equipment and professional knowledge can be laid to rest right here and now. It just isn't true. The cakes in this chapter are so little trouble to make, yet so much more delicious than even the best bakery product, there is no reason to settle for less—or to do more.

Any of the following basic cakes can be whipped up in 15 to 20 minutes. After that, you are free to relax (or clean up the kitchen) while the cake bakes. Once out of the oven, your cake can be wrapped and stored in the refrigerator or freezer until you're ready to use it. Then, with just a little extra effort and attention, you can transform what you've baked into a fabulous creation for any festive gathering—from that first happy birthday party to the most beautiful of wedding receptions.

For some reason, the thought of making a cake is intimidating, even to many otherwise excellent cooks; but it need not be. Only a few basic techniques are required, and they are easily mastered. Once you've learned to prepare one cake, very much the same procedure can be used to make any other.

It's as easy as this:

1. Read the recipe all the way through. If you don't understand a particular direction, turn to the Glossary of Techniques on page 2.
2. Make sure you have all the ingredients you will need, as well as the necessary equipment (especially the right size baking pans).
3. If the instructions call for eggs to be separated, remove them from the refrigerator and separate them at once. Eggs are much easier to separate when cold, but they beat more quickly at room temperature.
4. Unless otherwise directed, bring all the ingredients to room temperature, removing butter, eggs, milk, and so forth from the refrigerator at least half an hour before you begin. (Unwrap butter while it's still cold, so that none will stick to the paper.)
5. Make sure the oven racks are where you want them in the oven. Then preheat the oven to the temperature directed in the recipe.
6. Prepare the baking pans according to the directions.
7. Measure all the ingredients called for, then place them within easy reach on your work surface in the order listed in the recipe.

If the flour or other ingredients should be sifted, sift them at this time onto paper.

Now you are ready to begin! From this point on, it's one-two-three easy.

About Cake Ingredients

Flour. For this book, unless it is otherwise stated, I have used unbleached all-purpose flour instead of the bleached variety; I think it has a bit more flavor.

Sugar. I almost always use a superbly fragrant and flavorful sugar which I make myself with plain granulated sugar and vanilla beans (see directions following).

Eggs. The eggs I used were labeled large, not extra large or jumbo.

Butter or shortening. Because I don't believe salt belongs in dessert cookery, I definitely prefer unsalted butter; it seems to taste fresher and is usually of better quality than the salted variety. In some pastry recipes I have used vegetable shortening, but when I say butter, I mean butter—for which there is no substitute.

Chocolate. Depending on the recipe, I have used everything from the usual unsweetened, so-called "cooking" chocolate to the finest sweet and bittersweet chocolates.

Because no recipe is better than the ingredients in it, I always select the very best available and often add a not-so-basic ingredient. Expensive? Yes, of course, but then desserts are a luxury. While it is fine to be thrifty most of the time, when it comes to preparing a superb dessert, one should dismiss all practical thoughts and aim for the best.

Vanilla Sugar

Break a vanilla bean into several pieces and place it in an airtight container of granulated sugar. Allow it to steep until the sugar smells of vanilla, 2 to 3 days. You can use the same vanilla bean over and over again for at least a year, or until it is no longer fragrant.

Vanilla beans are available in supermarkets, as well as in gourmet stores. They come between 4 and 8 inches long, and the best-flavored ones are shiny and rather fat. The greatest thing about Vanilla Sugar is its superb fragrance and flavor, but it is also nice to know that it is less expensive to use than vanilla extract, as one bean can flavor many pounds of sugar.

Flour Arithmetic

1 cup self-rising cake flour = 1 cup cake flour + 1 1/2 tsp. baking powder + 1/4 to 1/2 tsp. salt (+ 1/4 tsp. baking soda, for a chocolate cake)

1 cup sifted cake flour = 1 cup + 2 1/2 Tbs. unsifted all-purpose flour

1 cup unsifted cake flour = 1 cup + 2 Tbs. unsifted all-purpose flour

Baking Powder Arithmetic

1 tsp. baking powder = 1/3 tsp. baking soda + 1/2 tsp. cream of tartar

1 tsp. baking powder = 1/4 tsp. baking soda + 1/2 cup buttermilk (and eliminate 1/2 cup of liquid called for in recipe)

About Preparing Cake Pans

Using a pastry brush especially reserved for this purpose, a small square of waxed paper, or your fingers, coat the pan(s) thoroughly with very soft, preferably unsalted butter. For pans with flat bottoms, cut a piece of waxed or parchment paper to fit, and press it over the butter. Then turn the paper buttered side up and sprinkle it with flour, sugar, or fine dry bread crumbs, depending on the type of cake you are going to bake. Rotate the pan and tap it briskly to distribute the coating evenly. Turn the pan upside down and dump out any excess.

To Fill and Frost Cake Layers

Cool the layers completely. (If they were prepared ahead and frozen, defrost them at room temperature or in the refrigerator.) If necessary, level each layer by slicing off its top horizontally. (Reserve slices to make trifle or to use as cake crumbs.) Spread a small amount of frosting in the center of a serving plate or platter. If desired, rim the plate or platter with four strips of foil or waxed paper. These can be removed after the cake is frosted, leaving the platter beautifully clean.) Place the first layer bottom side up on the plate, pressing it slightly into the frosting to secure it. Spoon the filling onto the center of the cake layer and spread it almost to the edge. Place the next layer on top, bottom side up, pressing it slightly into the filling. Repeat with any additional layers. Heap a large amount of frosting on top of the assembled cake. Push it over the edge and around the sides of the cake in a continuous motion. If necessary, add additional frosting to cover the top.

Elegant Génoise Cakes

Génoise Cake

This classic French sponge cake has a smooth texture and an elegant, subtle flavor that makes it a perfect foil for any number of different fillings and frostings, from very simple to elaborate. And, because Génoise can be baked in many differently shaped pans, it is also extremely versatile.

Despite this cake's elegance, it is made with such simple ingredients as flour, sugar, butter, and eggs, and it is surprisingly easy to prepare. As no leavening agent such as baking powder or baking soda is used, the only trick is in the beating. Sufficient air must be incorporated into the batter to achieve the final results: a cake with a velvetlike texture, firm, yet with unsurpassed lightness and purity of flavor.

1 cup cake flour
1/4 cup cornstarch
5 Tbs. unsalted butter
5 eggs
1 cup Vanilla Sugar, or 1 cup granulated sugar plus 1/2
    tsp. vanilla extract*
Dessert Syrup, optional (recipe follows)

Preheat oven to 325°F. Generously butter one 3- × 8-inch pan, two 8- or 9-inch layer-cake pans, or a 2-quart, round-bottomed, heat-proof bowl and sprinkle evenly with flour. Line flat pans with parchment or waxed paper, butter paper, and flour pans.

Sift flour with cornstarch onto waxed paper. Place sifter on a second sheet of paper and spoon in flour mixture. Do not sift; set aside. Melt butter in a small saucepan over low heat. Set aside. Combine eggs and Vanilla Sugar in a large, heat-proof mixing bowl. Place bowl over a pan of very hot water (water should not touch bottom of bowl). Beat with a whisk or electric hand beater until mixture is warm, remove bowl from water. Beat at high speed of an electric mixer until very pale, thick, and about triple in volume, about 5 minutes. Lower speed and beat for 1 minute to deflate mixture slightly. Sift flour mixture over egg mixture in three parts, folding after each addition until it has been thoroughly incorporated. Slowly pour in melted butter, leaving milky white sediment in bottom of pan, folding it into batter as added.

Bake in preheated oven for 40 to 45 minutes if in one pan or round-bottomed bowl; 25 to 30 minutes if in two pans; or until cake begins to pull away slightly from sides of pan(s) and it is very lightly browned. Cool cake(s) in pan(s) or bowl for about 2 minutes; run a spatula around edges and turn out onto rack(s). Cover loosely with a clean cloth; cool to room temperature. If desired, brush layers with Dessert Syrup before filling and frosting.

Dessert Syrup

This is the classic French dessert syrup for Génoise and other sponge-type cakes. It is also wonderful to have on hand for numerous other dessert creations.

1/2 cup granulated sugar
1/2 cup water
3 Tbs. rum, brandy, or liqueur

Combine sugar and water in a saucepan over medium heat. Cover and let simmer until sugar is dissolved, then uncover and bring to a full boil. Pour into a 2-cup measure. Stir in rum, brandy, or liqueur. Cool to room temperature before using. Syrup can be made ahead and stored in refrigerator until ready to use. Makes 1 generous cup of syrup.

Classic Génoise Layer Cake

The filling and frosting are variable, so you can confidently mix and match to your taste. No matter how you assemble the cake, it will be irresistibly good.

2 Génoise Cake* layers, cooled
Dessert Syrup*
Buttercream frosting (one possible recipe follows)
Topping, optional, such as Praline Powder (recipe
*   follows)*

Moisten cake layers with Dessert Syrup, then fill and frost with buttercream. Sprinkle with desired topping. Serves 6 to 8.

Golden Satin Buttercream Filling and Frosting

5 egg yolks
1/2 cup light corn syrup
1 cup (2 sticks) butter, softened
1 1-lb. box confectioners' sugar
Additional sugar as needed

In a large mixing bowl, beat yolks at medium speed of an electric mixer until very light and lemony, about 2 to 3 minutes. Place corn syrup in a small saucepan over medium heat until simmering; add to beaten yolks in a thin, steady stream, beating as added. Add butter about 2 tablespoons at a time, beating well after each addition. Beat until smooth; fold in 1 pound of confectioners' sugar; if necessary, add sufficient additional confectioners' sugar to bring mixture to spreading consistency.

Praline Powder

Softened butter
2 cups granulated sugar
1 cup almonds, slivered and toasted

Cover a flat baking sheet with foil and coat with butter. Place sugar in a large, heavy skillet over medium heat. Cook, stirring constantly, until dissolved to a deep golden, bubbly, caramel-like syrup. Stir in almonds. Immediately pour onto buttered foil. Cool until hardened, about 30 minutes. Peel off foil; break into small pieces. Place a few at a time in the work bowl of a food processor; process until finely ground.

Golden Génoise

2 Génoise Cake* layers, cooled
Dessert Syrup*, flavored with brandy
White Satin Buttercream Filling and Frosting* (recipe
*   follows), flavored with brandy*
1 cup Caramel Gold Dust (recipe follows)

Brush each cake layer generously with Dessert Syrup. Cut a round cardboard base the same size as cake layers. Spread center with a little buttercream frosting. Place one layer on cardboard; spread top and sides with buttercream. Top with second cake layer; frost with buttercream. With one hand, hold cake up on cardboard round; with other hand, slightly cupped, gently press Gold Dust into sides of cake. Sprinkle top with remaining Gold Dust. Serves 6 to 8.

White Satin Buttercream Filling and Frosting

3/4 cup milk
1/4 cup unsifted all-purpose flour
1/2 cup (1 stick) butter, room temperature
1/4 cup brandy, rum, or liqueur
1 cup granulated sugar

Place milk and flour in a small saucepan; beat with a whisk until smooth. Place over medium heat; cook, stirring constantly, until mixture comes to a full boil and thickens. Remove from heat; cool to room temperature. In a large mixing bowl, combine butter and sugar; beat until sugar has dissolved and mixture is very light and fluffy. Stir in brandy, rum, or liqueur. Slowly add cooled milk mixture, beating as added. Continue to beat at medium speed until frosting is smooth. If necessary, refrigerate until frosting thickens to spreading consistency.

Caramel Gold Dust

This is a very simple recipe for a glittery topping to sprinkle over cakes, ice cream, or any dessert that you feel needs a bit of glamour. Made ahead, it can be stored in an air-tight jar at room temperature to be used as needed.

Softened butter
2 cups granulated sugar

Cover a flat baking sheet with foil and coat with butter. Place sugar in a large, heavy skillet over medium heat. Cook, stirring constantly, until dissolved to a deep golden, bubbly, caramel-like syrup. Immediately pour onto buttered foil. Cool until hardened, about 30 minutes. Peel off foil; break into small pieces. Place a few at a time in work bowl of a food processor; process until finely ground. Makes about 2 cups.

Tropical Pineapple Génoise

2 Génoise Cake* layers, cooled
Dessert Syrup*, flavored with rum
Pineapple Rum Filling (recipe follows)
White Satin Buttercream Frosting*, flavored with rum
Pineapple slices, broken into crescents
Almonds, toasted and slivered

Brush each cake layer with Dessert Syrup. Place one layer on a cake plate; cover with Pineapple Rum Filling. Top with second layer. Cover top and sides of assembled cake with frosting. Garnish with pineapple crescents and slivered almonds. Serves 6 to 8.

Pineapple Rum Filling

1/2 cup granulated sugar
3 Tbs. cornstarch
1 1-lb. can crushed pineapple, drained
3 Tbs. rum
1 Tbs. butter

In a saucepan, mix sugar and cornstarch. Stir in pineapple; add rum. Cook over medium heat, stirring constantly, until liquid thickens and becomes transparent. Stir in butter; remove from heat. Cool to room temperature before using.

Ambassador Cake

This elegant French cake seems to have as many variations as there are pastry chefs in Paris, yet the basic ingredients remain the same: moist Génoise layers put together and iced with rich pastry cream and chopped candied fruit flavored with liqueur.

1/2 cup mixed candied fruit, finely chopped
1/4 cup brandy or orange liqueur
Custard Cream Filling and Frosting (recipe follows)
2 Génoise Cake* layers, cooled

In a small bowl, combine candied fruit and liqueur. Cover; let stand at room temperature. Several hours before assembling cake, prepare Custard Cream. Set aside. Drain fruit from liqueur through a fine sieve set over a bowl. Set drained fruit aside. Brush or drizzle both Génoise layers with drained liqueur. Cover one layer with Custard Cream and sprinkle with about three-fourths of fruit. Cover with remaining layer. Frost top and sides of cake with remaining Custard Cream. Sprinkle remaining fruit on top. Refrigerate until ready to serve. Serves 6 to 8.

Custard Cream Filling and Frosting

1 cup milk
4 egg yolks
1/2 cup granulated sugar
1 Tbs. cornstarch
2 Tbs. butter, room temperature
1 tsp. grated lemon zest
1/2 cup heavy (whipping) cream
1 Tbs. confectioners' sugar

Pour milk into a saucepan over medium heat. Bring just to boiling point. While milk heats, combine egg yolks and granulated sugar in a large bowl. Beat at high speed of an electric mixer until very thick. Fold in cornstarch. Slowly add hot milk, beating mixture as added. Pour into saucepan and cook over medium heat, stirring constantly from bottom of pan, until mixture is sufficiently thick to coat spoon. Remove from heat; stir in butter and lemon zest. Pour immediately into a storage bowl. Cover surface with plastic wrap. Cover bowl; refrigerate until custard is cold. Beat cream in a chilled bowl with chilled beaters until soft peaks form. Fold in confectioners' sugar. Stir about 2 tablespoons of whipped cream into chilled custard mixture, then fold in remaining whipped cream. Makes about 2 cups.

Cherries Jubilee Génoise

2 Génoise Cake* layers, cooled
Dessert Syrup*, flavored with Cherry Heering or kirsch
Tart Red Cherry Filling (recipe follows)
White Satin Buttercream Frosting*, flavored with Cherry
     Heering or kirsch
Candied cherries

Brush each cake layer with Dessert Syrup. Place one layer on a cake plate; cover with Tart Red Cherry Filling. Top with second layer. Cover top and sides of assembled cake with frosting. Garnish with candied cherries. Serves 6 to 8.

Tart Red Cherry Filling

1 10-oz. package frozen dark cherries in syrup
2 Tbs. Cherry Heering or kirsch
2 Tbs. cornstarch
1 Tbs. butter

Place frozen cherries in a colander over a bowl until thawed. Pour juice drained from cherries into a measuring cup; add Cherry Heering or kirsch and sufficient water to make 1/2 cup liquid. Combine with cornstarch in a saucepan and stir until smooth. Cook over low heat until thick and clear. Add cherries and cook 1 minute longer. Stir in butter; remove from heat. Cool before using.

Royal Raspberry Cake

Génoise layers, lavishly brushed with raspberry syrup, put together with raspberry buttercream and iced with—what else—raspberry-flavored whipped cream. Aristocratic and fabulously flavorful!

1 10-oz. package frozen raspberries in syrup
6 Tbs. raspberry brandy or kirsch
3 egg yolks
6 Tbs. granulated sugar
5 Tbs. water
1/2 cup (1 stick) butter, room temperature
1/2 pint heavy (whipping) cream
2 Tbs. confectioners' sugar
2 8- or 9-inch Génoise Cake* layers, cooled

Place frozen block of raspberries in a colander set over a bowl until berries are thawed and syrup has drained into bowl. Set raspberries aside. Stir raspberry liqueur or kirsch into syrup. Set aside. Place egg yolks in a large, heat-proof mixing bowl. Set bowl over (not in) simmering water. Beat with a whisk until yolks are slightly thickened and warm to the touch. Remove bowl from water and continue to beat until very thick. In a small saucepan, combine sugar and water. Place over low heat and stir until sugar has dissolved. Increase heat to medium high; boil until mixture registers 235°F. on a candy thermometer. Remove from heat; add to beaten yolks in a thin, steady stream, beating as added. Continue beating until mixture is slightly cooled.

Beat in butter, about a tablespoon at a time. Add 2 tablespoons of the raspberry syrup mixture and beat to a smooth custard. Sprinkle Génoise layers with 2 tablespoons of the raspberry syrup. Spread custard mixture over surface of one cake layer. Sprinkle with about three-fourths of thawed, drained raspberries. Cover with second cake layer. In a chilled bowl with chilled beaters, beat cream until stiff peaks form. Fold in remaining raspberry syrup mixture and confectioners' sugar; spread over top and on sides of assembled cake. Sprinkle top with remaining berries. Refrigerate until ready to serve. Serves 6 to 8.

Almond Meringue Cake

An astonishingly beautiful cake—and astonishingly easy to prepare.

> *1/2 cup granulated sugar*
> *1/2 cup water*
> *2 small lemon wedges*
> *1 Génoise Cake*, baked in a 3- × 8-inch round pan,*
> *   cooled*
> *1/2 cup apricot jam*
> *1/3 cup more granulated sugar*
> *1/2 cup confectioners' sugar*
> *3 egg whites*
> *2 Tbs. more granulated sugar*
> *1/2 cup almonds, slivered and toasted*

In a saucepan, combine 1/2 cup granulated sugar and water. Bring to a boil. Reduce heat to low; add lemon wedges and let simmer for about 10 minutes. Cool to room temperature. Remove and discard lemon wedges. With a serrated knife, cut Génoise cake horizontally into two even layers. Drizzle each with cooled lemon syrup. Place one layer, cut side up, on a heat-proof platter. Spread with apricot jam and cover with second layer, cut side down. Preheat oven to 475°F. Sift 1/3 cup granulated sugar with 1/2 cup confectioners' sugar. Set aside. In a large bowl, beat egg whites until frothy. Beat, adding 2 tablespoons granulated sugar, until soft peaks form. Continue to beat, adding sifted sugars, to a very stiff and glossy meringue; immediately spread over top and on sides of assembled cake. Sprinkle with slivered almonds. Place in preheated oven; bake for about 10 minutes, or until meringue is pale golden brown with deep brown peaks. Serves 6 to 8.

Note: Let cake stand at room temperature until ready to serve; or place on a flat surface in freezer for several hours, and then let stand at room temperature for about an hour before serving.

Baked Alaska Cake

A show-stopper!

> *1 Génoise Cake*, baked in a 2-quart, oven-proof,*
> *   round-bottomed bowl, cooled*
> *1 Tbs. currant jelly*
> *1 pint ice cream, softened*
> *Swiss Meringue with Walnuts (recipe follows)*

Cut a 1/2-inch slice from top of cooled cake and scoop out center, leaving a shell about 1 inch thick. Reserve center of cake for crumbs or other use. Spread cut side of top slice with jam. Pack shell with softened ice cream, filling it to rim. Cover with top slice, jam side down. Holding cake firmly together, invert it, rounded side up, onto a heat-proof platter. Place in freezer until ice cream is very firm. Preheat oven to 475°F. Cover frozen cake completely with Swiss Meringue. Use tines of a fork to create peaks and swirls. Immediately bake in preheated oven for 10 minutes, or until meringue peaks are lightly browned. Serve immediately, or return cake to freezer until ready to serve. Serves 6 to 8.

Swiss Meringue with Walnuts

1/2 cup confectioners' sugar
1/3 cup granulated sugar
3 egg whites
2 Tbs. more granulated sugar
3 oz. walnuts, finely ground

Sift confectioners' sugar with granulated sugar onto paper. In a large bowl, beat egg whites until frothy. Continue to beat, adding 2 tablespoons granulated sugar, until soft peaks form. Fold in sifted sugars, a little at a time, and beat to a very glossy, stiff meringue. Fold in chopped walnuts.

Génoise Sherry Custard Trifle

Serve this beautiful dessert in your best clear-glass bowl.

1 Génoise Cake*, baked in a 3- × 8-inch pan, cooled
2 Tbs. semisweet sherry
1 pint strawberries, hulled and cut lengthwise in half
6 large kiwis, peeled and cut across into slices
Sherry Custard (recipe follows)
1 cup heavy (whipping) cream
1 Tbs. confectioners' sugar
1 tsp. more semisweet sherry
Additional sliced or whole strawberries and sliced kiwis,
optional

With a serrated knife, cut Génoise Cake horizontally into two equal layers. Sprinkle cut side of each layer with 2 tablespoons sherry. Place one layer, cut side up, in a deep, clear-glass serving bowl. Arrange a circle alternating strawberries, cut side out, and kiwi slices against bowl around edges of cake. Spoon in about half of Sherry Custard. Top with remaining layer. Surround edge with another circle of fruit, and top with remaining custard. In a chilled bowl with chilled beaters, beat cream with confectioners' sugar and remaining sherry until soft peaks form. Spoon over custard and spread out evenly. Cover bowl; refrigerate until trifle is chilled. If desired, garnish just before serving with additional strawberries and kiwi slices. Serves 8 to 10.

Sherry Custard

> 1/2 cup granulated sugar
> 2 Tbs. cornstarch
> 2 cups light (or half-and-half) cream
> 3 egg yolks, lightly beaten
> 2 Tbs. semisweet sherry

Sift sugar and cornstarch into a large saucepan. Stir in cream and egg yolks. Cook, stirring constantly, until mixture is sufficiently thick to coat spoon. Remove from heat and continue to stir until slightly cooled. Stir in sherry. Pour into a bowl. Cover surface of custard with plastic wrap. Cover bowl, and refrigerate until chilled.

Chocolate Mousse–Filled Génoise

A dramatic finale to any meal.

> 1 Génoise Cake*, baked in a round-bottomed bowl, cooled
> Double Chocolate Filling (recipe follows)
> Coffee Whipped Cream Frosting (recipe follows)

Holding cake on its side, cut a 1/2-inch slice from bottom. Set bottom slice aside. Scoop out center of cake, leaving a shell about 1 inch thick. Reserve center for crumbs or other use. Spoon filling into shell, filling to rim. Cover with bottom slice. Holding cake firmly together, place it, round side up, on a serving platter. Frost with Coffee Whipped Cream. Sprinkle with grated chocolate. Refrigerate cake for several hours or until ready to serve. Serves 8 to 10.

Double Chocolate Filling

1/2 cup heavy (whipping) cream
1/4 cup granulated sugar
3 1-oz. squares semisweet chocolate, coarsely chopped
1 tsp. instant coffee
4 Tbs. (1/2 stick) butter, softened

In a heavy saucepan, combine cream and sugar. Place over medium heat; stir until mixture comes to a boil, then reduce heat to low. Let simmer, without stirring, for 4 to 5 minutes. Remove from heat; add chocolate and instant coffee. Stir until mixture is smooth and cooled slightly. Transfer to a bowl. Add butter 1 tablespoon at a time, beating well after each addition. Continue to beat until light and fluffy. Refrigerate, covered, until ready to use.

Coffee Whipped Cream Frosting

1/2 pint heavy (whipping) cream
3 Tbs. confectioners' sugar
1 tsp. instant coffee

In a chilled bowl with chilled beaters, beat cream until soft peaks form. Fold in confectioners' sugar and instant coffee. Beat to spreading consistency.

Soufflé Cake,
Filled and Rolled Cakes,
Oblong Layer Cakes,
Individual Cake Squares,
and More

Soufflé Cake

This soufflé-like batter makes a light, versatile, sponge cake that can be rolled up, jelly-roll fashion, for a classic Bûche de Noël or a Lemon Meringue Log, as well as any number of other jelly-roll-type cakes. It can also be cut across into three equal layers for an Italian Cassata, French Pauvé, and other elegant oblong cakes.

> 6 eggs
> 3 Tbs. butter
> 3/4 cup cake flour
> 1 Tbs. granulated sugar
> 1/2 cup more granulated sugar
> 1/2 tsp. vanilla or almond extract, optional
> Dessert Syrup*, optional

Preheat oven to 425°F. Butter a 10 1/2- × 15 1/2-inch jelly-roll pan; line with parchment or waxed paper cut to fit. Butter paper. Separate eggs, placing yolks in one large mixing bowl, whites in another. Place butter in a small saucepan over very low heat until melted. Cool to room temperature. Spoon flour into sifter. Do not sift. Beat egg whites until frothy; add 1 tablespoon sugar and continue to beat until stiff peaks form. Set aside. Add remaining sugar to yolks. Beat until sugar has dissolved, and mixture is very thick and about triple in volume.

Sift flour over yolk mixture, in three parts, folding it in after each addition. Fold in beaten egg whites. If desired, fold in vanilla or almond extract. Fold in cooled, melted butter, leaving any sediment in bottom of pan. Spoon batter into prepared pan.

Bake in preheated oven for 10 minutes, or until cake is lightly browned. Do not overbake. Turn cake out onto a clean dish towel. Brush paper lightly with cold water. Let stand about 2 minutes, then peel off paper. Cover cake with a clean cloth to prevent drying out; cool to room temperature. If desired, brush with Dessert Syrup. Cake is now ready to be filled and rolled into a jelly roll or cut across into equal slices for an oblong layer cake. Makes one 10 1/2- × 15 1/2-inch cake.

Cassata à la Siciliana

A Sicilian classic that is positively addictive.

> *Zest from 1 small lemon*
> *1/2 cup granulated sugar*
> *1 cup water*
> *2 Tbs. kirsch or other liqueur*
> *1 Soufflé Cake*, cooled*
> *Ricotta Cheese Filling (recipe follows)*
> *Chocolate Glaze (recipe follows)*

Cut lemon zest into julienne strips; cut strips across into tiny cubes. Place in a saucepan; add sugar and water. Cover pan, bring mixture to full boil, and boil until sugar is dissolved. Uncover, reduce to very low heat, and let mixture simmer gently for about 1/2 hour. Remove from heat. Pour syrup through a fine sieve into a small bowl or measuring cup with a pouring lip; add kirsch. Place lemon zest in a second small bowl. Set both aside. With a serrated knife, cut prepared cake into three equal slices. Drizzle or brush each slice with lemon syrup. Spread one slice with half of Ricotta Cheese Filling to about 1/4 inch of edge. Cover with a second slice and top with remaining filling. Top with third slice of cake. Gently press down on layers with palms. Cover cake with an oblong weight, such as a small wooden chopping board or an oblong glass baking dish. Refrigerate for about an hour, or until ready to cover with glaze. If necessary, remove any filling that has escaped from between layers. Spoon warm chocolate glaze over top and down sides. Use a small metal spatula to spread it evenly. Refrigerate until glaze hardens. Keep refrigerated until ready to serve. Serves 8 to 10.

Note: This cake really should be allowed to "mellow" in the refrigerator for at least several hours; it will taste even better if prepared a day ahead.

Ricotta Cheese Filling

1 15- or 16-oz. carton skim milk ricotta cheese
2 Tbs. kirsch or other liqueur
4 Tbs. confectioners' sugar
Candied lemon zest (reserved from cake preparation)
2 1-oz. squares bittersweet chocolate, coarsely grated or
*   finely chopped*

In a mixing bowl, combine ricotta cheese, kirsch, and sugar; blend well. Stir in candied lemon peel and chocolate.

Chocolate Glaze

8 1-oz. squares bittersweet chocolate, coarsely chopped
2 tsp. instant coffee
1/2 cup heavy (whipping) cream

Combine ingredients in top half of a double boiler. Place over simmering water until chocolate has partially melted. Remove pan from water, and stir until mixture is smooth. Place pan in cold water, and stir until glaze is cooled to room temperature.

Braco de Gitano

A Spanish-style jelly roll, with a rich sherry custard filling. *Braco de gitano* means, literally, "arm of a gypsy." Why this particular cake should be so named is a mystery to me, but it is delicious, quite rich, and elegant, especially when served with a fine Oloroso sherry.

> *4 Tbs. currant jelly*
> *1/4 cup semisweet or sweet (Oloroso) sherry*
> *1 Soufflé Cake*, cooled*
> *Sherry Custard, chilled (recipe follows)*
> *Confectioners' sugar*

In a small saucepan, combine jelly and sherry; stir over low heat until smooth. Brush evenly over entire surface of Soufflé Cake. With a whisk, beat chilled Sherry Custard to consistency of whipped cream. Spread evenly over cake, leaving a 1/2-inch border around edge. Roll cake, jelly-roll fashion, from long side. Transfer, seam side down, to an oblong serving platter. Refrigerate until ready to serve. Just before serving, sprinkle generously with confectioners' sugar. Serves 6 to 8.

Sherry Custard

> *1/4 cup semisweet sherry*
> *1 envelope unflavored gelatin*
> *1 cup light (or half-and-half) cream*
> *1 vanilla bean*
> *4 egg yolks*
> *1/2 cup granulated sugar*
> *1/4 cup all-purpose flour*
> *1 Tbs. butter, softened*

Combine sherry and gelatin in a small bowl; stir once, then set aside until softened and ready to use. Place cream and vanilla bean in a small saucepan over low heat; bring to a simmer. Remove from heat; remove vanilla bean. With a small, sharp knife, split bean lengthwise in half; scrape seeds back into cream. (Blot cream from pods, let stand at room temperature until dry, and reserve for other use.) In a mixing bowl, beat eggs with sugar until very thick. Stir in flour, and beat until smooth. Slowly add hot cream, stirring as added. Pour mixture back into saucepan; place over low heat and cook, stirring constantly from bottom and around sides of pan, until sufficiently thick to coat spoon. Stir in gelatin mixture. Remove from heat, and stir until gelatin has dissolved. Stir in softened butter. Pour into a storage bowl. Cover surface with plastic wrap. Refrigerate until cold and firm. Just before using, beat custard with a whisk to consistency of whipped cream.

Strawberry Cream Cake Squares

Four thin layers of Soufflé Cake put together with fresh strawberry cream filling, topped with confectioners' sugar, garnished with fresh strawberries, and cut into individual squares.

> 1 Soufflé Cake*, cooled
> 4 Tbs. kirsch
> 2 pints strawberries, hulled
> 1/4 cup boiling water
> 1 envelope unflavored gelatin
> 3/4 cup confectioners' sugar
> 1 pint heavy (whipping) cream
> 2 Tbs. currant jelly

With a serrated knife, cut cake across into equal halves. Cut each half horizontally into two thin layers. Brush cut side of layers with kirsch. Set aside. Cut in half and set aside three large strawberries for garnish.

Processor Method: Pour boiling water into work bowl of a food processor; sprinkle with gelatin. Let stand for about 2 minutes, then process until gelatin has dissolved. Add remaining berries to gelatin mixture in processor. Process until puréed. Add confectioners' sugar and continue to process until sugar is dissolved, about 30 seconds.

Hand Method: Pour boiling water into a mixing bowl; sprinkle with gelatin. Stir until dissolved. Purée remaining berries. Stir into gelatin mixture. Add confectioners' sugar and stir to blend.

In a chilled bowl with chilled beaters, beat cream until soft peaks form. Gently fold in puréed strawberry mixture. Spread cut side of one cake layer with about a third of the strawberry cream. Repeat with second and third layers. Top with remaining layer, cut side down. Refrigerate cake until filling is firm, about 2 hours. To serve, sift confectioners' sugar evenly over top of cake. Cut cake lengthwise in half and then across into 6 servings. Place a strawberry half in center of each. Melt jelly in a small saucepan over low heat; brush over each strawberry half. Serves 6.

Brandied Peach Pauvé

Make this beautiful cake at the height of peach season.

>   1 Soufflé Cake*, cooled
>   3 Tbs. peach brandy
>   1 cup peach jam
>   1/4 cup brown sugar, firmly packed
>   2 Tbs. more peach brandy
>   4 to 6 medium-to-large, fresh, ripe peaches
>   1/2 pint heavy (whipping) cream
>   2 Tbs. confectioners' sugar
>   1 Tbs. more peach brandy
>   2 or 3 more medium-to-large peaches
>   2 Tbs. lemon juice

With a serrated knife, cut cake across into three equal slices. Sprinkle each slice with 1 tablespoon peach brandy. Set aside. In a saucepan, blend jam, brown sugar, and 1/4 cup brandy. Cook, stirring, over medium heat until mixture thickens. Transfer to a storage bowl. Refrigerate until cool. Peel, pit, and chip 4 to 6 peaches. Stir into cooled jam mixture; return mixture to refrigerator until ready to use. In a chilled bowl with chilled beaters, beat cream with confectioners' sugar until soft peaks form. Fold in remaining peach brandy.

Place 1 cake slice on an oblong platter. Spread top with jam mixture. Cover with second layer; spread with jam. Top with remaining layer. Cover top and sides of cake with brandy-flavored whipped cream. Refrigerate until ready to serve. Peel, pit, and slice remaining peaches. Place in a small bowl and toss with lemon juice. Refrigerate until ready to use. Just before serving, drain sliced peaches and arrange on top of cake in slightly overlapping rows, covering it completely. Serves 8 to 10.

Midsummer Fresh Fruit Cake

A bountiful, beautiful, easily served creation—perfect for a midsummer buffet.

> *1/2 cup granulated sugar*
> *2 Tbs. cornstarch*
> *1 1/2 cups orange juice*
> *1/4 cup currant jelly*
> *3 or 4 ripe peaches or nectarines*
> *1 Tbs. lemon juice*
> *1/2 pint fresh raspberries*
> *1 pint fresh blackberries, or 1 10-oz. package frozen*
> *   berries without sugar*
> *1 Soufflé Cake*, cooled*
> *Lightly sweetened whipped cream, optional*

In a saucepan, combine sugar and cornstarch; stir in orange juice. Place over medium heat and cook, stirring constantly, until mixture thickens and boils, about a minute. Remove from heat; stir in jelly. Cover saucepan and refrigerate until mixture is chilled, about an hour. Plunge each peach or nectarine into a large pan of boiling water; hold under cold running water and slip off skins. Cut each into halves; cut halves into wedges, letting them drop into a bowl containing lemon juice. Toss to coat. Wash berries only if they seem dusty; blot dry. Add berries to peaches and refrigerate until ready to use. Place cake on an oblong serving platter; top with about half of chilled orange juice mixture. Arrange peaches and berries in an attractive design over entire surface of cake. Brush or drizzle fruit with remaining orange juice mixture. Serve with lightly sweetened whipped cream, if desired. Serves 12 to 14.

Zuppa Inglese with Marrons

An Italian version of English trifle; a marvelous layering of sponge cake, rich custard, marrons in heavy syrup, and light, airy meringue.

> *1 Soufflé Cake*, cooled*
> *1 cup marron pieces in heavy syrup*
> *2 cups milk*
> *1/2 cup granulated sugar*
> *1/2 cup flour*
> *1/4 tsp. salt*
> *4 eggs, separated*
> *1/8 tsp. cream of tartar*
> *1/4 cup more granulated sugar*

Let Soufflé Cake stand at room temperature several hours or overnight to dry out. With a serrated knife, cut into thin slices. Place slices in a single layer on a long, shallow baking sheet. Set aside. Drain syrup from marrons; spoon syrup over cake slices. Reserve marron pieces. Pour milk into a heavy saucepan; place over moderate heat until small bubbles appear around edges. While milk heats, combine sugar, flour, and salt in top half of a double boiler. Add egg yolks; beat with a whisk until mixture is blended and smooth. Slowly add hot milk, beating vigorously as added. Place over, not touching, very gently simmering water. Stir, scraping sides and bottom of pot, until mixture thickens to a soft custard and coats spoon. Pour immediately into a bowl, preferably one with a pouring lip. Cool to room temperature, stirring occasionally to keep a skin from forming on top. Arrange about three-fourths of cake slices in slightly overlapping circles on bottom and around sides of a 1 1/2-quart soufflé dish. Pour in about two-thirds of custard. Sprinkle surface with reserved marron pieces. Arrange remaining cake slices over top and cover with remaining custard. Set aside.

Preheat oven to 425°F. In a large bowl, beat egg whites with cream of tartar until frothy. Continue to beat, adding remaining sugar about a tablespoon at a time, until meringue holds stiff, glossy peaks. Cover zuppa with meringue and swirl around with tines of a fork to form peaks. Bake in preheated oven for 8 to 10 minutes, or until peaks of meringue are a deep, golden brown. Serve immediately, or refrigerate until ready to serve. Serves 10 to 12.

Chestnut Roll

1 cup canned chestnut purée
1/4 cup heavy (whipping) cream
6 Tbs. confectioners' sugar
1 Tbs. rum
1 Soufflé Cake*, cooled
3/4 cup more heavy cream
4 Tbs. more confectioners' sugar
Chocolate Glaze (recipe follows)

In a small bowl, stir and mash chestnut purée until smooth and spreadable. In a chilled bowl with chilled beaters, beat 1/4 cup cream with 6 tablespoons confectioners' sugar until stiff peaks form. Fold in chestnut purée. Sprinkle rum over Soufflé Cake; spread with chestnut purée mixture. Roll up, jelly-roll fashion, from long side. Refrigerate until chilled or until about an hour before serving. In a chilled bowl with chilled beaters, beat remaining cream until soft peaks form. Fold in remaining confectioners' sugar and continue to beat until stiff. Cover chilled chestnut roll with whipped cream mixture. Drizzle glaze over top. Serves 8 to 10.

Chocolate Glaze

1 1-oz. square unsweetened chocolate
1/4 tsp. vegetable shortening

Melt chocolate with vegetable shortening in top half of a double boiler over hot, not boiling, water. Stir to blend. Use while warm.

Chocolate Sponge Cakes

Chocolate Arithmetic
3 Tbs. unsweetened cocoa + 1 Tbs. butter = 1 oz. melted unsweetened chocolate
6 Tbs. unsweetened cocoa + 7 Tbs. granulated sugar + 1/4 cup butter = 6 oz. semisweet chocolate
3 Tbs. unsweetened cocoa + 1/4 cup granulated sugar + 2 Tbs. butter = 4 oz. sweet cooking chocolate

Chocolate Decorations
Grated Chocolate: Work with a large slab of semisweet or bittersweet chocolate. A large piece is easier to grate than a small one,

and darker chocolate looks more appetizing.) Place a hand grater on foil or waxed paper, holding it at an angle. Rub the chocolate through the coarse side, letting it fall onto the paper. Grate only the amount you want to use, reserving the remaining chocolate for another use. Use a spoon to sprinkle the grated chocolate over the dessert.

Chocolate Leaves: Be certain to use nonpoisonous leaves that have not been sprayed with plant food or insect repellent. Rose, geranium, and ivy leaves work especially well. Rinse each leaf under cold running water; blot thoroughly dry with paper towels. To prepare 10 to 15 chocolate leaves, place 4 ounces of bittersweet or semisweet chocolate in a small, heat-proof bowl. Place the bowl over, not in, very hot water until the chocolate is partially melted. Remove the bowl from the heat and stir until the chocolate is smooth. With a pastry brush, spread a layer of melted chocolate about 1/8 inch thick on the back of each leaf just to the edge, making sure chocolate does not run onto the front side of the leaf. Place on a baking sheet lined with foil or waxed paper. Refrigerate until the chocolate has set, about 5 minutes. Spread another thin layer of melted chocolate over the first layer on each leaf. Refrigerate until the chocolate is firm. Carefully peel off the leaves, beginning at the stem ends. Refrigerate the chocolate leaves until ready to use.

Chocolate Slabs: Line a long, flat baking sheet with waxed paper or foil. Place 3 ounces of chopped bittersweet or semisweet chocolate in a small, heat-proof bowl. Place the bowl over, not in, hot water until the chocolate is partially melted. Remove the bowl from the heat and stir until the chocolate is completely melted and smooth. Pour onto a prepared baking sheet and use a long, narrow, metal spatula to spread it very thin. Place the sheet in the freezer or refrigerator until the chocolate is firm. Use the tip of the spatula to break the firm chocolate into irregular slabs. Using the spatula rather than your hands, pick up each slab and let it fall directly onto the dessert. Drop slabs haphazardly on top of an iced cake before the icing has hardened. Or use them to decorate whipped-cream-topped desserts or ice cream.

Chocolate Curls: Unwrap an 8-ounce bar of bittersweet or semisweet chocolate and place it on foil in a gas oven with the pilot light on (or in an electric oven that has been warmed slightly, then turned off), until it is slightly softened. The chocolate should be just slightly warmed, so that the curls will not crack as they are made. Line a flat baking sheet with foil. Holding the bar of chocolate over it, shave the smooth side of the chocolate from top to bottom with a swivel-bladed vegetable peeler, letting the curled shavings drop onto the sheet. Move the bar after making each curl so that the curls are evenly spaced and not touching. Place the baking sheet in the refrigerator or freezer until the curls are firm or until you are ready to use them. Use a spatula to transfer the curls from the sheet to the dessert.

Chocolate Sponge Cake

Light, spongy layers, perfect for rich fillings and frostings.

> *1 1/2 cups cake flour, sifted*
> *1 tsp. baking powder*
> *2 Tbs. cocoa, firmly packed*
> *1/4 tsp. salt*
> *5 eggs, separated*
> *1 cup Vanilla Sugar*, or 1 cup granulated sugar plus*
> *1 tsp. vanilla extract*

Preheat oven to 325°F. Butter two 9-inch round pans. Line with parchment or waxed paper cut to fit; butter and flour paper. Sift flour, baking powder, cocoa, and salt onto waxed paper. Place sifter on a second sheet of paper and spoon in mixture; do not sift. Set aside.

Beat egg whites until they stand up in soft peaks. Beat in 1/4 cup of Vanilla Sugar, 1 tablespoon at a time. Continue beating until mixture is very stiff. In another bowl, beat yolks until thick and lemony colored. Gradually beat in remaining 3/4 cup Vanilla Sugar. Spoon this mixture over beaten whites and fold gently together. Sprinkle flour mixture over egg mixture and fold together only until no streaks of white can be seen. Spoon into prepared pans. Bake in preheated oven for 15 to 20 minutes, or until cakes are dry on top and start to shrink away from sides of pans. Cool cakes in pans for about 2 minutes, then turn out onto racks. Cover loosely with a clean cloth; cool to room temperature. If desired, brush layers with Dessert Syrup before filling and frosting. Makes two 9-inch layers.

Chocolate Sponge Cake with Rum Cream

A classic cake that, when sprinkled with Praline Powder or Caramel Gold Dust, dazzles, glitters, and pleases the eye as well as the palate.

1 envelope unflavored gelatin
1/4 cup water
4 egg yolks
3/4 cup granulated sugar
1/4 cup light rum
1/2 cup (1 stick) butter, very soft
1 cup heavy (whipping) cream
4 Tbs. Dessert Syrup*, flavored with rum
2 Chocolate Sponge Cake* layers, cooled
Caramel Gold Dust* or Praline Powder*, optional

Sprinkle gelatin over water in a small saucepan. Place over low heat and stir until gelatin has dissolved and mixture is clear. Place egg yolks and sugar in a large, heat-proof bowl. Place bowl over, not in, a pan of simmering water. With a wire whisk or hand electric mixer, beat yolks with sugar until very pale and thick. Stir in gelatin mixture and rum. Remove bowl from water and continue to beat mixture until cooled to room temperature. Add butter, about a tablespoon at a time, beating to incorporate thoroughly. Cover, and refrigerate until chilled. In a separate chilled bowl with chilled beaters, beat cream until stiff peaks form; fold in chilled gelatin mixture. Moisten each cake layer with Dessert Syrup. Spread one layer with about a fourth of rum cream mixture; cover with second layer. Spread remaining mixture on top and sides of assembled cake. Serves 6 to 8.

Chocolate Sponge Cake with Lemon Custard Filling and Chocolate Buttercream

Chocolate Sponge Cake layers put together with a tart and tangy lemon custard filling and frosted with a Classic Chocolate Buttercream.

> *1 large lemon*
> *Orange liqueur or fresh orange juice*
> *1 Tbs. cornstarch*
> *1/2 cup granulated sugar*
> *5 egg yolks*
> *4 Tbs. butter, room temperature*
> *2 Chocolate Sponge Cake* layers, cooled*
> *Classic Chocolate Buttercream (recipe follows)*
> *1/4 cup Candied Lemon Rind**

Grate zest from lemon. Squeeze lemon juice into a 1-cup measure. Add sufficient orange liqueur or orange juice to make 1/2 cup liquid. In top half of a double boiler, combine cornstarch and sugar. Add egg yolks and butter; beat until smooth. Place over simmering water and add lemon juice mixture, blending well. Cook, stirring constantly from bottom and around sides of pan, until custard is sufficiently thick to coat spoon. Remove from heat and beat with a whisk until cool. Spread one cake layer with cooled lemon custard filling; top with second layer. Spread sides and bottom of cake with Chocolate Buttercream. Sprinkle top with Candied Lemon Rind. Serves 6 to 8.

Classic Chocolate Buttercream

6 1-oz. squares bittersweet chocolate
8 Tbs. light cream
1/2 cup granulated sugar
3 eggs
1 cup (2 sticks) butter, room temperature

Place chocolate and cream in top half of a double boiler, over simmering water, until chocolate is partially melted. Remove pan from water and stir until mixture is smooth. In a large bowl, beat sugar and eggs at high speed of an electric mixer until very pale and thick. Fold in chocolate mixture, then add butter in four parts and continue to beat until smooth. Refrigerate until thickened to spreading consistency.

Frozen Black Forest Cake

A sumptuous version of an international favorite.

1 8-oz. jar maraschino cherries in syrup
1 Tbs. kirsch or cherry-flavored brandy
2 Chocolate Sponge Cake* layers, cooled
1 pint Maraschino Ice Cream* or commercially prepared
   cherry ice cream, softened
1/2 pint heavy (whipping) cream
2 Tbs. confectioners' sugar, sifted
Chocolate Curls*

Drain cherries through a sieve set over a small bowl. Set cherries aside. Stir kirsch or cherry brandy into syrup. Brush each cake layer with all but 1 tablespoon of mixture. Wrap each airtight and place in freezer. Line a layer cake pan (same size as cake layers) with plastic wrap. Spoon in softened ice cream and spread out evenly. Cover and wrap pan in foil; place in freezer until very firm. Place one frozen cake layer on a 10-inch corrugated cardboard cake support (or on a 10-inch round of cardboard wrapped in foil). Unwrap pan of ice cream and invert it over cake layer. Remove pan and peel off plastic wrap. Place a second cake layer over ice cream layer. Return assembled cake to freezer.

In a chilled bowl with chilled beaters, beat cream until soft peaks form; fold in confectioners' sugar and remaining cherry syrup mixture. Take cake from freezer and quickly cover sides and top with whipped cream. Garnish with Chocolate Curls. Return cake to freezer until whipped cream is firm, then wrap entire cake loosely in foil. To serve, unwrap cake and place it on a serving platter (no need to remove it from its cardboard support). Cut with a wet knife into thick slices. Serves 8 to 10.

Mocha Mousse Cake

The most chocolaty chocolate cake ever.

2 Chocolate Sponge Cake* layers, cooled
4 Tbs. Dessert Syrup*, flavored with coffee liqueur
Mocha Mousse Filling (recipe follows)
Chocolate Buttercream Frosting (recipe follows)

Moisten one cake layer with 2 tablespoons of Dessert Syrup. Butter a 9-inch layer cake pan and cover bottom with waxed or parchment paper. Fit cake layer into pan and cover with prepared mousse filling. Cover filling surface with plastic wrap. Refrigerate until filling is firm, about 6 to 8 hours. When ready, place remaining cake layer on a cardboard disk or dessert platter and moisten with remaining Dessert Syrup. Remove layer with mousse topping from refrigerator; run knife around edge to loosen mousse, then unmold by turning upside down onto first cake layer. Remove paper. Cover top and sides of assembled cake with Chocolate Buttercream Frosting. Serves 8 to 10.

Mocha Mousse Filling

4 egg yolks
3/4 cup light cream
6 oz. semisweet chocolate morsels
1/4 cup brandy

In a mixing bowl, beat yolks until very pale and lemony, about 5 minutes. Set aside. Combine cream and chocolate in heavy-bottomed saucepan. Cook, stirring constantly, over medium heat until mixture begins to boil. Remove from heat and stir in brandy. Add to yolks in a thin, steady stream, stirring as added. Continue to stir until mixture thickens. Let stand until cooled to room temperature before using.

Chocolate Buttercream Frosting

2 cups granulated sugar
2 Tbs. white corn syrup
3/4 cup milk
1/4 cup brandy
1/4 tsp. salt
2 oz. unsweetened chocolate, grated
2 Tbs. butter
Light cream, heated, optional

Place sugar, corn syrup, milk, brandy, salt, and chocolate in a heavy-bottomed saucepan. Stir to blend. Cook over low heat, stirring occasionally, until mixture reaches soft ball stage (230°F. on a candy thermometer). Remove from heat; add butter, and beat until cooled. If mixture becomes too stiff, add hot cream, about 1 tablespoon at a time, until desired spreading consistency is obtained.

Creole Chocolate Cakes

Creole Chocolate Cake

Buttermilk gives these not-too-sweet chocolate cake layers extra flavor.

>*2 ozs. chopped chocolate*
>*1 cup very hot, freshly brewed coffee, preferably dark*
>   *roast*
>*1 3/4 cup unsifted all-purpose flour*
>*1 tsp. baking powder*
>*1 tsp. baking soda*
>*1/2 tsp. salt*
>*1/2 cup (1 stick) butter, room temperature*
>*2 cups Vanilla Sugar*, or 2 cups granulated sugar plus*
>   *1 tsp. vanilla extract*
>*3 eggs*
>*1 cup buttermilk*

Preheat oven to 350°F. Butter three 8- or 9-inch layer cake pans. Sprinkle with granulated sugar and rotate pans to spread evenly. Place chopped chocolate in a 1-cup measure. Pour in hot coffee; stir until chocolate has melted. Set aside until cooled to room temperature. Sift flour, baking powder, soda, and salt onto paper. In large bowl of an electric mixer, combine butter, Vanilla Sugar, and eggs; beat at high speed until light and fluffy, about 5 minutes. (Or place butter and sugar in a large mixing bowl and beat with a whisk until light and fluffy; add eggs one at a time, beating well after each addition.)

Fold flour mixture into beaten egg mixture in four parts alternately with buttermilk, folding only until ingredients are incorporated. Fold in chocolate mixture. Spoon batter into prepared pans, dividing evenly. Bake in preheated oven for 25 to 30 minutes, or until a cake tester inserted into center of cake comes out clean. Cool layers in pans on a rack for about 10 minutes; invert and remove pans. Cool layers completely before filling and frosting. Makes three 8- or 9-inch layers.

Chocolate Temptation

3 Creole Chocolate Cake* layers, cooled
6 Tbs. coffee liqueur or coffee
2 Tbs. apricot jam
Sour Cream Frosting (recipe follows)
Chocolate Curls*, made from bittersweet chocolate,
    optional

Moisten each cake layer with 2 tablespoons of liqueur. Spread one layer with jam and then with a thin layer of Sour Cream Frosting. Cover with second layer and repeat. Top with third layer; cover top and sides of assembled cake with remaining frosting. If desired, garnish with Chocolate Curls. Serves 8 to 10.

Sour Cream Frosting

2 3-oz. packages cream cheese, softened
1/2 cup (1 stick) butter, softened
1 1-lb. package confectioners' sugar, sifted
4 Tbs. sour cream

In a large bowl, beat cream cheese with butter until light and fluffy. Stir in confectioners' sugar, a little at a time, and beat until smooth. Add sufficient sour cream to bring mixture to spreading consistency. Makes enough frosting for one 8- or 9-inch two-layer cake.

Chocolate Layer Cake with White Icin'

A Southern classic.

> *3 Creole Chocolate Cake* layers, cooled*
> *6 Tbs. apricot liqueur or kirsch*
> *4 Tbs. apricot preserves*
> *Southern-Style White Icin' (recipe follows)*
> *Chocolate Glaze (recipe follows)*

Moisten each cake layer with 2 tablespoons of liqueur. Spread one layer with apricot preserves and then with a thin layer of frosting. Cover with second layer and repeat. Top with third layer. Spread remaining frosting over top and sides of assembled cake. Pour warm glaze in swirls over top. Serves 8 to 10.

Southern-Style White Icin'

> *4 cups granulated sugar*
> *3/4 cup water*
> *1/2 cup light corn syrup*
> *6 egg whites*
> *6 Tbs. confectioners' sugar*

In a large saucepan, combine sugar, water, and corn syrup. Cover; cook over medium heat until mixture comes to a boil. Uncover and simmer, stirring occasionally, until mixture comes to 238°F. on a candy thermometer. While syrup simmers, beat egg whites in a large bowl until soft peaks form. Slowly add syrup, beating as added. Add confectioners' sugar in four parts, beating well after each addition. Continue to beat until mixture holds stiff peaks.

Chocolate Glaze

*1 3-oz. bar bittersweet chocolate (such as Lindt or
    Tobler), chopped*
1 tsp. vegetable shortening

Place chocolate and shortening in top half of a double boiler until chocolate is partially melted. Remove from water and stir until mixture is smooth.

Creole Chocolate Cake with Bourbon Buttercream

3 Creole Chocolate Cake* layers, cooled
2 Tbs. currant jelly
Bourbon Buttercream Frosting (recipe follows)

Spread one cake layer with currant jelly and buttercream; top with second layer and repeat. Cover with third layer. Frost top and sides with remaining buttercream. Serves 8 to 10.

Bourbon Buttercream Frosting

1 cup (2 sticks) butter, softened
4 egg yolks
1/4 cup granulated sugar
1/4 cup light cream
2 Tbs. bourbon whiskey

Place butter in a large mixing bowl. Beat until light and fluffy. Set aside. Place eggs, sugar, and cream in top half of a double boiler over simmering water and cook, stirring constantly, until mixture is thick and smooth. Remove from heat and stir until cooled to room temperature. Stir in bourbon. Slowly add to butter in mixing bowl, beating as added. Continue to beat until mixture is smooth. Refrigerate until thickened to spreading consistency.

Roz Cole's Rocky Road Cake

A cake for when too much is never enough.

3 Creole Chocolate Cake* layers, cooled
2 Tbs. red currant jelly
Rocky Road Frosting (recipe follows)

Spread one cake layer with currant jelly and then with a layer of Rocky Road Frosting. Cover with second layer and repeat. Top with third layer. Spoon remaining frosting over top of assembled cake. Serves 8 to 10.

Rocky Road Frosting

2 3-oz. bars Tobler or Lindt dark chocolate, chopped
4 Tbs. butter, softened
2 1/2 cups sifted confectioners' sugar
3 Tbs. light cream
1 tsp. vanilla
1 egg
1 1/2 cups miniature marshmallows
1 cup coarsely chopped walnuts

Place chocolate in a large, heat-proof bowl. Place bowl over, not in, a pan of simmering water until chocolate is partially melted. Remove bowl from water and stir until chocolate is smooth. Add butter, sugar, cream, and vanilla; blend thoroughly. Beat in egg and continue to beat until mixture is firm enough to hold its shape. Fold in marshmallows and chopped walnuts.

Devil's Food Cakes

Devil's Food Cake

It's hard to believe something so inexpensive and easy to prepare can be so devilishly delicious.

> *1 1/2 cups all-purpose flour*
> *1/2 cup cocoa*
> *1 tsp. baking soda*
> *1/4 tsp. salt*
> *1/2 cup (1 stick) butter, softened*
> *1 1/4 cup granulated sugar*
> *2 large eggs*
> *1/2 tsp. vanilla*
> *1/2 tsp. Angostura bitters, optional*
> *1/4 tsp. coarsely ground black pepper*
> *1 cup boiling water*

Preheat oven to 350°F. Butter two 8- or 9-inch layer cake pans. Line bottom of each with parchment or waxed paper; butter paper and flour pans. Sift flour with cocoa, baking soda, and salt onto waxed paper. Set aside. In a large bowl, cream butter with sugar until light and fluffy. Add eggs one at a time, beating well after each addition. Stir in vanilla, Angostura bitters, and pepper. Dump sifted ingredients over surface. Without stirring, pour in boiling water, then beat vigorously until batter is smooth. Spoon into prepared pans, dividing evenly. Bake in preheated oven for 25 to 30 minutes, or until sides of cakes spring away from edges of pans and cake testers inserted in centers come out clean. Turn layers out onto racks. Cool to room temperature. Makes two 8- or 9-inch layers.

Lemony Chocolate Layer Cake

Devil's Food Cake layers put together with a tart and tangy lemon curd custard and frosted with Classic Chocolate Buttercream.

> *1 large lemon*
> *Orange liqueur*
> *1 Tbs. cornstarch*
> *1/2 cup granulated sugar*
> *5 large egg yolks*
> *4 Tbs. (1/2 stick) butter, room temperature*
> *2 Devil's Food Cake* layers, cooled*
> *Classic Chocolate Buttercream**
> *1/4 cup Candied Lemon Rind**

Grate zest from lemon. Squeeze lemon juice into a 1-cup measure. Add sufficient orange liqueur to make 1/2 cup liquid. In top half of a double boiler, combine cornstarch and sugar. Add egg yolks and butter; beat until smooth. Place over hot water and add lemon juice mixture, blending well. Cook, stirring constantly from bottom and around sides of pan, until custard is sufficiently thick to coat spoon. Remove from heat and beat with a whisk until cool. Spread one cake layer with lemon custard filling and top with second cake layer. Spread sides and top of assembled cake with Classic Chocolate Buttercream. Sprinkle top of cake with Candied Lemon Rind. Serves 8 to 10.

Chocolate Lovers' Lane Cake

A fabulous combination.

> *2 cups sour cream*
> *1 tsp. vanilla extract*
> *3 cups shredded coconut*
> *1 cup chopped walnuts*
> *1 cup mixed candied fruit, finely diced*
> *1 1/2 cups confectioners' sugar, sifted*
> *2 Devil's Food Cake* layers, preferably baked in 8-inch*
> *   square pans, cooled*
> *4 Tbs. kirsch or orange liqueur*

In a large bowl, mix sour cream, vanilla, coconut, walnuts, and candied fruit. Stir in confectioners' sugar. Brush each cake layer with 2 tablespoons of kirsch or orange liqueur. Spread one layer with half of sour cream mixture. Cover with second layer and spread with remaining mixture, leaving sides of cake unfrosted. Serves 6 to 8.

Plum Beautiful Devil's Food Cake

> *2 Devil's Food Cake* layers, cooled*
> *4 Tbs. Mirabelle liqueur*
> *1 1-lb., 14-oz. can whole purple plums*
> *1/2 cup seedless raisins*
> *1/2 cup chopped pecans or walnuts*
> *1/4 cup granulated sugar*
> *Mirabelle Whipped Cream (recipe follows)*
> *Additional chopped pecans or walnuts, optional*

Moisten each cake layer with 2 tablespoons of liqueur. Drain and pit plums, reserving 2 tablespoons liquid. Place plums in work bowl of a food processor or blender; process or blend until smooth. In a saucepan, combine plum pulp, raisins, nuts, sugar, and reserved plum liquid. Place over medium heat and bring to a boil. Cook, stirring, until mixture is thick, about 5 minutes. Cool to room temperature. Cover one cake layer with plum filling; top with second layer. Cover top and sides of assembled cake with Mirabelle Whipped Cream. If desired, sprinkle with chopped nuts. Refrigerate until ready to serve. Serves 6 to 8.

Mirabelle Whipped Cream

1/2 pint heavy (whipping) cream
2 Tbs. Mirabelle liqueur

In a chilled bowl with chilled beaters, whip cream until stiff peaks form. Fold in Mirabelle liqueur.

Chocolate Caramel Rum Cake

2 Tbs. granulated sugar
1/4 cup dark rum
2 Devil's Food Cake* layers, cooled
Caramel Rum Filling and Frosting (recipe follows)
Caramel Gold Dust*, optional

In a small skillet, combine sugar and rum. Place over low heat and stir until sugar has dissolved. Remove from heat and cool to room temperature. Pierce surface of each cake layer with tines of a fork; drizzle with rum mixture. Spread one layer with about a third of Caramel Rum Frosting. Top with second layer. Spread top and sides with remaining frosting. If desired, sprinkle top with Caramel Gold Dust. Serves 6 to 8.

Caramel Rum Filling and Frosting

1/2 cup granulated sugar
1/2 cup boiling water
1/2 cup (1 stick) butter, softened
1 16-oz. package confectioners' sugar
2 Tbs. dark rum

Place granulated sugar in a large skillet over low heat. Stir until melted to a pale amber syrup; remove from heat. Slowly stir in boiling water and continue to stir until sugar has dissolved. Set aside until cooled. In a large mixing bowl, beat butter until creamy. Stir in confectioners' sugar alternately with syrup and rum. Beat until smooth.

Chocolate Cheese Pudding Cake

We're not sure if this is a cake or a pudding—nonetheless, by either name, it is a rich and intensely flavored dessert.

1 lb. farmer's cheese
4 Tbs. sour cream
2/3 cup granulated sugar
4 eggs
1 tsp. almond extract
Batter for Devil's Food Cake*
Chocolate Cream Cheese Frosting (recipe follows)

Preheat oven to 350°F. Butter a 9- × 13- × 2-inch baking pan. In a mixing bowl, combine farmer's cheese, sour cream, and sugar; beat until blended. Add eggs; continue to beat until mixture is smooth. Stir in almond extract. Set aside. Prepare batter for Devil's Food Cake. Pour half into prepared pan. Spoon cheese mixture over surface;

spread out evenly. Cover with remaining batter. Bake in preheated oven for 40 to 45 minutes, or until top of cake springs back when lightly touched with fingertips. Cool cake in pan on rack for about 10 minutes. Cool to room temperature. Cover completely with Chocolate Cream Cheese Frosting. Serves 8 to 10.

Chocolate Cream Cheese Frosting

4 Tbs. butter
1 3-oz. package cream cheese, softened
1/3 cup sour cream
3 cups confectioners' sugar
1/2 cup cocoa
1 tsp. almond extract
Pinch of salt
Additional confectioners' sugar

Melt butter in a small skillet over low heat; cool to room temperature and set aside. In a mixing bowl, beat cream cheese with sour cream until light and fluffy. Stir in confectioners' sugar, cocoa, almond extract, salt, and melted butter. Beat until smooth. If necessary, add additional confectioners' sugar to bring to spreading consistency.

Chocolate Nut Tortes

Chocolate Nut Torte

This is a very rich, dark chocolate cake made with ground nuts instead of flour. When baked, the layers will be thin, slightly moist in the center, with tops that are fragile and crackly. When put together with filling, covered with icing or frosting, then allowed to mellow in the refrigerator for several hours, the cake can be cut into thin, moist, and densely delicious slices.

> *6 1-oz. squares bittersweet chocolate, coarsely chopped*
> *6 eggs, separated*
> *1/2 cup (1 stick) butter*
> *1 cup granulated sugar*
> *1 1/4 cups (6 ozs.) finely ground hazelnuts, walnuts, or*
>   *almonds*
> *1 Tbs. more granulated sugar*

Preheat oven to 375°F. Butter two 8- or 9-inch layer cake pans; line bottom of each with waxed or parchment paper cut to fit. Butter paper and flour pans. Place chocolate in top half of a double boiler over very hot water until partially melted. Remove from water and stir until smooth. Cool slightly. Add egg yolks one at a time, beating well after each addition. In a large mixing bowl, cream butter with sugar until light and fluffy. Add chocolate mixture, scraping it from pan with a rubber spatula. Beat until well blended. Fold in ground nuts; blend thoroughly. In a second bowl, beat egg whites until frothy. Continue to beat, adding sugar a little at a time, until whites hold a definite shape and are stiff but not dry. Stir a large spoonful of whites into chocolate mixture. Fold in remaining whites.

Pour batter into prepared pans, dividing evenly. Bake in pre-heated oven for 25 to 30 minutes, or until cake pulls slightly from sides of pan. Cool in pans on racks for about 5 minutes. Loosen sides of cake with spatula. Invert layers onto racks. Cool completely before filling and frosting. Makes two 8- or 9-inch layers.

Brownies Napoleon

This elegant aristocrat of the brownie family is a variation of a recipe from the Diamond Walnut people.

1/2 cup (1 stick) cold butter, cut into small cubes
2 1-oz. squares unsweetened chocolate, chopped
2 eggs
1 cup Vanilla Sugar*, or 1 cup granulated sugar plus
    1 tsp. vanilla extract
1/2 cup sifted cake flour
1 cup coarsely chopped walnuts
Buttercream Frosting (recipe follows)
Chocolate Glaze (recipe follows)

Butter an 8-inch square baking pan and dust lightly with sugar. Preheat oven to 350°F. Place butter and chocolate in a large, heat-proof mixing bowl. Place bowl over, not in, simmering water until chocolate is partially melted. Remove bowl from water and stir until mixture is smooth. Let cool to room temperature. Add eggs one at a time, beating after each addition. Add Vanilla Sugar, and continue to beat until well blended. Fold in flour, then walnuts. Spoon into prepared pan and bake in preheated oven for 20 minutes, or until a cake tester inserted near center comes out clean. Center will remain slightly soft—do not overbake. Cool cake on a rack in pan for about 30 minutes. Turn out onto a second cake rack, then turn right side up and spread with Buttercream Frosting. Let stand until frosting has set, then spoon Chocolate Glaze over surface. Cut into bite-size squares or bars. Serves 8 to 10.

Buttercream Frosting

2 Tbs. butter, softened
2 cups confectioners' sugar, sifted
2 Tbs. light cream
2 Tbs. brandy

In a mixing bowl, combine butter, sugar, cream, and brandy. Stir to blend.

Chocolate Glaze

3 1-oz. squares semisweet chocolate, chopped
2 tsp. butter

Place chocolate and butter in top half of a double boiler over hot water. Stir until chocolate has dissolved and mixture is smooth. Remove pan from water, and let mixture cool to room temperature before using.

Mocha Mousse Torte

2 Chocolate Nut Torte* layers, cooled
Mocha Mousse (recipe follows)
Bittersweet Chocolate Glaze (recipe follows)
Walnut halves, optional

Place one cake layer on an 8-inch cardboard cake support or a round of cardboard wrapped in foil, and place it on a rack supported over a flat baking sheet to catch drippings from glaze. Spread with Mocha Mousse and cover with second layer. Pour tepid glaze over center of assembled cake and quickly spread it onto sides with a metal spatula. If desired, garnish cake with walnut halves. When glaze is firm, transfer cake on cardboard support to a serving platter. Serves 8 to 10.

Mocha Mousse

6 ozs. bittersweet chocolate, chopped
3 Tbs. very strong coffee or coffee liqueur
3 egg yolks
1 cup heavy (whipping) cream

Place chocolate and coffee in top half of a double boiler over simmering water until chocolate has partially melted. Remove from heat and stir mixture until smooth. Add egg yolks one at a time, beating well after each addition. Continue to beat until mixture is thoroughly cooled. In a chilled bowl with chilled beaters, beat cream until soft peaks form when beaters are lifted from bowl. Fold into chocolate mixture. Refrigerate for 30 minutes or until ready to use.

Bittersweet Chocolate Glaze

1 cup heavy (whipping) cream
1/4 cup light corn syrup
6 1-oz. squares bittersweet chocolate

In a small, heavy saucepan, combine cream and corn syrup. Bring to a full boil; add chocolate, and immediately remove from heat. Cover pan and let mixture stand for 5 minutes, then stir gently until smooth. Let stand until just slightly warm and thickened before using.

Creole Nut Layer Cake with Cream Cheese Pecan Frosting

A rich nut cake layer sandwiched between two creole chocolate layers, covered with a rich cream cheese nut frosting.

2 1-oz. squares unsweetened chocolate
1/4 cup very hot coffee, preferably dark roast, freshly
*   brewed*
1 3/4 cup unsifted all-purpose flour
1 tsp. baking powder
1 tsp. baking soda

1/4 tsp. salt
1/2 cup (1 stick) butter, room temperature
2 cups Vanilla Sugar*, or 2 cups granulated sugar plus
    1 tsp. vanilla extract
3 eggs
1 cup buttermilk
1/2 cup chopped pecans
Cream Cheese Nut Frosting (recipe follows)

Preheat oven to 350°F. Grease three 8- or 9-inch layer cake pans. Sprinkle each lightly with sugar, rotating pans to spread sugar evenly. Place chocolate in a small bowl and add hot coffee; stir until chocolate has dissolved. Cool to room temperature. Sift flour, baking powder, soda, and salt onto paper. Set aside. In large bowl of an electric mixer, combine butter, Vanilla Sugar, and eggs. Beat at high speed until thoroughly blended and fluffy, about 5 minutes. (Or place butter and sugar in a large mixing bowl and beat with a whisk until light. Add eggs one at a time, beating well after each addition.) Add flour to batter alternately with buttermilk, blending just until smooth. Measure 1 1/2 cups batter into a small bowl. Stir in chopped nuts; pour into a prepared pan. Add chocolate mixture to remaining batter; mix until smooth. Spoon into remaining pans, dividing evenly.

Bake layers 25 to 30 minutes, or until cake testers inserted in centers come out clean. Cool cakes in pans on racks for about 10 minutes. Invert and remove pans. Cool layers completely. Spread one chocolate layer with cream cheese frosting. Top with nut layer; spread with frosting and cover with remaining chocolate layer. Spread remaining frosting on sides and top of cake. If desired, garnish with pecan halves. Serves 8 to 10.

Cream Cheese Nut Frosting

1/2 cup (1 stick) butter, room temperature
1 8-oz. package cream cheese, room temperature
2 tsp. vanilla extract
1 1-lb. box confectioners' sugar
1 cup chopped pecans

In a large bowl, beat butter and cream cheese until light and fluffy. Fold in vanilla. Add confectioners' sugar in four parts, blending well after each addition. Beat until smooth. Fold in chopped pecans.

Chocolate Nut Cake with Currant Jelly and Ricotta Whipped Cream Frosting

4 Tbs. currant jelly
2 Tbs. kirsch
2 Chocolate Nut Torte* layers, cooled
Ricotta Whipped Cream (recipe follows)
1/2 cup finely chopped walnuts

Stir 1 tablespoon kirsch into currant jelly. Spread on one cake layer; cover with about a fourth of Ricotta Whipped Cream. Top with second layer and moisten with remaining kirsch. Spread top and sides of cake with remaining Ricotta Whipped Cream. Press chopped nuts into sides of cake. Refrigerate cake several hours before serving. Serves 8 to 10.

Ricotta Whipped Cream

1 tsp. unflavored gelatin
1/4 cup milk
4 Tbs. ricotta cheese
4 Tbs. confectioners' sugar
1/4 tsp. vanilla extract
1/2 pint heavy (whipping) cream

In a small saucepan, sprinkle gelatin over milk. Place over low heat, stirring, until gelatin has dissolved. Pour into a mixing bowl; stir in ricotta cheese, sugar, and vanilla. In a chilled bowl with chilled beaters, beat cream until stiff peaks form. Fold in ricotta mixture. Refrigerate until thickened to spreading consistency.

Old-Fashioned Southern Chocolate Cakes

Old-Fashioned Southern Chocolate Cake

A wonderfully versatile, moist, and light chocolate cake.

1 3/4 cups all-purpose flour
2 tsp. baking powder
1/2 tsp. salt
4 1-oz. squares unsweetened chocolate, chopped
5 Tbs. coffee, freshly brewed, or coffee liqueur
3/4 cup (1 1/2 sticks) butter, softened
1 1/2 cups Vanilla Sugar*, or 1 1/2 cups granulated sugar
*   plus 1 tsp. vanilla extract*
3 large eggs, separated
1/2 cup milk

Preheat oven to 350°F. Butter a 9- × 13- × 2-inch baking pan. Line bottom with parchment or waxed paper. Butter paper and flour pan. Sift flour, baking powder, and salt onto waxed paper. Place chocolate and coffee or coffee liqueur in top of a double boiler over, not in, simmering water until chocolate is partially melted. Remove pan from water and stir until mixture is smooth. Set aside, stirring occasionally, until ready to use. In a large mixing bowl, beat butter with sugar until very light and fluffy. Add egg yolks in four parts, beating well after each addition. Fold in chocolate mixture until no streaks of chocolate remain.

Add flour mixture alternately with milk, beginning and ending with flour. Beat egg whites until soft peaks form. Stir one-fourth into batter, then fold in remainder. Spoon batter into prepared pan; bake in preheated oven for 20 minutes, or until a cake tester inserted in center comes out clean. Let cool in pan on a rack for about 5 minutes. Turn out on a lightly greased rack; brush lining paper lightly with cold water, then peel off paper. Place a second rack over cake and invert. Cool to room temperature. Makes one 9- × 13- × 2-inch cake.

Note: This cake can be cut across into two equal halves, then each half can be split lengthwise for a total of 4 layers. Or it can be cut into individual servings, split, and filled with any number of great things. It's also good simply topped with confectioners' sugar.

Cherry Cheese Chocolate Cake

1 Old-Fashioned Southern Chocolate Cake*, cooled
1 8-oz. package cream cheese, softened
2 Tbs. light (or half-and-half) cream, or sour cream
1/4 cup granulated sugar
1/4 tsp. almond or vanilla extract
Cherry Jubilee Sauce (recipe follows)

In a mixing bowl, beat cream cheese with cream and sugar until blended and smooth. Stir in almond or vanilla extract. Cut cooled cake into six equal squares. With a serrated knife, cut each square in half horizontally. Spread bottom halves with cream cheese mixture, dividing evenly. Cover each with top cake layer. Place on individual dessert plates. Spoon warm Cherry Jubilee Sauce over each and serve at once. Serves 6.

Cherry Jubilee Sauce

1 16-oz. can pitted dark sweet cherries
1/4 cup granulated sugar
2 Tbs. cornstarch
2 Tbs. kirsch, cherry brandy, or liqueur

Drain cherries, reserve juice. Set cherries aside. In a saucepan, blend sugar and cornstarch; gradually add cherry juice, blending well. Cook, stirring, over medium heat, until mixture thickens. Remove from heat. Stir in kirsch, brandy, or liqueur; add cherries. Serve warm over cake squares.

Mocha Cream–Filled Cake Squares

1 Old-Fashioned Southern Chocolate Cake*, cooled
1 1/2 cups light (or half-and-half) cream
1 3 3/4-oz. package instant vanilla pudding
Whipped cream, lightly sweetened
1 Tbs. instant coffee
Additional instant coffee, optional

Cut baked cake into 6 or 8 equal squares; split each square horizontally into 2 layers. Set aside. In a large mixing bowl, combine cream, pudding mix, and instant coffee. Beat with a whisk until well blended. Refrigerate until ready to use. Spread filling on bottom half of each cake square, dividing evenly; cover with top halves. Just before serving, spoon sweetened whipped cream over each and, if desired, sprinkle with instant coffee. Serves 6 or 8.

Very American Layer Cakes

Special Frostings for Old-Fashioned Layer Cakes

Rum Buttercream Frosting

Creamy, rich, and very spreadable.

> *1 cup light cream*
> *1/4 cup all-purpose flour*
> *1 egg yolk*
> *1 cup (2 sticks) butter, softened*
> *1 cup confectioners' sugar*
> *1 Tbs. dark or light rum*
> *Additional confectioners' sugar as needed*

In a saucepan, combine cream and flour. Place over medium heat and cook, stirring constantly, until mixture thickens. Remove from heat; fold in egg yolk. Cool to room temperature, stirring occasionally. In a large mixing bowl, cream butter with sugar until very light and fluffy. Fold in rum, then cooled flour mixture. Continue to beat at medium speed until sugar is completely dissolved and frosting is very light and fluffy. Add additional confectioners' sugar as needed to bring mixture to spreading consistency. Sufficient to fill and frost two 8- or 9-inch cake layers.

Uncooked Buttercream Frosting with Liqueur

Soak cake layers with Dessert Syrup* flavored with liqueur, then use the same liqueur in this frosting.

1/2 cup (1 stick) butter, softened
1/3 cup light corn syrup
1 lb. confectioners' sugar, sifted
2 Tbs. liqueur

In a large mixing bowl, cream butter with corn syrup until light and fluffy. Add sugar, about 1/4 cup at a time, alternately with liqueur, about 1 teaspoon at a time, beating well after each addition. Then add sufficient additional sugar to bring mixture to spreading consistency. Sufficient to fill and frost two 8- or 9-inch cake layers.

Mocha Buttercream

A smooth and glossy, deep chocolate frosting.

1 cup granulated sugar
1/2 cup water
1/4 tsp. cream of tartar
4 egg yolks
1 1/2 cups (3 sticks) butter, softened
6 1-oz. squares bittersweet chocolate, chopped
4 Tbs. water
1 Tbs. instant coffee

Combine sugar, water, and cream of tartar in a saucepan. Cover; bring to a boil over medium heat. Boil until sugar has dissolved. Uncover and continue to cook until mixture reaches 234°F. on a candy thermometer. In large mixing bowl of an electric mixer, beat yolks at medium speed until about triple in volume. Add sugar syrup in a thin, steady stream, beating constantly. Continue to beat until mixture is very thick. Add butter about a tablespoon at a time, beating well after each addition. Combine chocolate and water in top half of a double boiler over simmering water; stir until chocolate has partially melted. Remove from heat and stir until smooth. Stir in instant coffee. Fold into yolk mixture, blending well. Refrigerate until desired consistency is obtained. Sufficient to fill and frost two 8- or 9-inch cake layers.

Tropical Fruit Layer Cake

1 Tbs. cornstarch
1/2 cup rum or water
1 1 lb., 4-oz. can crushed pineapple
1/2 cup light brown sugar, firmly packed
1 cup diced mixed candied fruit
1/2 tsp. vanilla
1/2 tsp. ground cinnamon
1/4 tsp. ground ginger
1/2 cup chopped walnuts
1/2 cup shredded coconut
2 Classic American Cake* layers, cooled
Sweetened whipped cream, optional

In a small bowl, stir cornstarch into rum or water until smooth. In a saucepan, combine pineapple, sugar, and candied fruit; stir in vanilla, cinnamon, and ginger. Cook, stirring, over medium heat until mixture simmers; stir in cornstarch mixture. Add walnuts and coconut. Simmer, stirring occasionally, until mixture thickens. Cool to room temperature. Place one cake layer on a decorative cake plate and spread with about half of tropical fruit mixture. Cover with second cake layer; spoon remaining mixture over surface. If desired, frost sides of cake with sweetened whipped cream. Serves 6 to 8.

Classic American Cake

Could anything be better?

2 cups cake flour
2 tsp. baking powder
1/4 tsp. salt

1/2 cup (1 stick) butter, softened
1 cup Vanilla Sugar*, or 1 cup granulated sugar plus
    1 tsp. vanilla extract
3 eggs
3/4 cup milk

Preheat oven to 350°F. Butter two 8- or 9-inch round cake pans; line with parchment or waxed paper cut to fit. Butter paper and flour pans. Sift flour, baking powder, and salt onto paper. In a large mixing bowl, cream butter with Vanilla Sugar until light and fluffy. Add eggs one at a time, beating well after each addition. Fold in flour mixture alternately with milk, beginning and ending with flour.

    Spoon batter into prepared pans, dividing evenly. Bake in preheated oven for 25 to 30 minutes, or until cake testers inserted in centers come out clean. Cool on racks in pans for about 5 minutes, then invert onto racks. Cool completely. Fill and frost as desired. Makes two 8- or 9-inch layers.

Chocolate Chip Cake with Snow Leopard Cream

Batter for Classic American Cake*
3/4 cup semisweet miniature chocolate chips
Snow Leopard Cream (recipe follows)

Preheat oven to 350°F. Butter two 8- or 9-inch layer cake pans; line with parchment or waxed paper cut to fit; butter paper and flour pans. Fold chocolate chips into cake batter. Spoon into prepared pans. Bake in preheated oven for 25 to 30 minutes, or until cake testers inserted in centers come out clean. Cool on racks in pans for about 5 minutes, then invert onto racks. Cool completely. Fill and frost with Snow Leopard Cream. Serves 6 to 8.

Snow Leopard Cream

1 tsp. unflavored gelatin
3 Tbs. water
1/2 pint heavy (whipping) cream
1 Tbs. granulated sugar
3/4 cup semisweet miniature chocolate chips

In a very small saucepan, sprinkle gelatin over water. Stir over low heat until gelatin dissolves and mixture is clear. Set aside until cool. In a chilled bowl with chilled beaters, beat cream until stiff peaks form; sprinkle with sugar. Add dissolved gelatin mixture. Beat until stiff; fold in chocolate chips.

California Layer Cake

Cake layers rich with walnuts and raisins, frosted with sunny Orange Buttercream.

Batter for Classic American Cake*, substituting 2 tsp.
orange extract for vanilla
1/2 cup golden seedless raisins
1/2 cup chopped walnuts
1/4 cup minced Candied Orange Rind*
Orange Buttercream (recipe follows)
Additional slivered Candied Orange Rind

Preheat oven to 350°F. Butter two 8- or 9-inch layer cake pans; line with parchment or waxed paper cut to fit. Butter paper and flour pans. Fold raisins, walnuts, and orange peel into cake batter. Spoon batter into prepared pans, dividing evenly. Bake in preheated oven for 25 to

30 minutes, or until cake testers inserted in centers come out clean. Cool in pans for about 5 minutes, then invert onto racks and cool completely. Fill and frost with Orange Buttercream; garnish top with slivered candied orange peel. Serves 6 to 8.

Orange Buttercream

2 3-oz. packages cream cheese, softened
1/2 cup (1 stick) butter, softened
1 1-lb. package confectioners' sugar, sifted
4 Tbs. freshly squeezed orange juice
1 tsp. grated orange rind

In a large bowl, beat cream cheese and butter until light and fluffy. Stir in sugar a little at a time, and beat until smooth. Add orange juice and grated rind and blend well. Add additional orange juice if necessary to bring mixture to spreading consistency.

Heavenly Angel Cakes

Angel Food Cake

An all-American favorite, this light and airy cake is a perfect foil for a fruit glaze or a delicate whipped cream filling and frosting.

1 1/4 cup sifted cake flour
1/2 cup super fine granulated sugar
12 egg whites

1/2 tsp. almond extract
1/4 tsp. cream of tartar
1 1/2 cups more super fine granulated sugar

Preheat oven to 325°F. Sift flour and 1/2 cup sugar onto paper. Set aside. In a large bowl, beat egg whites with an electric mixer at high speed until foamy. Add almond extract and cream of tartar. Continue to beat until soft peaks form. Gradually add 1 1/4 cups sugar, and continue to beat until mixture is very glossy and stiff peaks form when beater is lifted from bowl. Fold in flour mixture in three parts, folding only until blended. Spoon batter into a 10-inch ungreased tube pan. Bake in preheated oven for 1 hour, or until a cake tester inserted in center comes out clean. Cake should be lightly browned, and sides should pull away from pan. Invert pan and let cake stand until cooled to room temperature. Remove from pan. Makes one 10-inch tube cake.

Angel Food Cake with Madeira Glaze

Madeira and lemon juice make a luscious glaze to transform a plain angel cake into pure heaven.

1 Angel Food Cake*, cooled
1 cup sifted confectioners' sugar
1/4 cup dry Madeira wine
1/4 cup fresh lemon juice

Place cooled cake on a large platter with a slight rim. In a small bowl, combine remaining ingredients and stir until blended. With a fork, pierce top of cake at 1-inch intervals. Slowly spoon glaze over top, letting it soak in and run down sides and onto plate. Let stand at room temperature until ready to serve. To serve, cut cake with a serrated knife into thick slices and place on rimmed dessert plates. Spoon a little of glaze that has not soaked into cake over each slice. Serves 6 or 8.

Candy Flower Garland Cake

Festive and fun—perfect for a child's birthday party.

> *1 Angel Food Cake*, cooled*
> *Fluffy Pink Frosting (recipe follows)*
> *Candy Flower Garlands (recipe follows)*

Cover top and sides of cake with frosting. Refrigerate until frosting is firm. Just before serving, arrange a candy flower garland around top edge of cake; surround base with a second flower garland.

Fluffy Pink Frosting

> *1 3-oz. package cream cheese, softened*
> *1/2 cup confectioners' sugar*
> *1/4 cup light cream*
> *1/4 tsp. almond extract*
> *1/2 pint heavy (whipping) cream*
> *1 to 2 drops red food coloring, optional*

In a large mixing bowl, beat cream cheese until light and fluffy. Fold in confectioner's sugar, light cream, almond extract, and, if desired, red food coloring. In a chilled bowl with chilled beaters, whip heavy cream until soft peaks form; fold into cream cheese mixture.

Candy Flower Garlands

12 or 16 large green gumdrops
Confectioners' sugar
12 or 16 additional gumdrops in various colors (other
than green)
Jellybeans in assorted colors

Cut green gumdrops across into thin slices. Sprinkle work surface with sugar to avoid sticking. Flatten gumdrop slices with rolling pin until no more than 1/4 inch thick, coating well. Cut with a sharp knife into leaves and flower petals. With kitchen shears, cut remaining gumdrops into small rounds. Arrange leaves alternately with petals grouped around gumdrop center to resemble flowers on top edge of cake and around base.

The Best Pound Cakes

Classic Pound Cake

This velvety-textured cake combines the most straightforward ingredients to produce a cake that is exceptionally light without relying upon chemical leavening agents such as baking soda or baking powder. It's a great cake to make in advance, as it improves and ripens if allowed to remain in the refrigerator for several days. Also, it may be frozen to reappear whenever a great dessert is wanted.

2 3/4 cups all-purpose flour
1/4 cup cornstarch
1/2 tsp. mace

1 1/4 cup (2 1/2 sticks) butter, softened
1 1-lb. box confectioners' sugar
6 eggs
1 tsp. vanilla extract
1/2 tsp. almond extract, optional

Preheat oven to 325°F. Coat two 9 1/4- × 5 1/4-inch loaf pans generously with butter, then line bottom of each with waxed or parchment
paper cut to fit. Sprinkle paper and sides of pans with granulated
sugar. Rotate pans to distribute sugar evenly; shake out excess. Sift
flour with cornstarch and mace onto paper. Set aside.

In a large mixing bowl, beat butter with sugar until very light and
fluffy. Add 2 eggs, one at a time, beating well after each addition, then
fold in 1 cup of flour mixture. Repeat with 2 more eggs and 1 more
cup of flour, then repeat again with remaining eggs and flour. Fold in
vanilla and, if desired, almond extract. Spoon batter into prepared
pans, dividing evenly. Bake in preheated oven for 1 hour and 15
minutes, or until tops of cakes spring back easily when lightly pressed
with fingertips. Cool cakes in pans on racks for 10 minutes, then turn
out onto racks and immediately turn top side up. Cool to room temperature before slicing or storing. Makes two 9 1/4- × 5 1/4-inch loaf
cakes, one to glaze and one to serve plain. Each loaf will serve 6 to 8.

Note: A nice way to keep these cakes until ready to use is to wrap
them in two or three thicknesses of cheesecloth and sprinkle cheesecloth liberally with bourbon, dry sherry, or brandy. Wrap in foil and
refrigerate for 2 or 3 days or in freezer for up to 6 weeks.

Buttered Rum Pound Cake

Batter for Classic Pound Cake*
1/2 cup chopped walnuts
2 tsp. all-purpose flour
Buttered Rum Glaze (recipe follows)

Preheat oven to 325°F. Butter a 10-inch tube or 12-inch Bundt pan. Mix nuts with flour, coating evenly; fold into cake batter. Spoon batter into prepared pan. Bake in preheated oven for 1 hour and 30 minutes, or until a cake tester inserted in center comes out clean. Cool cake on a rack in pan for 10 minutes. Invert onto rack. Cover bottom of cake with a round, rimmed platter and turn it right side up. While still warm, prick top of cake at 1-inch intervals with tines of a fork. Spoon about a fourth of glaze over cake; allow to soak in. Repeat until all of glaze is used. Serves 10 to 12.

Buttered Rum Glaze

1/2 cup (1 stick) butter
3 Tbs. water
1 cup granulated sugar
4 Tbs. dark Jamaican rum
1/2 cup chopped walnuts

Combine butter, water, sugar, and rum in a small saucepan; bring to a boil. Boil mixture, stirring constantly, for 1 to 2 minutes. Remove from heat and stir in walnuts. Makes enough glaze for one 10- or 12-inch cake.

Lemon Pound Cake

Chopped lemon zest makes this pound cake very fragrant and doubly delicious.

Zest from 1 large unblemished lemon (sufficient to make about 2 Tbs. chopped zest)
3 cups all-purpose flour
1/2 tsp. baking powder

1/8 tsp. salt
1 1/2 cups (3 sticks) butter, softened
3 cups Vanilla Sugar*, or 3 cups granulated sugar plus
*   1 tsp. vanilla extract*
5 eggs
1 cup milk

Preheat oven to 325°F. Butter a 10- × 4-inch tube pan; line bottom with parchment or waxed paper cut to fit. Butter paper and dust it lightly with granulated sugar; tilt pan back and forth to distribute sugar evenly. Invert pan; shake out excess. Finely chop lemon zest into tiny cubes (don't grind or grate) and place them in a saucepan. Cover with water, and simmer over low heat for about 15 minutes. Drain into a colander, blot dry, then let stand for about 30 minutes at room temperature to dry thoroughly. Sift flour onto paper, then spoon it back into sifter. Add baking powder and salt, and sift once more onto paper. Set aside.

In a large mixing bowl, cream butter with Vanilla Sugar until light and fluffy. Add eggs one at a time, beating well after each addition. Fold in flour mixture in four parts alternately with milk, blending well. Stir in chopped lemon zest. Spoon batter into prepared pan. Place in preheated oven; cover loosely with a sheet of aluminum foil and bake for about 30 minutes. Remove foil and continue to bake an additional hour, or until a cake tester inserted in center comes out clean. Cool cake in pan on a rack for about 10 minutes. Loosen sides with a small spatula; invert and turn out on a second rack. Remove paper and turn cake right side up. Cool at room temperature. Makes one 10-inch pound cake.

Pound Cake with Bourbon Glaze

1 Classic Pound Cake*, fresh from the oven
1/2 cup granulated sugar
1/4 cup bourbon whiskey

Turn out pound cake while warm onto a rack, then place right side up in a glass baking dish. In a small saucepan, combine sugar with bourbon. Stir over low heat only until sugar has dissolved. Spoon warm glaze over top of warm cake. Let stand for several hours or overnight before serving.

Walnut or Pecan Pound Cake

Prepare Classic Pound Cake* as directed, first folding 1/2 cup chopped walnuts or pecans into flour mixture.

Bourbon Pound Cake with Walnuts and Butterscotch Sauce

The heady richness of bourbon enhances this Southern specialty.

> *2 1/2 cups all-purpose flour*
> *2 tsp. baking powder*
> *1/4 tsp. salt*
> *1 3-oz. package chopped walnuts*
> *1 cup (2 sticks) unsalted butter, softened*
> *1 cup granulated sugar*
> *5 eggs, separated*
> *1/4 cup bourbon whiskey*
> *Butterscotch Sauce with Bourbon and Walnuts (recipe follows)*

Preheat oven to 350°F. Coat a 9- × 5-inch loaf pan with soft butter, and line bottom with parchment or waxed paper cut to fit. Do not butter paper. Sift flour with baking powder and salt onto paper. In a small bowl, combine 2 tablespoons of flour mixture with nuts; set aside. In a large mixing bowl, cream butter with sugar until light and fluffy. Add egg yolks one at a time, beating well after each addition. Fold in flour alternately with bourbon, taking care not to overmix. Fold in nuts.

In a second bowl, beat egg whites until very stiff but not dry; fold into batter. Spoon batter into prepared pan and bake in preheated oven for 55 to 60 minutes, or until a cake tester inserted near center comes out clean. Do not overbake. Let cake cool in pan for about 10 minutes, then turn out onto a rack and cool completely. Serve thick slices in individual dessert bowls; top with Butterscotch Sauce. Makes 12 to 14 individual servings.

Butterscotch Sauce with Bourbon and Walnuts

1/2 cup light brown sugar, firmly packed
3 Tbs. butter
Pinch of salt
1 cup heavy (whipping) cream
2 Tbs. bourbon whiskey

Combine sugar, butter, salt, and cream in a saucepan. Place over low heat, and stir until sugar has dissolved. Let simmer for about 10 minutes. Stir in bourbon and cook, stirring for a final 2 minutes. Serve warm or at room temperature. Makes about 1 1/2 cups sauce.

Chocolate Pound Cake

A rich, dense cake that can be served without further embellishment or, for true chocoholics, covered with thick Chocolate Fudge Frosting.

3 cups all-purpose flour
1/4 tsp. salt
1/2 tsp. baking powder
1/2 cup cocoa
1 cup (2 sticks) butter
1/2 cup vegetable shortening
3 cups Vanilla Sugar*, or 3 cups granulated sugar plus
    1 tsp. vanilla extract
5 eggs
1 cup milk
1/4 cup dark rum
Confectioners' sugar or Chocolate Fudge Frosting (recipe
    follows), optional
Walnut or pecan halves, optional

Preheat oven to 325°F. Generously butter a 10-inch tube pan. Sift flour with salt, baking powder, and cocoa onto waxed paper. Set aside. In a large bowl, cream butter with shortening. Add Vanilla Sugar, and continue to beat until light and fluffy. Add eggs one at a time, beating well after each addition. Fold in flour mixture alternately with milk and rum. Spoon batter into prepared pan. Bake in preheated oven for 1 hour and 20 minutes, or until a cake tester inserted in center comes out clean. Cool cake in pan for about 5 minutes, then run a knife around edge and invert onto a cake rack. Let stand until cooled. Just before serving, sprinkle cake with sifted confectioners' sugar, or, if desired, cover with Chocolate Fudge Frosting and garnish with walnut or pecan halves. Serves 10 to 12.

Chocolate Fudge Frosting

1/2 cup (1 stick) butter
2 1-oz. squares unsweetened chocolate
2 cups Vanilla Sugar*, or 2 cups granulated sugar plus
    1 tsp. vanilla extract
1/2 cup heavy (whipping) cream

In a large, heavy saucepan, melt butter with chocolate over low heat. Add remaining ingredients; increase heat to high. Bring mixture to a full boil, stirring constantly. Boil for 2 minutes. Remove from heat; let stand without stirring until cooled. Beat to spreading consistency; immediately spread over top and on sides of cake. (Work quickly—this icing thickens as it cools.) Makes sufficient frosting for one 10-inch tube cake.

Marie Antoinette's "Bread Pudding"

"Let them eat cake," this lady said when told the populace lacked bread. A royal idea for a pudding!

> *8 to 10 1/2-inch slices toasted Classic Pound Cake**
> *About 3 Tbs. softened butter*
> *1/2 cup diced mixed candied fruit, raisins, or chopped*
> *   dates*
> *4 large eggs*
> *1/2 cup granulated sugar*
> *3 1/2 cups milk or light cream*
> *1/2 cup sweet or semisweet sherry*
> *Sherry Whipped Cream (recipe follows), optional*

Preheat oven to 325°F. Generously butter a long, shallow (2-quart) baking dish. Butter one side of each toasted cake slice. Place, slightly overlapping, in a single layer in baking dish. Sprinkle with candied fruit, raisins, or dates. In a mixing bowl, beat eggs with sugar until blended. Whisk in milk and sherry; pour evenly over cake slices in dish. Let stand at room temperature until liquid is almost absorbed, about 30 minutes. Cover dish and seal with foil. Bake in preheated oven for 30 minutes; remove foil and continue to bake until top of pudding is lightly browned. Serve warm or at room temperature, topped with Sherry Whipped Cream, if desired. Serves 8 to 10.

Sherry Whipped Cream

1/2 pint heavy (whipping) cream
2 Tbs. confectioners' sugar
1 Tbs. sweet or semisweet sherry

In a chilled bowl with chilled beaters, beat cream until soft peaks form. Fold in sugar and sherry; continue to beat until stiff. Refrigerate until ready to use.

Treasure Chest Pound Cake

1 Classic Pound Cake*, cooled
1 cup Praline Powder*
1/2 cup apricot jam, melted and strained
1/2 cup heavy (whipping) cream
1 Tbs. confectioners' sugar
1 Tbs. strawberry liqueur or kirsch
1/2 pint fresh strawberries, washed and hulled
1 8-oz. can pineapple chunks, drained

Slice a 1/4-inch-thick layer from top of cake, for lid of chest. With a sharp knife, cut an oblong all around inside of cake 1/2 inch from sides and carefully scoop out center with fork, to form chest. Brush outside of chest and top of lid with all but 2 tablespoons of melted and strained jam. Pat Praline Powder onto sides of chest and top of lid, covering completely. No more than 2 hours before serving, beat cream in a chilled bowl with chilled beaters until stiff. Fold in sugar and liqueur or kirsch. Spoon into bottom of chest. Cover with a mixture of strawberries and pineapple, mounding them high. Brush fruit with remaining melted jam. Slant lid over fruit, holding it up with concealed toothpicks. Serves 8 to 10.

Sophisticated Ginger Cakes

Candied Ginger Cake

Like gingerbread, but more sophisticated and complex in flavor than its country cousin.

> *1 tsp. vinegar*
> *1 cup milk*
> *2 cups all-purpose flour*
> *1 cup chopped walnuts or pecans*
> *2 ozs. candied ginger, finely chopped*
> *1 Tbs. cocoa*
> *1 tsp. baking soda*
> *1 tsp. baking powder*
> *1 1/2 tsp. salt*
> *1/2 cup (1 stick) butter*
> *1 cup granulated sugar*
> *2 eggs*
> *3/4 cup molasses*
> *1/4 cup dark rum*
> *Applesauce Whipped Cream (recipe follows), optional*

Preheat oven to 350°F. Butter and flour a 12- × 8- × 2-inch baking pan. Stir vinegar into milk. Set aside. In a bowl, combine 1/4 cup flour with nuts and ginger; stir to coat evenly. Sift remaining flour, cocoa, soda, baking powder, and salt onto waxed paper. In a large bowl, beat butter until light and fluffy. Add sugar in four parts, beating well after each addition. Beat in eggs. Add molasses and rum; beat until blended. Add flour alternately with milk, blending well after each addition. Fold in ginger and nuts. Pour batter into prepared pan. Bake in preheated oven for 25 to 30 minutes, or until a cake tester inserted in center comes out clean. Cool on a rack in pan. To serve, cut into squares in pan. If desired, serve with Applesauce Whipped Cream or with slightly sweetened sour cream. Serves 8.

Applesauce Whipped Cream

1/2 pint heavy (whipping) cream
2 Tbs. confectioners' sugar
1/4 cup applesauce
1 Tbs. rum

In a chilled bowl with chilled beaters, beat cream until soft peaks form. Fold in sugar, applesauce, and rum.

Beer Batter Gingerbread with Sour Cream Hardsauce

This recipe promotes gingerbread from first grade into the adult class.

2 1/2 cups all-purpose flour
1 tsp. baking soda
1/2 tsp. cinnamon
1/2 tsp. ground ginger
1/4 tsp. salt
1 tsp. coarsely ground black pepper
1/2 cup (1 stick) butter, room temperature
2 Tbs. granulated sugar
1 egg
1 cup light or dark molasses
1 cup dark beer
Sour Cream Hardsauce (recipe follows)

Preheat oven to 325°F. Butter a 12- × 8- × 2-inch baking pan. Sprinkle lightly with fine, dry bread crumbs. Rotate pan to distribute crumbs evenly. In a mixing bowl, cream butter with sugar until light and fluffy. Add eggs, and beat until smooth. Stir in molasses and beer. Fold in flour mixture in four parts. Stir only until blended. Spoon batter into prepared pan. Bake in preheated oven for 45 to 50 minutes, or until a cake tester inserted in center comes out clean. Cool cake on a rack in pan. When ready to serve, cut into 6 or 8 squares; place each on a small dessert plate, and top with Sour Cream Hardsauce. Serves 6 to 8.

Sour Cream Hardsauce

1 cup sour cream
3 Tbs. confectioners' sugar
1/2 tsp. vanilla extract

Combine all ingredients in a mixing bowl; beat with a whisk until well blended. Refrigerate until chilled or until ready to use. Makes about 1 1/4 cups sauce.

Millionaire's Gingerbread

A darkly delicious, Texas-rich date-nut cake spiked with ginger.

3/4 cup hot, strong coffee
3/4 cup chopped prunes
1/4 cup dark rum
2 cups all-purpose flour
1/2 cup chopped walnuts
1 1/2 tsp. baking powder
1/4 tsp. baking soda

1 tsp. ground ginger
1/2 tsp. salt
6 Tbs. butter, softened
1 cup granulated sugar
2 eggs
Caramel Frosting (recipe follows)

Preheat oven to 350°F. Butter two 8- or 9-inch layer cake pans. Sprinkle pans lightly with sugar; rotate pans to distribute evenly. In a small bowl, pour hot coffee over prunes; add rum. Set aside until cool. Mix 2 tablespoons flour with walnuts, coating evenly. Sift remaining flour, baking powder, soda, ginger, and salt onto waxed paper. In a large mixing bowl, cream butter with sugar until light and fluffy. Add eggs one at a time, beating well after each addition. Add flour mixture alternately with prune mixture, blending well. Fold in flour-coated nuts. Pour batter equally into prepared pans. Bake in preheated oven for 20 to 25 minutes, or until cake testers inserted in centers come out clean. Cool cakes in pans on racks for about 10 minutes. Loosen sides and invert onto racks. Cool completely. Spread one layer with about one-fourth of Caramel Frosting; cover with second layer. Spread top and sides of assembled cake with remaining frosting. Serves 8 to 10.

Caramel Frosting

1 1/2 cups light brown sugar, firmly packed
1/2 cup heavy (whipping) cream
3 Tbs. butter
Pinch of salt
1 Tbs. dark rum

Combine sugar and cream in a saucepan over low heat; stir until sugar is dissolved. Increase heat to medium. Cook, stirring constantly, until mixture comes to a boil; boil for 1 minute. Remove pan from heat. Add butter and rum. Beat until thickened to spreading consistency.

Epicurean Cheese Cakes

New York Deli-Style Cheese Cake

Just as they like it on Broadway: an especially light, velvety cheese cake with just a hint of crust.

> *4 8-oz. packages cream cheese, at room temperature*
> *1 1/2 cups Vanilla Sugar*, or 1 1/2 cups granulated sugar*
> *plus 1 tsp. vanilla extract*
> *1 tsp. finely grated lemon zest*
> *3 Tbs. lemon juice*
> *3 egg yolks*
> *5 egg whites*
> *1/2 cup graham cracker crumbs*
> *Fruit sauce, optional (recipes follow)*

Preheat oven to 300°F. Spread insides of an 8-inch cheese cake pan (a 3-inch-deep cake pan) very heavily and all the way to rim with soft, preferably unsalted, butter. In a large mixing bowl, beat cream cheese with an electric beater at high speed until very light and smooth. Add Vanilla Sugar and beat until blended. Fold in lemon zest and juice. Add egg yolks one at a time, beating well after each addition. In a separate bowl, beat egg whites until very soft peaks form; fold into cheese mixture. Pour batter into prepared pan. Gently smooth out top with back of a spoon; sprinkle with about half of graham cracker crumbs.

   Bake in preheated oven for 1 1/2 to 2 hours, or until top of cake is lightly brown and feels dry to the touch. (Center will remain soft.) Place cake in pan on a rack and let stand at room temperature until thoroughly cooled, about 2 hours. Place a flat plate on top, invert, and lift off pan; sprinkle bottom of cake with remaining graham cracker crumbs. Place a second plate over top and invert cake once again.

Refrigerate 6 to 8 hours or overnight; or freeze until firm, then wrap and store in freezer until ready to serve. Serves 8 to 10.

Note: This is a wonderful cake to serve as a late dessert several hours after a hearty meal. Make plenty of hot coffee and serve as is or with a fruit sauce. Here are two of my favorites.

Mandarin Orange Sauce

3/4 cup fresh orange juice
Juice from 1/2 lemon (about 1 Tbs.)
1/2 cup granulated sugar
1 tsp. cornstarch
1/4 cup orange liqueur, or golden rum
1 8-oz. can mandarin orange sections, drained

In a saucepan, combine orange juice, lemon juice, and sugar. Place over low heat and stir until sugar has dissolved. Let simmer gently for 2 to 3 minutes, stirring occasionally. In a small bowl, stir cornstarch into liqueur; stir into simmering orange syrup mixture. Remove from heat. Add mandarin orange sections. Cool to room temperature or refrigerate until ready to serve. Makes about 1 1/2 cups sauce.

Cherry Sauce

1 16-oz. can dark sweet cherries
1/4 cup granulated sugar
1/4 cup kirsch or cherry-flavored brandy
2 Tbs. cornstarch
1/2 tsp. almond extract

Drain cherries through a colander set over a saucepan. Set cherries aside. Over medium heat bring cherry liquid to a full boil. Stir in sugar. Lower heat and let simmer. Sprinkle cornstarch over kirsch or brandy and stir until smooth. Stir into simmering liquid; cook, stirring constantly, until mixture thickens. Remove from heat; stir in almond extract and reserved cherries. Cool to room temperature or refrigerate until ready to use. Makes about 2 cups sauce.

Miniature Cheese Cakes

Bite-size and delicious—and they couldn't be easier!

1 cup chocolate wafer crumbs
2 8-oz. packages cream cheese, softened
3/4 cup Vanilla Sugar*, or 3/4 cup granulated sugar plus
*   1/2 tsp. vanilla extract*
3 eggs, separated
Sour Cream Filling (recipe follows)
Additional chocolate wafer crumbs

Generously butter 1 1/2-inch muffin tins; sprinkle evenly with chocolate wafer crumbs. Set aside. In a large mixing bowl, mix cream cheese with Vanilla Sugar until light and fluffy. Fold in egg yolks, blending well. In a separate bowl, beat egg whites until stiff peaks form; fold into egg yolk mixture. Spoon into muffin tins, filling them about 3/4 full. Bake in preheated oven for about 20 minutes. Cool for 10 to 15 minutes (centers will fall, forming indentations). Carefully remove from muffin tins. Spoon about 1 teaspoon of Sour Cream Filling into each indentation. Sprinkle each with chocolate wafer crumbs. Refrigerate until ready to serve. Makes 4 dozen.

Sour Cream Filling

1 cup sour cream
4 Tbs. confectioners' sugar
1 tsp. grated lemon zest

In a mixing bowl, combine sour cream with sugar and lemon zest. Stir until blended.

Creamy Cheese Cake with Chocolate Cookie Crumb Crust

One of the easiest of all cheese cakes to make, yet sensationally rich and flavorful.

1 1/2 cups chocolate cookie crumbs
1/2 cup granulated sugar
1/2 cup (1 stick) butter, melted and cooled
12 ozs. farmer's (pot) cheese, room temperature
3/4 cup more granulated sugar
1 Tbs. all-purpose flour
Pinch of salt
1/2 pint sour cream
2 eggs, separated
1 whole egg
1 Tbs. lemon juice
1/2 tsp. almond extract
1/2 pint heavy (whipping) cream

Place the cookie crumbs and sugar in a mixing bowl; slowly pour in melted butter while stirring with a fork. Remove about one-fourth of mixture; set aside for topping. Generously butter bottom and sides of an 8-inch springform pan; pour in crumb mixture. Press it firmly against bottom and sides of pan with back of a large spoon. Chill in refrigerator for 1 hour or longer. Preheat oven to 400°F. Carefully fit a piece of aluminum foil over crust to prevent it from scorching. Bake in preheated oven for about 5 minutes. Transfer to a rack to cool in pan before filling. (Cake will stiffen as it cools.) Place farmer's cheese, sugar, flour, and salt in a large mixing bowl; beat until mixture is well blended and smooth. Add sour cream, egg yolks, whole egg, lemon juice, and almond extract. Beat until blended, scraping down sides of bowl and turning as necessary. In a separate bowl, beat egg whites until soft peaks form; fold into sour cream mixture. Pour batter into prepared cookie crumb crust.

Reduce oven temperature to 325°F. Place cheese cake in center of oven and bake for about 1 hour, or until center is almost set but still jiggles slightly when oven rack is gently moved. Turn off oven; let cake stand in oven with door slightly open until bottom and sides of pan are completely cooled to room temperature. Refrigerate cake uncovered in pan until firm, 6 to 8 hours or overnight. To serve, remove sides of pan. Place cake on a serving plate with bottom of pan intact. Beat cream until soft peaks form. Spread evenly over top of cheese cake. Sprinkle with remaining crumb mixture. Serves 8 to 10.

Italian Cheese Cake with Two Cheeses

1/4 cup (1/2 stick) butter, softened
16 shortbread cookies
1 16-oz. package cream cheese, softened
1 15-oz. carton skim milk ricotta cheese
1 cup granulated sugar
4 eggs, separated
1 Tbs. Galliano liqueur or orange liqueur
2 Tbs. more granulated sugar
1 Tbs. more Galliano liqueur
Orange Glaze (recipe follows)

Preheat oven to 350°F. Spread butter in a thick layer on bottom and up sides of a 9-inch springform pan. Place shortbread cookies in work bowl of a food processor or blender, process or blend to fine crumbs. Spoon into buttered pan. Tap pan and shake back and forth until it is completely covered with crumbs, then invert it over paper and shake out excess crumbs. Reserve excess crumbs for topping. Set pan aside. In a large bowl, beat cream cheese until light and fluffy. Fold in half of ricotta cheese. Add 1 cup sugar and egg yolks, blend thoroughly. Stir in 1 tablespoon Galliano.

In a separate bowl, beat egg whites until stiff peaks form. Fold into cream cheese mixture. Turn into prepared pan. Bake in pre-heated oven for 40 minutes, or until mixture is firm. Remove from oven. Increase oven temperature to 475°F. Mix remaining ricotta cheese with 2 tablespoons of sugar and remaining Galliano; blend thoroughly. Spread evenly over top of cheese cake. Sprinkle with any reserved cookie crumbs. Bake in preheated 475°F oven for 5 minutes. Transfer to a wire rack; cool to room temperature. Refrigerate for at least 6 hours to allow flavors to mellow. If desired, top with Orange Glaze. Serves 10 to 12.

Orange Glaze

1 cup orange marmalade
3 Tbs. Galliano liqueur

Place marmalade in a small saucepan; add liqueur. Stir over medium heat until it comes to a full boil. Cool slightly; pour evenly over top of cheese cake.

Key West Cheese Cake

Brazil Nut Cookie Crust (recipe follows)
1 12-oz. can mango nectar
1 envelope unflavored gelatin
2 8-oz. packages cream cheese, softened

1/2 cup granulated sugar
1 tsp. grated lemon rind
1 Tbs. lemon juice
1 Tbs. vanilla extract
1/2 cup heavy (whipping) cream
1 Tbs. granulated sugar
1 Tbs. cornstarch
1 Tbs. light or dark rum
1/2 cup more heavy (whipping) cream
1 Tbs. confectioners' sugar
1 tsp. more rum
Chipped Brazil nuts for garnish

Prepare Brazil Nut Cookie Crust; set aside. Place 3/4 cup of mango nectar in a small saucepan; sprinkle with gelatin. Let stand until softened. Stir over low heat until gelatin dissolves. Cool to room temperature. Beat cream cheese, 1/2 cup granulated sugar, lemon rind, juice, and vanilla in large mixing bowl until smooth. Stir in gelatin mixture; beat until light and fluffy. In a chilled bowl with chilled beaters, beat 1/2 cup cream until soft peaks form; fold into cream cheese mixture, blending well. Pour over prepared crust. Refrigerate, uncovered, until set, about 4 hours. Mix 1 tablespoon sugar and cornstarch in a small saucepan. Gradually blend in remaining mango nectar. Cook, stirring, over medium heat until mixture boils. Remove from heat; stir in rum, and continue to stir until mixture cools slightly. Spread evenly over cheese cake. Refrigerate until topping is firm, about 30 minutes. Just before serving, remove sides of pan. Beat remaining cream until stiff peaks form; fold in remaining sugar and rum. Spread over top of cheese cake; sprinkle with nuts. Serves 6 to 8.

Brazil Nut Cookie Crust

1 cup finely ground shortbread cookie crumbs
1/4 cup finely chopped Brazil nuts
3 Tbs. butter, melted and cooled to room temperature

Preheat oven to 350°F. Combine crumbs and nuts in a mixing bowl. Drizzle with melted butter. Stir and toss until well mixed; press evenly over bottom of an ungreased 8-inch springform pan. Bake crust in preheated oven until lightly browned, about 5 minutes. Cool on a wire rack for about 30 minutes before filling.

The Ultimate Raspberry Cheese Cake

The flavor and color of this rich, smooth cheese cake are gorgeous. And it takes only about 10 minutes to prepare.

>*1/2 cup graham cracker crumbs*
>*1 8-oz. package cream cheese*
>*1 cup sifted confectioners' sugar*
>*1/2 pint heavy (whipping) cream*
>*2 cups plus 1 Tbs. water*
>*1 6-oz. package raspberry-flavored gelatin*
>*2 ozs. frozen raspberries*
>*Lightly sweetened whipped cream, optional*

Butter insides of an 8-inch-wide, 3-inch-deep round cake pan. Sprinkle with graham cracker crumbs and shake crumbs around bottom and sides until coated. Shake out excess; set aside. In a large mixing bowl, beat cream cheese with confectioners' sugar until light and fluffy. Set aside. In a separate bowl, beat heavy cream until soft peaks form. Stir about 2 tablespoons of beaten cream into cream cheese mixture; fold in remaining beaten cream. Spoon into prepared pan and smooth out evenly. In a saucepan, heat water to boiling. Remove from heat and stir in gelatin; when dissolved, add frozen raspberries. Stir until berries separate. Let stand for about 10 minutes. Pour on top of cheese mixture in pan. Refrigerate until chilled. If desired, garnish with mounds of sweetened whipped cream. Serves 10 to 12.

Cakes for Special Occasions

White Christmas Log

Coconut, candied cherries, and whipped cream are the filling and frosting for this light and airy holiday cake roll.

> *3/4 cup cake flour*
> *3/4 tsp. baking powder*
> *1/4 tsp. salt*
> *4 large eggs*
> *3/4 cup Vanilla Sugar*, or 3/4 cup granulated sugar plus*
> *   1 tsp. vanilla extract*
> *confectioners' sugar*
> *1 1/2 cups heavy (whipping) cream*
> *1 Tbs. confectioners' sugar*
> *1/2 cup chopped candied green and red cherries*
> *1/2 cup shredded or flaked coconut*
> *1 Tbs. additional coconut*

Preheat oven to 400°F. Butter a 10- × 15-inch jelly-roll pan. Line bottom with parchment or waxed paper cut to fit; generously butter paper. Sift flour with baking powder and salt onto paper. Set aside. In a large bowl, combine eggs and Vanilla Sugar. Beat at high speed of an electric mixer until very pale, thick, and about triple in volume. Fold in flour mixture in three parts. Spoon batter into prepared pan; tilt pan to spread evenly. Bake in preheated oven for 13 to 14 minutes. Sprinkle a clean dishcloth evenly with confectioners' sugar. Turn cake out onto cloth. Brush paper lightly with cold water. Let stand for about 2 minutes. Peel off paper. Cut off any crisp edges of cake, then roll cake up in cloth. Let stand on a cake rack for about 30 minutes.

In a chilled bowl with chilled beaters, beat cream with 1 tablespoon confectioners' sugar until soft peaks form. Mixture should be thick but still glossy. Do not overbeat. Unroll cake. Spread with about half of whipped cream. Sprinkle with cherries and about half of coconut, and roll again. Fold remaining coconut into remaining whipped cream. Spread cake with mixture. Use tines of a fork to create swirls and peaks. Sprinkle lightly with additional coconut. Refrigerate cake until ready to serve. Serves 8 to 10.

Twelfth Night Cake

Rich mincemeat laced with rum and walnuts forms the topping for this impressive, festive cake. Serve it warm, topped with scoops of vanilla ice cream.

1 1-lb., 12-oz. jar mincemeat
1/3 cup dark rum
1/2 cup (1 stick) butter
1 cup brown sugar
1 cup coarsely chopped walnuts
1/2 cup (1 stick) more butter, softened
2 cups granulated sugar
3 eggs
1 tsp. vanilla
1 cup milk
1/2 cup more dark rum
1 1/2 cups all-purpose flour
1 1/2 cups wholewheat flour
1/4 tsp. salt
1/2 tsp. nutmeg
1 Tbs. baking powder

Preheat oven to 325°F. In a small bowl, combine mincemeat and 1/3 cup rum; stir to blend; set aside for 30 minutes to 1 hour. Cut 1/2 cup of butter into small pieces; place in a 9- × 13-inch baking pan. Place pan in oven until butter is melted; remove and tilt so butter coats all surfaces. Stir in brown sugar, and spread mixture evenly over bottom of pan. Sprinkle with walnuts. Spoon mincemeat mixture over walnuts and spread it out evenly over bottom of pan; set aside. In a large mixing bowl, cream butter with sugar until very light and fluffy. Beat in eggs one at a time, beating well after each addition. Add vanilla, milk, and remaining rum; blend well. Sift flour, salt, nutmeg, and baking powder onto waxed paper. Add in four parts to creamed mixture. Pour batter evenly over mincemeat mixture.

Bake in preheated oven for 1 hour. Loosen sides of cake by running a knife around edges of pan. Invert and turn cake upside down onto a baking sheet. Arrange broiler rack about 4 inches under heat. Preheat broiler to high. Place cake on a baking sheet under broiler heat until topping is lightly browned. Use two spatulas to transfer cake to a rack to cool. Transfer to a large serving plate; serve at room temperature. Serves 12 to 16.

Passover Cake with Fruit Sauce

1 large, unblemished lemon
6 eggs, separated
1 cup granulated sugar
1 cup matzoh meal
1/8 tsp. salt
Rich Vanilla Ice Cream*, optional
Fruit Sauce (recipe follows), optional

Preheat oven to 350°F. Grate zest from lemon; set aside. Cut lemon in half. Squeeze juice; measure 1/4 cup for cake. (Reserve any remaining juice for other use.) Place yolks in a large mixing bowl; beat until thick and pale lemon yellow in color, about 1 minute. Slowly add sugar, beating as added. Continue to beat until mixture is thickened, about 5 minutes. Stir in lemon juice. Fold in matzoh meal and grated lemon rind. In a second bowl, beat egg whites with salt until stiff peaks form when beater is lifted from bowl. Stir about one-fourth of whites into yolk mixture, then fold in remaining beaten whites. Pour batter into an ungreased, loose-bottomed 9- × 3 1/2-inch tube pan.

Bake in preheated oven for 1 hour, or until top of cake springs back when lightly pressed with fingertips. Cover top of cake lightly with aluminum foil during last 15 minutes of baking, to prevent over-browning. Invert cake, in pan; let stand until cool. Gently loosen sides and invert onto a serving plate. Slice and serve with ice cream topped with Fruit Sauce, if desired. Serves 6 to 8.

Fruit Sauce

> 1 cup fruit preserves
> 1 Tbs. water
> 1/4 cup fruit brandy of your choice

Place preserves and water in a small skillet over low heat. Cook, stirring, until mixture comes to a boil. Remove from heat; stir in desired fruit brandy. Serve warm or at room temperature. Makes 1 generous cup of sauce.

Note: Sauce will be chunky with fruit from preserves. If you prefer a smooth sauce, press mixture through a fine strainer before serving.

Fresh Fruit Fruitcake

This is far and away my favorite fruitcake. No glacéd fruit is used, so the fresh fruit flavor comes through in every bite. Bathing it in brandy or rum makes it extra special.

> 1 large seedless orange
> 1 small lemon
> 1 cup dried apricots

3 cups all-purpose flour
1 Tbs. baking powder
1/2 tsp. baking soda
1/2 tsp. salt
2 small to medium tart, crisp apples, peeled, cored, and
    cubed
1 ripe pear, peeled, cored, and cubed
1/2 cup whole fresh cranberries
1/2 cup (1 stick) butter
1 cup granulated sugar
3 large eggs
1 cup raisins
1 cup chopped walnuts or pecans
1/2 cup brandy or rum
Additional brandy or rum as needed

Peel zest from orange and lemon; cut it into small cubes. Place in a saucepan; add apricots, and cover with water by about 1 inch. Simmer over low heat until apricots are quite tender and all but about 1 tablespoon of liquid has been absorbed. Set aside. Working over a bowl, cut peeled orange into cubes; add two thin slices of lemon. (Reserve remaining lemon for other use.) Add apricot mixture. Preheat oven to 350°F. Butter and flour a 10-inch tube pan. Sift flour, baking powder, soda, and salt onto waxed paper. Place fruit mixture in work bowl of a food processor or blender. Process or blend until mixture is a chunky purée. Add apples, pears, and cranberries; process for about 5 seconds more. In a large mixing bowl, cream butter with sugar until light and fluffy. Add eggs one at a time, beating well after each addition. Stir in puréed fruit mixture, raisins, and nuts. Fold in dry ingredients alternately with 1/2 cup brandy or rum, blending well.

Pour batter into prepared pan. Bake for 60 to 70 minutes, or until a cake tester inserted in center comes out clean. Place cake on a rack in pan. Spoon about 2 tablespoons of brandy or rum over surface. Let stand for about 5 minutes, then turn it out onto a greased rack and brush with about 2 tablespoons more brandy or rum. Cool to room temperature. Wrap cake in several layers of cheesecloth and soak cloth with as much brandy or rum as it will absorb. Overwrap in foil or plastic wrap to keep moisture in. Store cake in a cool place for 1 to 2 weeks; then check to see if cheesecloth is dry. If so, drizzle a little more brandy or rum on it. Replace foil or plastic wrap and store cake for another 1 to 2 weeks, or until you are ready to serve it. Serves 10 to 12.

California Gold Coast Christmas Cake

Candied orange peel and apricots are the fruit for this golden cake. This recipe makes sufficient batter for two 6-cup fluted molds or Bundt pans—one to give and one to serve.

> *3 1/2 cups all-purpose flour*
> *1/2 tsp. salt*
> *3/4 cup milk*
> *1/4 cup brandy*
> *1/2 tsp. almond extract*
> *1/2 tsp. vanilla extract*
> *1 1/2 cups (3 sticks) butter*
> *2 cups granulated sugar*
> *6 eggs, separated*
> *1 cup coarsely chopped blanched almonds, lightly toasted*
> *1 cup chopped dried apricots*
> *1 cup chopped Candied Orange Peel**
> *1 cup golden raisins*
> *1/2 tsp. cream of tartar*
> *1 cup more brandy*
> *Additional brandy, optional*

Preheat oven to 275°F. Butter and flour two 6-cup molds or Bundt pans. Sift flour with salt onto paper. In a 2-cup measure, combine milk, brandy, almond extract, and vanilla extract. In a large mixing bowl, beat butter with sugar until light and fluffy. Add egg yolks one at a time, beating well after each addition. Add flour mixture alternately with milk mixture and stir to a smooth batter. Fold in nuts and fruit. In a separate bowl, beat egg whites and cream of tartar until stiff but not dry. Fold whites into batter gently but thoroughly.

Pour mixture into prepared pans. Bake in preheated oven for 2 1/2 to 3 hours, or until a cake tester inserted in center comes out clean. Cool cakes in pans on racks for about 30 minutes, then invert and remove pans. Pierce top of each cake with tines of a fork at 1-inch intervals. Spoon remaining brandy slowly over each, dividing evenly. Wrap each cake in foil, and refrigerate or freeze until ready to give or serve. You can make these cakes up to 1 month ahead, remoistening with brandy and then rewrapping 3 or 4 times. Makes two cakes. Each cake will serve 6 to 8.

The Most Beautiful Wedding Cake

Yes, you can do it yourself! You can make the most important cake of your life—a cake that will be truly better, in many different ways, than anything the best bakery in town can deliver. The cake itself is deliciously buttery, with a velvety-smooth texture. Because the batter will "hold up" in the refrigerator, you need only bake the number of layers your own oven will successfully accommodate at one time. Also, all layers can be baked ahead and frozen until you are ready to assemble, frost, and decorate the cake. The satiny-smooth frosting is not only delicious—totally unlike the usual flat-tasting commercially prepared kind—it is also easy to make. There are no tricks or techniques to be mastered—it simply cannot fail. And there is this bonus too: the cake may be frozen for several weeks after it has been frosted and decorated, leaving you free to concentrate on other wedding preparations. And oh how truly beautiful it is; a cake you will always remember.

> *4 cups sifted cake flour*
> *1 Tbs. baking powder*
> *1/2 tsp. salt*

2 cups (4 sticks) butter, softened
2 1/2 cups granulated sugar
6 eggs
1 tsp. lemon extract
1 tsp. vanilla extract
1 cup milk
Never-Fail Buttercream Frosting (recipe follows)

Preheat oven to 350°F. Butter one 10-inch round layer cake pan, one 8-inch round layer cake pan, and one 6-inch round layer cake pan. Line each pan with waxed paper cut to fit. Sift flour, baking powder, and salt onto paper. Set aside. In large bowl of an electric mixer, beat butter until very light and fluffy. Add sugar about 1/2 cup at a time, beating well after each addition. Add eggs one at a time, again beating well after each is added. Blend in extracts. Beat for a final 5 minutes. Add flour mixture in five parts alternately with milk, beginning and ending with flour. Spoon batter into pans you plan to bake immediately, filling them about 1/2 full. Refrigerate any remaining batter until ready to use.

Bake layers for 25 to 30 minutes, or until a cake tester inserted in center comes out clean. Cool in pans on racks for 10 minutes. Turn out onto racks and carefully remove waxed paper lining. Cool completely before filling and frosting.

Never-Fail Buttercream Frosting

1 1/2 to 2 lbs. confectioners' sugar
10 egg yolks
1 cup corn syrup
1 1/2 lbs. (6 sticks) butter, softened

Sift confectioners' sugar through a large, fine sieve. Do not force it through; simply shake sieve and let sugar fall onto a large sheet of paper. Set aside. In large bowl of an electric mixer, beat egg yolks at high speed until a very pale lemony yellow. Pour corn syrup into a small, heavy saucepan; place over high heat and bring to a full boil, stirring constantly. Remove from heat and let stand until boiling stops. With mixer still on high speed, gradually add syrup to egg yolks in a thin, steady stream, pouring it into side of bowl and not on beaters. Continue beating until outside of bowl is cool to touch. Add butter a few tablespoons at a time, and beat until smooth and creamy. Spoon in confectioners' sugar about 1/2 cup at a time, beating after each addition, adding only enough sugar to bring mixture to a smooth spreading consistency. Makes about 10 cups.

Note: Frosting may be made ahead and kept in the refrigerator for about 3 weeks or frozen in tightly sealed container for up to 6 months. Thaw in refrigerator overnight before using.

To Assemble, Frost, and Decorate the Cake for the Wedding

Cut two waxed paper circles, using 8- and 6-inch pans for guides; then cut two cardboard circles of the same sizes.

If cake layers were frozen, defrost in refrigerator or at room temperature. Before frosting, level each layer by slicing off top of layer horizontally.

Spread a small amount of Buttercream Frosting in center of a large cake plate or decorative cake stand. (If desired, rim plate or stand with four strips of waxed paper or foil.) Place 10-inch cake layer in center over frosting and press it down lightly to hold it in place. Heap a large amount of frosting between center and edge of layer, then push it over edges and around sides of cake in a flowing, continuous motion. Add more frosting to center of cake and smooth it out to cover completely. (Using a large amount of frosting prevents crust from separating from cake so crumbs don't get in frosting. Excess frosting can be easily removed.) Using a hot knife (dip it in very hot water and shake off all excess water), smooth sides and top of frosted layer; then place 8-inch waxed paper circle in center. Spread a small amount of frosting on 8-inch cardboard circle. Press 8-inch cake layer on cardboard. Place on top of waxed paper on 10-inch layer. Frost top and sides of this layer. Repeat with remaining waxed paper and cardboard and 6-inch layer.

To smooth frosting, hold blade of hot knife against sides of cake; move it around sides in a flowing, continuous motion, stopping as necessary to remove excess frosting from knife and redip it in hot water to reheat. Smooth top edge of each layer by placing knife blade at top edge of cake horizontally, and moving it up toward center of cake. Smooth top with hot knife by moving it across cake. Remove strips of waxed paper or foil if used, or clean edge of plate with a warm, damp paper towel.

Complete cake decoration with a spiral of same fresh flowers used in bride's bouquet and place a small duplicate of bridal bouquet itself on top layer of cake.

Buche de Noël

A new and delicious but super-easy version of a French Christmas yule log.

> 1 cup chopped walnuts
> 1/4 cup all-purpose flour
> 1/4 cup cocoa
> 5 eggs, separated
> 1/4 tsp. cream of tartar
> 1/3 cup Vanilla Sugar*, or 1/3 cup granulated sugar plus
>   1/2 tsp. vanilla extract
> 1/3 cup more Vanilla Sugar
> Confectioners' sugar
> Cherry Whipped Cream (recipe follows)
> Rich Chocolate Frosting (recipe follows)
> Additional confectioners' sugar

Preheat oven to 350°F. Butter a long, shallow (10- × 15- × 1-inch) baking pan and line with waxed or parchment paper cut to fit. Butter pan and sprinkle evenly with sugar. Place chopped walnuts and flour in work bowl of a food processor; process until walnuts are finely ground. Add cocoa and process briefly to mix. (Or, put chopped walnuts through a grinder; combine with flour and cocoa.) Set aside. In a large mixing bowl, beat egg whites with cream of tartar until soft peaks form. Fold in 1/3 cup Vanilla Sugar about 1 tablespoon at a time, and continue to beat until stiff peaks form.

In a second large mixing bowl, beat yolks with remaining Vanilla Sugar until thick; gently fold into whites. Fold in walnut mixture. Spoon batter into prepared pan and bake in preheated oven for 18 to 20 minutes, or until top springs back when lightly touched. Turn cake out onto a cloth and sprinkle thickly with confectioners' sugar. Roll up loosely in cloth. When cold, unroll; spread with Cherry Whipped Cream; reroll. Cut off both ends of filled cake diagonally; place on top of cake to simulate wood knots. Cover entire cake with chocolate frosting, using tines of a fork to simulate texture of bark. Refrigerate cake until ready to serve. Just before serving, sprinkle with confectioners' sugar to simulate snow. Serves 6 to 8.

Cherry Whipped Cream

1/4 tsp. unflavored gelatin
1/4 cup maraschino syrup, or milk plus 1 or 2 drops red food coloring
1/2 pint heavy (whipping) cream
1/2 cup chopped red and green candied cherries

In a small saucepan, sprinkle gelatin over syrup or milk plus food coloring. Stir over low heat until gelatin has dissolved. In a chilled bowl with chilled beaters, beat cream until soft peaks form. Fold in gelatin mixture and candied cherries. Refrigerate for about 30 minutes before using.

Rich Chocolate Frosting

6 cups sifted confectioners' sugar
1/2 cup cocoa
1/4 cup milk
1/4 cup brandy
1/2 cup (1 stick) butter

Sift sugar with cocoa onto paper. Set aside. In a saucepan, combine milk and brandy. Place over low heat until steamy hot. In a mixing bowl, cream butter until light and fluffy; gradually add half of sugar mixture, blending well. Add remaining sugar mixture alternately with hot milk and brandy, beating after each addition until smooth.

Christmas Apple-Mincemeat Squares with Whipped Cream and Lemon Sauce

1/2 cup (1 stick) butter
1 cup finely chopped pecans
1 cup self-rising flour
1 1-lb. can prepared mincemeat
1 1-lb. can apple pie filling
2 Tbs. rum
1 tsp. grated lemon rind
1 Tbs. lemon juice
1 Tbs. light brown sugar
1 Tbs. cornstarch
3/4 cup more self-rising flour
3/4 cup sugar
1 egg, beaten
3 Tbs. more butter, melted and cooled
Whipped Cream (recipe follows)
Old-Fashioned Lemon Sauce (recipe follows)

In a medium skillet, melt butter over low heat. Remove skillet from heat; stir in nuts and 1 cup flour. Stir to mix. Spoon into bottom of a 9- × 13- × 2-inch baking pan and spread out evenly. Place pan about 3 inches under high broiler heat for 2 to 3 minutes, or until mixture is lightly crusted but not browned. Remove from heat and allow to cool at room temperature. Preheat oven to 375°F. In a bowl, combine mincemeat, pie filling, rum, lemon rind, lemon juice, and sugar. Sprinkle cornstarch over surface; stir to blend thoroughly. Spoon over crust and spread out evenly.

In a second bowl, combine remaining flour with sugar; mix thoroughly. Add beaten egg, and stir with a fork until mixture resembles small peas. Sprinkle evenly over mincemeat mixture. Drizzle with remaining melted butter. Place in center rack of preheated oven and bake for 30 to 35 minutes, or until topping is lightly browned. Cool in pan on a rack to room temperature. Use a spatula to cut into squares. When ready to serve, place squares on dessert plates, top with whipped cream, and pour lemon sauce over cream, letting it drizzle down. Serves 12.

Whipped Cream

1/2 cup heavy whipping cream
1 Tbs. confectioners' sugar
1 Tbs. light rum

In a chilled bowl with chilled beaters, beat very cold cream until soft peaks form. Fold in sugar and rum. Refrigerate until ready to serve. Makes about 1 1/2 cups.

Old-Fashioned Lemon Sauce

1/2 cup granulated sugar
1 Tbs. cornstarch
1/8 tsp. salt
1 cup hot water
3 Tbs. unsalted butter, at room temperature
1 tsp. finely grated lemon rind
2 Tbs. lemon juice, or to taste

In a saucepan, mix sugar, cornstarch, and salt. Gradually stir in hot water. Place over medium heat and cook, stirring constantly, for about 5 minutes, or until mixture comes to a boil and becomes thick and clear. Remove from heat and continue to stir with a rubber spatula from bottom of pan for about 2 minutes. Stir in butter, lemon rind, and juice. Continue to stir until butter has melted and mixture is smooth. Serve warm, at room temperature, or chilled. If made ahead, refrigerate until ready to use. Sauce will keep for about 1 week in refrigerator. It can be reheated in top of a small double boiler over hot water. Makes about 1 1/2 cups.

Patisserie Perfection

*Starts with simple, but simply splendid,
American pies and ends with elegant French
dessert quiche and sweet Italian pizzas.*

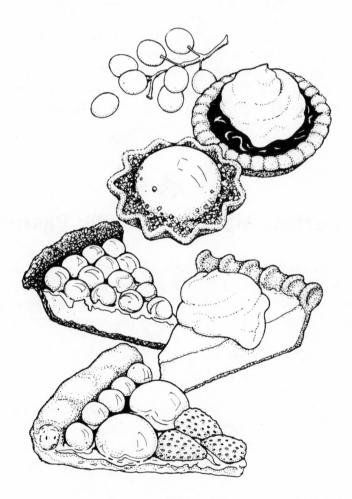

About Pie and Pastry Dough

There is no excuse for soggy, miserable pastry under a delectable filling. Good pastry should be the rule and not the exception. Thank goodness the rules for making a great pastry are easy to keep.

1. Chill all ingredients to be used, including the flour.
2. When adding the fat (butter, shortening, etc.) to the flour, remember the point is not to create a homogenized mixture but to cut the fat into tiny particles, each coated with flour.
3. Add the chilled liquid ingredients sparingly—you can always add more—to bring the flour-coated fat particles together without breaking them down. Mix quickly with a fork and form into a soft ball.
4. For tender, flaky, crisp crust, wrap the ball of dough in waxed paper or plastic wrap and refrigerate for at least 1 hour. This congeals the butter in the dough so that it can be rolled out easily; it also allows the water to be absorbed by the flour so that the pastry shell will bake properly, without shrinking.

Perfect Make-Ahead Pie Pastry

This is an old-fashioned pie dough recipe that is indeed "never-fail perfect." In old-fashioned generosity, it makes five 9-inch pie crusts, which can be wrapped and stored in the refrigerator or freezer, ready to use. With pastry on hand, a great pie can be made in short order.

> *4 cups all-purpose flour*
> *1 Tbs. granulated sugar*
> *2 tsp. salt*
> *1 1/2 cups vegetable shortening, firmly chilled and cut*
> *   into small pieces*
> *1/4 cup butter, firmly chilled and cut into small pieces*

1 large egg
1 Tbs. cold vinegar
1/2 cup ice water

To Prepare:

Hand Method: In a mixing bowl, combine flour, sugar, and salt. Place in freezer for 5 to 10 minutes, until chilled. Add shortening and butter; work into flour with fingertips until mixture forms small, flaky granules, like oatmeal. In a measuring cup or a small bowl with a pouring lid, beat together egg, vinegar, and ice water. Add to flour mixture and stir with a fork only until dough holds loosely together. Dough should feel moist but not sticky. If too dry, sprinkle with a few drops of water; if too sticky, add a teaspoon or two of flour.

Food Processor Method: In a mixing bowl, combine flour, sugar, and salt. Place in freezer for 5 to 10 minutes, until chilled. Transfer to work bowl of a food processor. Add chilled shortening and butter. Process for 8 to 10 seconds, turning motor on and off until mixture forms very small, flaky granules, like oatmeal. In a measuring cup or a small bowl with pouring lip, beat together egg, vinegar, and ice water; pour through feed tube of food processor over flour mixture. Process until a ball of dough forms on top of blade, about 15 seconds. If dough is too moist, add 1 to 2 teaspoons of flour; if too dry, add 1 to 2 teaspoons of water and process an additional 5 to 6 seconds, until ball of dough forms.

Turn dough out onto a lightly floured work surface. Separate into five equal portions. Form each portion into a ball and flatten into a disk; wrap in waxed paper. Refrigerate until chilled, about 1/2 hour.

To Store:

Place each disk of dough in a zip-lock freezer storage bag and seal. Store in refrigerator or freezer until ready to use.

To Use:

Unwrap each round of dough as needed. Let dough stand at room temperature until sufficiently softened to roll out but still cold. Roll out on a lightly floured work surface or floured pastry cloth, working from center of disk only in one direction, not back and forth. Stop just short of edge to obtain an even circle 11 to 12 inches in diameter, about 1/8 inch thick. Roll dough up loosely over rolling pin; lift, then unroll carefully over pan. Lift up edges of dough, then let it fall gently into place, patting it lightly into bottom of pan without forcing or stretching it. Trim edges with a sharp knife or scissors, allowing an overlap of 1/4 to 1/2 inch. Crimp overlap to form a firm fluted edge.

When using a tart pan with a removable bottom, be sure that dough is pushed well, without stretching, into fluted sides of pan. Be certain also that it is completely sealed and free of cracks, so filling will not leak. If pastry breaks while lining pan, just patch it by pressing edges together. Patch any holes with trimmings, and seal with moist fingertips. Place dough-lined pan in refrigerator or freezer for 5 to 10 minutes before baking.

To Bake:

After years of making and baking pies, I have found the most common failing is a soggy crust. The trick to a crisp one is very simple: the pastry is partially baked before it is filled and then brushed with either egg yolk or egg white or spread with a thin layer of tart-sweet jelly, which adds an extra dimension of flavor to any pie. The result is a perfectly crisp bottom crust.

For a partially baked shell: Preheat oven to 425°F. Line shell with foil and weight it down with pie weights, dry beans, or raw rice (which may be kept in a jar and used repeatedly). Or simply line shell with foil, shiny side down, pressing it into pastry. Bake in preheated oven for 14 to 16 minutes, until bottom is set and dough is very lightly colored. Remove shell from oven and remove lining and any weights you have used. Brush bottom with beaten yolk, white, or jelly and return it to oven for about 2 minutes to seal bottom. Pastry will finish cooking when it is baked with filling.

For a fully baked shell: Bake for about 20 minutes, or until lightly browned. Brush with egg glaze or jelly and dry out for 2 minutes in oven.

Ten-Minute Pie Pastry

Although this pastry should rest in the refrigerator for about an hour before it is rolled out, it takes only about 10 minutes to put together.

> *1 cup cake flour*
> *Pinch of salt*
> *2 Tbs. butter*
> *1 Tbs. vegetable shortening or lard*
> *2 to 3 Tbs. ice water*

Combine flour and salt in a bowl. Add butter and shortening and cut it into flour with a pastry blender or fingertips until mixture resembles coarse meal. Add 2 tablespoons water, 1 tablespoon at a time, and toss with flour mixture to distribute evenly. Add additional ice water if necessary, to form a soft dough. Form dough into a ball, wrap in waxed paper, and chill for about 1 hour in refrigerator before rolling out. Roll out, following directions for Perfect Make-Ahead Pie Pastry*. Makes one 9-inch pie or 10-inch tart shell.

Old and New American Pies

Brandy-Glazed Apple Pie

1 1/4 cups unsweetened apple juice
3/4 cup granulated sugar
7 or 8 tart, crisp apples, such as McIntosh or Granny
*   Smith, peeled, cored, and cut into wedges*

1/4 cup apple brandy or applejack
3 Tbs. cornstarch
1 Tbs. butter
1/2 cup currant jelly
1 Tbs. more apple brandy or applejack
1 9-inch pie shell, baked and cooled
Whipped cream, lightly sweetened, optional

In a large saucepan over medium heat, combine apple juice and sugar; bring to a boil and add chopped apples. Cover and let simmer for 4 to 5 minutes, or until apples are tender but not too soft. With a slotted spoon, transfer apples from liquid to a colander. Set aside to drain. In a small bowl, stir brandy into cornstarch until smooth; add to liquid in saucepan. Cook, stirring, until thick and bubbly. Remove from heat; stir until slightly cooled. Stir in butter. Cover and let stand for about 30 minutes, or until thickened to a smooth custard. In a small saucepan, melt jelly over low heat. Stir in remaining brandy or applejack. Cool slightly. Brush bottom of baked pie shell with about one-fourth of mixture. Cover with cooled custard. Arrange apple slices in a circle over surface. Brush evenly with remaining jelly mixture. Cover and refrigerate until chilled. If desired, garnish with sweetened whipped cream. Serves 6 to 8.

Sour Cream Apple Pie with Walnuts

This is a pie of such depth of flavor and crunchy generosity it deserves to be the star of the meal. Serve with a large pot of fresh coffee, with plenty for seconds.

1/4 cup brown sugar
1/2 cup chopped walnuts
1/4 cup all-purpose flour
4 Tbs. butter, melted

3/4 cup Vanilla Sugar, or 3/4 cup granulated sugar plus
    1/2 tsp. vanilla extract
1 1/2 Tbs. cornstarch
1 egg, lightly beaten
1/4 cup sour cream
1/4 tsp. nutmeg
1/4 tsp. cinnamon
5 large apples, or sufficient to make 3 1/2 cups peeled,
    cored, and diced
1 9-inch pie shell, partially baked*

Preheat oven to 425°F. In a mixing bowl, combine brown sugar, walnuts, flour, and melted butter; stir to blend. Set aside. In a second, larger bowl, combine Vanilla Sugar, cornstarch, egg, sour cream, nutmeg, and cinnamon. Beat with a whisk until blended. Peel and core apples and cut into small dice, adding them as diced to sour cream mixture. Stir to blend. Pour into partially baked pie shell. Top evenly with walnut mixture. Place in preheated oven and bake for 15 minutes. Reduce oven temperature to 350°F. Bake for a final 45 minutes to 1 hour, or until juices bubble up through topping. Remove from oven; place on a rack to cool. Serve warm or at room temperature. Serves 6 to 8.

Key West Crème de Menthe Pie

An inspired variation of Key Lime Pie.

*1 3-oz. package lime gelatin
1 cup boiling water
1 to 2 tsp. grated lemon zest
1/2 cup Crème de Menthe liqueur
1 egg yolk, lightly beaten
1 14-oz. can sweetened condensed milk*

1/2 tsp. Angostura bitters
1/2 cup heavy (whipping) cream
1 9-inch pie shell, baked and cooled
Lemon Whipped Cream (recipe follows)

In a large bowl, sprinkle gelatin over boiling water. Stir until dissolved. Add grated lemon zest and liqueur; cool to room temperature. Add egg yolk and beat until blended. Stir in condensed milk and bitters. Refrigerate until mixture has slightly thickened. In a chilled bowl with chilled beaters, beat cream until stiff peaks form; fold into thickened gelatin mixture. Spoon into baked pie shell; chill until firm, 3 to 4 hours. Top with Lemon Whipped Cream. Serves 6 to 8.

Lemon Whipped Cream

2 Tbs. frozen lemon juice concentrate
1/2 cup heavy (whipping) cream, chilled

Place frozen lemon juice concentrate in a large mixing bowl. Beat until mushy; add cream. Beat until soft peaks form.

Tropical Fruit Pies

The alluring mix of fresh tropical fruit creates a flavor excitement in these light and airy pies.

1 envelope unflavored gelatin
1/2 cup peach or other brandy
1 1-lb. can crushed pineapple in heavy syrup, undrained
1/4 cup all-purpose flour
1 cup granulated sugar
1 cup orange juice

1 3-oz. package chopped walnuts
1 1/2 cups any combination of the following fresh fruits:
  pitted fresh cherries; seedless grapes; peeled and
  sliced kiwi fruit; melon balls or cubes; peeled and
  sliced bananas; peeled, pitted, and sliced peaches,
  apricots, nectarines, or mangoes
2 9-inch pie shells, baked and cooled
Whipped cream, lightly sweetened, optional

In a small bowl, sprinkle gelatin over brandy. Set aside. Combine pineapple, flour, and sugar in a saucepan. Stir over medium heat until thick and bubbly. Add gelatin mixture and stir until dissolved; remove from heat. Stir in orange juice. Transfer to storage bowl and refrigerate until mixture is slightly thickened. Fold in chopped nuts and fruits. Spoon into prepared pie shells, dividing evenly. Refrigerate until filling is firm. If desired, garnish with sweetened whipped cream. Makes two 9-inch pies.

Layered Apple Tart

With made-ahead pastry on hand, you can prepare this elegant Viennese-style torte in short order.

Unbaked pastry for 3 9-inch pies, prepared ahead,
  flattened into disks, and chilled
Brandied Apple Filling (recipe follows)
Sweetened whipped cream
Slivered almonds, optional

Preheat oven to 450°F. One at a time, roll each disk of pastry out into a 10-inch circle (use a 10-inch tart pan as a guide). Place one disk on a flat baking sheet and prick well with a fork. Bake in preheated oven for 12 to 15 minutes, or until lightly browned. Cool on a rack. Repeat with remaining pastry disks. Place one disk on an attractive serving platter. Spread with half of Brandied Apple Filling; cover with second layer and remaining filling. Top with third layer. Cover with mounds of whipped cream and garnish, if desired, with slivered almonds. Serves 8 to 12.

Brandied Apple Filling

1 cup granulated sugar
1 cup unsweetened apple juice
2 1/2 lbs. tart, crisp apples
1/2 cup apple jelly
2 Tbs. cornstarch
3 Tbs. applejack or apple brandy

Place sugar in a deep, heavy skillet and add apple juice. Place over medium heat, and let simmer until sugar has dissolved and mixture is reduced to a thin syrup. While syrup simmers, peel, core, and cut apples into small cubes; add to syrup. Cook, uncovered, until tender but not falling apart; with a slotted spoon, remove them to a bowl. To syrup add apple jelly, and stir until dissolved. In a 1-cup measure, sprinkle cornstarch over applejack or apple brandy; mix to a paste, then add mixture into simmering syrup. Cook, stirring, until thickened; pour over apple cubes. Cool to room temperature before using.

Southern Comfort Peach Pie

Just scrumptious, y'all!

1 9-inch pie shell, partially baked
2 Tbs. peach jam
3 medium-sized ripe peaches
3 eggs

1/2 cup granulated sugar
1 cup light cream
1/4 cup Southern Comfort
Sweetened whipped cream, optional

Preheat oven to 400°F. Brush bottom of pie shell evenly with peach jam. Bake in preheated oven for 2 minutes. Remove from oven; cool to room temperature. Reduce oven temperature to 350°F. Plunge each peach into boiling water, hold under cold water, and slip off skin. Cut each in half and remove pits. Place halves, cut side down, in bottom of pie shell about 1 inch from rim. In a bowl, beat eggs with sugar until blended; stir in cream and Southern Comfort. Pour over peaches in shell. Bake in preheated oven until a knife inserted in center of custard comes out clean. Refrigerate until chilled. If desired, garnish with sweetened whipped cream. Serves 6 to 8.

Creole Pecan Pie

Slow baking gives this pie a divine texture.

1/2 cup (1 stick) butter, cut into small cubes
3 large eggs
1 cup Vanilla Sugar*, or 1 cup granulated sugar plus
*   1 Tbs. vanilla extract*
1 cup light corn syrup
1/4 cup coffee liqueur
1 1/4 cups chopped pecans
1 9-inch pie shell, partially baked
Whipped cream, lightly sweetened, optional

Preheat oven to 425°F. Place butter in a small skillet over low heat until melted and lightly browned. Do not allow to burn. Cool to room temperature. In a large mixing bowl, beat eggs with Vanilla Sugar until blended. Fold in corn syrup and liqueur. Stir in cooled, browned butter, then pecans. Place partially baked pie shell on a flat baking sheet; pour in pecan filling. Bake in preheated oven for 10 minutes. Lower heat to 325°F.; bake for 35 to 40 minutes, or until a knife inserted near center comes out clean. Cool pie on a rack. Serve at room temperature. If desired, top each serving lightly with whipped cream. Serves 6 to 8.

Chiffon and Whipped Cream Pies

Cookie Crumb Crust

If you don't have time to make pastry for pie, make a cookie crumb crust. It's quick, and a fine beginning for many delicious fillings, from fluffy chiffon to fresh fruit and ice cream. It's so easy because almost all of the baking has already been done. Though the crust does go into the oven for just a few minutes, it's not to bake the crumbs, but to allow them to absorb the butter and hold together. High on the preferred list are graham cracker crust and vanilla or chocolate wafer crumb crust. They really are delicious, but even more so when you add an extra, surprise ingredient for additional flavor.

Chocolate Cookie Crumb Crust

1/2 cup (1 stick) butter, cubed
1 1/2 cups chocolate wafers (sometimes called ice box cookies)
1/2 cup granulated sugar
1 tsp. instant coffee

Graham Cracker Crumb Crust

1/2 cup (1 stick) butter, cubed
1 1/2 cups graham cracker crumbs
1/2 cup granulated sugar
1/2 tsp. cinnamon
1/4 tsp. ground ginger
1/4 tsp. ground allspice or mace

Lemony Vanilla Crumb Crust

1/2 cup (1 stick) butter, cubed
1 1/2 cups fine vanilla wafer crumbs
1/2 cup granulated sugar
1 tsp. grated lemon or orange rind

Place butter cubes in a large, heavy skillet over low heat until melted. Remove skillet from heat and stir in remaining ingredients, blending thoroughly. Transfer crumb mixture to pie plate. Using fingertips, distribute it evenly over sides and bottom of pan. Then use palms to press crust firmly and evenly in place, being careful that top edge of crust is not too thin. Another pie pan can be fitted down over crumbs to help shape crust. Refrigerate until chilled, about 1 hour.

Preheat oven to 400°F. To prevent crumbs from scorching, carefully fit a piece of aluminum foil over crust. Do not fill with weights. Bake in preheated oven for 5 minutes. Cool on a rack before filling.

Nut Cookie Crumb Crust

1/4 cup (1/2 stick) butter
1 1/2 cups vanilla cookie crumbs
1/2 cup finely chopped walnuts or pecans

Preheat oven to 400°F. In a large, heavy skillet, melt butter over low heat. Remove skillet from heat; add cookie crumbs and nuts. Stir until evenly moistened. Press mixture against bottom and sides of a 9-inch pie plate. Bake in preheated oven for 8 to 10 minutes. Cool on a wire rack.

Christmas Egg Nog Pie

An old-timey, all-time Southern favorite.

1/4 cup granulated sugar
1 envelope unflavored gelatin
1/8 tsp. salt
1/8 tsp. mace
1/2 tsp. nutmeg
1/4 tsp. allspice
3/4 cup milk
1/4 cup bourbon whiskey
4 eggs, separated
1/4 cup more granulated sugar
1/2 cup heavy (whipping) cream
1/2 cup finely chopped walnuts
1 3-oz. bar bittersweet chocolate, chopped
1/4 cup drained and chopped maraschino cherries
1 9-inch Nut Cookie Crumb Crust*, baked and cooled
1/2 cup more heavy (whipping) cream
1 Tbs. confectioners' sugar
1 teaspoon more bourbon whiskey

In top half of a double boiler, combine sugar, gelatin, salt, mace, nutmeg, and allspice. Stir in milk and bourbon. Cook, stirring, over medium heat until mixture is steamy hot and sugar and gelatin have dissolved. In a mixing bowl, beat egg yolks until frothy. Slowly add hot milk mixture, beating with a whisk as added. Pour mixture back into top of double boiler. Place over simmering water and cook, stirring, until slightly thickened. Pour into a storage bowl. Refrigerate until cold and mixture mounds slightly. In another bowl, beat egg whites until soft peaks form. Fold in remaining sugar about 1 tablespoon at a time and beat to a very stiff, glossy meringue. With same beaters beat 1/2 cup cream until stiff peaks form; fold in sugar and bourbon. Fold meringue, beaten cream, walnuts, chocolate, and cherries into gelatin mixture. Spoon into prepared pie shell; chill for several hours. Whip remaining 1/2 cup cream with remaining sugar and bourbon until stiff. Swirl over pie just before serving. Serves 6 to 8.

Pineapple Cream Pie

Pineapple chunks and pineapple yogurt give tang and texture to this flavorful pie.

>*1 8-oz. can pineapple chunks in juice*
>*1 tsp. unflavored gelatin*
>*1/4 cup honey*
>*1 tsp. vanilla extract*
>*1/2 pint heavy (whipping) cream*
>*1 8-oz. carton pineapple yogurt*
>*1 9-inch Chocolate Cookie Crumb Crust*, baked and*
>   *cooled*

Drain pineapple; reserve chunks. Measure 1/3 cup of juice, adding water if necessary; pour into a small saucepan. Sprinkle gelatin over juice; let stand until softened. Stir over very low heat until mixture is clear. Add honey and vanilla extract; stir until smooth. Cool to room temperature. In a chilled bowl with chilled beaters, beat cream until stiff peaks form. Fold in pineapple yogurt; add juice mixture. Pour into prepared crumb crust. Refrigerate until filling has set. Just before serving, arrange reserved pineapple chunks over filling. Serves 6 to 8.

Chocolate Cherry Cream Pie

Brandied cherries taste great in this rich chocolate cream pie.

1 1-lb. can pitted black bing cherries
1/4 cup brandy or sherry
1 4-oz. bar German sweet chocolate
1/2 pint heavy (whipping) cream
1 Cookie Crumb Crust*, baked and cooled

Drain cherries and place them in a small storage bowl. Add brandy. Cover and refrigerate for 8 to 24 hours. Place chocolate in a saucepan. Drain cherries and add brandy to chocolate. Place over low heat and stir until chocolate has partially melted. Remove pan from heat and stir mixture until smooth. Cool, stirring occasionally. In a chilled bowl with chilled beaters, beat cream until stiff peaks form; fold in chocolate mixture and drained cherries. Spoon into prepared crumb crust. Refrigerate until chilled. Serves 6 to 8.

Green Grape and Sour Cream Pie

This easy-to-make sour cream pie is flavored with honey and fresh orange juice.

1 tsp. unflavored gelatin
1/3 cup water
1/3 cup honey
1/4 cup fresh orange juice
1/2 pint heavy (whipping) cream
1/2 pint sour cream
1 9-inch Nut Cookie Crumb Crust*, baked and cooled
2 cups seedless green grapes, washed and halved

In a small saucepan, sprinkle gelatin over water; let stand until softened. Stir over very low heat until gelatin has dissolved and mixture is clear; cool. In a mixing bowl, combine honey and orange juice; add gelatin mixture and stir until smooth. In a chilled bowl with chilled beaters, beat cream until stiff peaks form; fold in sour cream and gelatin mixture. Spoon into prepared crumb crust. Refrigerate until filling has set. Just before serving, cover filling with grape halves. Serves 6 to 8.

Daiquiri Pie

1 3-oz. package lemon pudding
1 3-oz. package lime gelatin
1/3 cup granulated sugar
1/2 cup water
2 eggs, slightly beaten
1 1/4 cup more water
1/4 cup lemon juice
1/2 cup light rum
1/2 pint heavy (whipping) cream
1 tsp. grated lemon zest
1 9-inch Cookie Crumb Crust*, baked and cooled
Whipped cream, lightly sweetened, optional
Candied Lemon Peel*, optional

Combine pudding, gelatin, and sugar in a saucepan. Stir in 1/2 cup water, add eggs, and blend well. Add remaining water and lemon juice. Stir over medium heat until mixture comes to a full boil. Remove from heat; stir in rum. Refrigerate until chilled. In a chilled bowl with chilled beaters, beat cream until stiff peaks form; fold into chilled pudding mixture. Fold in lemon zest. Spoon into pie shell. Refrigerate until firm or until ready to serve. If desired, garnish pie with sweetened whipped cream and Candied Lemon Peel. Serves 6 to 8.

Strawberry Cream Pie

If ever there was a party pie, this is it.

> *1 tsp. unflavored gelatin*
> *1/4 cup Cherri-Swiss liqueur or cherry-flavored brandy*
> *1/2 pint heavy (whipping) cream*
> *1/4 cup confectioners' sugar*
> *1 9-inch pie shell, baked and cooled*
> *1 pint large, fresh strawberries, washed, hulled, and cut*
>   *lengthwise in halves*
> *Strawberry Glaze (recipe follows)*

Sprinkle gelatin over liqueur or brandy in a small saucepan. Place over low heat and stir until gelatin has dissolved and mixture is clear. Set aside. In a chilled bowl with chilled beaters, beat cream until stiff peaks form; fold in confectioners' sugar, then dissolved gelatin. Heap into prepared pie shell and place in refrigerator. When cream has set, cover it with halved strawberries, placing them as close together as possible. Spoon thick, chilled glaze over pie, letting it completely cover berries. Return pie to refrigerator until glaze is firm. Serves 6 or 8.

Strawberry Glaze

> *1/2 tsp. unflavored gelatin*
> *2 Tbs. Cherri-Swiss liqueur or cherry-flavored brandy*
> *1/2 pint fresh strawberries, washed and hulled*
> *1/4 cup granulated sugar*

In a small bowl or 1-cup measure, sprinkle gelatin over liqueur or brandy. Set aside until softened. Place berries in work bowl of a food processor or blender, process or blend to a purée, or place berries in a bowl and mash with a fork. Transfer puréed berries to a saucepan and add sugar. Place over medium heat and bring to a simmer. Add softened gelatin and stir until dissolved. Pour mixture in a shallow pan and place in refrigerator until thick but not set.

Pumpkin Chiffon Pie

Like most, I hold with tradition for Thanksgiving dinner, but after turkey with all the trimmings, I prefer my pumpkin pie "chiffoned."

> *1 1-lb. can pumpkin purée*
> *1/2 cup light cream*
> *1 cup light brown sugar*
> *1/2 tsp. ground cinnamon*
> *1/4 tsp. ground ginger*
> *5 eggs, separated*
> *1 envelope unflavored gelatin*
> *1/4 cup light rum*
> *1/2 pint heavy (whipping) cream*
> *1 tsp. grated orange rind*
> *1 9-inch Graham Cracker Crumb Crust*, baked and*
>   *cooled*
> *Candied Orange Rind* or Praline Powder**

In a saucepan, combine pumpkin purée, light cream, sugar, cinnamon, nutmeg, and ginger. Stir over medium heat until bubbly hot. In a large mixing bowl, beat yolks until frothy. Add hot pumpkin mixture and beat until well blended. Pour mixture back into saucepan and cook, stirring, until thickened. Sprinkle gelatin over rum; let stand until softened. Add to hot pumpkin mixture and stir until dissolved. Cool until mixture begins to thicken, stirring occasionally. In a separate bowl, beat egg whites until stiff but not dry. Fold in pumpkin mixture. Refrigerate until chilled but not set. In a chilled bowl with chilled beaters, beat cream until stiff peaks form. Fold in grated orange rind. Fold into chilled mixture. Spoon into crumb crust, mounding it high. Refrigerate until chilled. Just before serving, sprinkle top of pie with Praline Powder or Candied Orange Rind. Serves 6 to 8.

Peach Melba Pie

Even more dramatic and delicious than the classic recipe that inspired it!

> *1 Tbs. fresh lemon juice*
> *4 cups peeled, pitted, and sliced peaches*
> *2 Tbs. cornstarch*
> *4 Tbs. water*
> *1/4 cup Cassis (commercially prepared black currant syrup)*
> *1 envelope unflavored gelatin*
> *1/4 cup boiling water*
> *4 Tbs. sour cream*
> *1/2 pint heavy (whipping) cream*
> *1/4 cup confectioners' sugar*
> *1 9-inch Cookie Crumb Crust*, baked and cooled*

In a large bowl, combine lemon juice with peaches. Place 1 cup of mixture in work bowl of a food processor or blender; process or blend until puréed. In a saucepan, sprinkle cornstarch over water; stir until smooth. Add puréed fruit and Cassis. Cook over medium heat, stirring constantly, until thickened. Transfer to a storage bowl; cover and refrigerate until cool. Fold in remaining peaches. In a bowl, sprinkle gelatin over boiling water. Stir until dissolved. Stir in sour cream; set aside. In a chilled bowl with chilled beaters, beat cream until stiff peaks form; fold in confectioners' sugar and sour cream mixture. Spread over bottom and up sides of cooled pie crust. Fill with fruit mixture. Refrigerate until ready to serve. Serves 6 to 8.

The Best of Tarts

Perfect Tart Shells

A crisp, firm pastry that complements numerous fillings.

> *2 cups all-purpose flour*
> *Pinch of salt*
> *1/4 cup (1/2 stick) butter, cut into small pieces*
> *1/3 cup vegetable shortening*
> *2 Tbs. lemon juice, strained*
> *6 to 8 Tbs. ice water*

Processor Method: Place flour and salt in work bowl of a food processor; add butter and vegetable shortening. Process, turning motor on and off, until mixture resembles coarse meal, about 5 seconds. Pour lemon juice and about 3 tablespoons of ice water through feed tube of processor; process only until mixture comes together. Add additional water only if dough will not form.

Hand Method: Combine flour and salt in a large bowl. Cut in butter and vegetable shortening until mixture resembles coarse meal. Blend in lemon juice and about 6 tablespoons ice water. Mix just until dough holds together, adding more water if necessary.

Turn dough out onto a lightly floured work surface. Shape into a flat disk. Wrap loosely in waxed paper and refrigerate until chilled, or wrap in airtight plastic freezer bags, seal, and store in freezer until ready to use. When ready to use, roll dough out on a lightly floured work surface to thickness of about 1/8 inch; cut into rounds about 1 inch larger than tart pans. Fit rounds into pans and crimp edges to form decorative rim. Makes 12 3-inch tart shells, or 36 miniature shells.

Buttery Nut Tart Shells

Crispy and crunchy.

> *1/2 cup all-purpose flour*
> *1 1/2 cups nut meal† (hazelnut or walnut)*
> *1 cup (2 sticks) butter, cut into small cubes*
> *1 egg, lightly beaten*
> *Ice water*

In a large mixing bowl, combine flour and nut meal. Add butter cubes; cut in with pastry cutter or fingers until mixture resembles coarse meal. Stir in beaten egg and sufficient ice water to form a firm dough. Wrap in waxed paper and refrigerate until chilled, about 1 hour. Preheat oven to 425°F. Place about 2 tablespoons of dough in each of twelve 3-inch tart pans. Press dough evenly over bottom and up sides of each pan. Prick bottom of dough with tines of a fork. Bake in preheated oven 8 to 10 minutes, or until lightly brown. Makes 12 3-inch tarts.

Almond Custard Tart with Kiwis

> *1 4 3/4-oz. package vanilla custard mix*
> *1 3/4 cup light cream*
> *1/4 cup Amaretto liqueur*
> *12 3-inch tart shells, baked and cooled*
> *3 or 4 kiwis, peeled and cut crosswise into slices*

Prepare custard according to package directions, substituting light cream and liqueur for other liquid. Cool slightly, then spoon into tart

† Available at gourmet food shops.

shells, dividing evenly. Arrange kiwi slices in circles on top of custard, and spoon glaze over fruit. Makes 12 3-inch tarts.

Apricot Glaze

1 cup apricot preserves
1 Tbs. Amaretto liqueur

Place preserves into a small saucepan, and stir over low heat until melted. Pour through a fine sieve into a small bowl. Stir in liqueur.

Green Grape Tarts with Red Currant Glaze

Lovely for a midsummer luncheon. The pastry shells can be made ahead, and it takes only a few minutes to assemble the tarts.

1 tsp. unflavored gelatin
1/4 cup kirsch or other liqueur
1 cup red currant jelly
12 3-inch tart shells, baked and cooled
1/2 pint sour cream
1 lb. seedless green grapes, washed and stemmed
Sweetened whipped cream

In a saucepan, sprinkle gelatin over kirsch; let stand until softened, then stir over low heat until gelatin has dissolved. Add jelly and stir to a smooth glaze. Spoon a little glaze into each tart shell and spread it out evenly. Cover with a thick layer of sour cream and top with seedless grapes, mounding them slightly. Brush lavishly with glaze.

The tarts look so beautiful as is, don't mask them with whipped cream, but, if you like, serve a bowl of sweetened whipped cream separately to be spooned over each tart. Makes 12 tarts.

Praline Tarts

Deliciously rich.

> *1 cup brown sugar, firmly packed*
> *3/4 cup light corn syrup*
> *2 large eggs*
> *1/4 cup butter, room temperature*
> *1/2 tsp. vanilla*
> *1/2 cup chopped pecans*
> *12 Buttery Nut Tart Shells*, partially baked*

Preheat oven to 400°F. Cream butter with sugar until light and fluffy. Add corn syrup and eggs; beat until mixture is smooth. Add vanilla; fold in chopped pecans. Spoon into prepared tart shells, dividing evenly. Bake in preheated oven for 5 minutes. Reduce heat to 350°F. and bake until filling is firm, about 20 minutes. Cool on racks. Serve at room temperature. Makes 12 3-inch tarts.

Deep South Chocolate Pecan Tarts

Positively addictive.

> *3/4 cup granulated sugar*
> *1 cup molasses*
> *3 1-oz. squares bittersweet chocolate, chopped*

3 Tbs. butter, softened
3 eggs
2 Tbs. bourbon whiskey
1 1/2 cups coarsely chopped pecans
12 3-inch tart shells, partially baked
12 pecan halves

Preheat oven to 375°F. In a saucepan, combine sugar and molasses; place over medium heat until sugar has dissolved. Bring mixture to a full boil. Reduce heat and let simmer for about 2 minutes, stirring constantly. Stir in chocolate and butter, then immediately remove pan from heat and continue to stir until mixture is smooth. In a large mixing bowl, beat eggs until frothy; then add chocolate mixture and beat until blended. Add bourbon and pecans, stirring well to blend. Allow mixture to cool slightly. Spoon into tart shells, dividing evenly and making sure nuts are evenly distributed. Top each tart with a pecan half. Bake in preheated oven for 40 to 45 minutes, or until filling has set. Cool before serving. Makes 12 3-inch tarts.

Pineapple-Cranberry Tarts

Serve these colorful tart-sweet pastries as dessert for a Thanksgiving or Christmas buffet.

1 8-oz. can pineapple tidbits in juice
1 envelope unflavored gelatin
2 cups fresh or dry-frozen cranberries
1 cup granulated sugar
4 Tbs. currant jelly
12 3-inch tart shells, baked and cooled
Lightly sweetened whipped cream

Drain pineapple tidbits; set tidbits aside. Pour 1/2 cup of juice into a 1-cup measure and sprinkle with gelatin. Set aside. In a saucepan, combine pineapple tidbits, cranberries, sugar, and jelly. Place over moderate heat and cook, stirring frequently, until cranberry skins begin to burst, about 15 minutes. Remove pan from heat and stir in softened gelatin, stirring until dissolved. Cool to room temperature. Spoon into baked tart shell, dividing evenly. Refrigerate until chilled or ready to serve. Just before serving, top each tart with a dollop of sweetened whipped cream. Makes 12 3-inch tarts.

Fresh Strawberry Tarts with Strawberry Glaze

Only the freshest, ripest berries belong in these summertime tarts.

12 Buttery Nut Tart Shells*, baked and cooled
Cream Cheese Pastry Cream (recipe follows)
1 pint fresh ripe strawberries, washed and hulled
Strawberry Glaze (recipe follows)

Fill each tart shell with Cream Cheese Pastry Cream. Top with fresh whole strawberries. Spoon Strawberry Glaze over each.

Cream Cheese Pastry Cream

1 8-oz. package cream cheese
1/2 cup granulated sugar
2 Tbs. strawberry-flavored brandy or kirsch
2 Tbs. light cream or milk

In a large mixing bowl, combine ingredients; beat until fluffy and smooth.

Strawberry Glaze

1 pint strawberries, hulled and sliced
1 cup granulated sugar
3 Tbs. cornstarch
3 Tbs. strawberry brandy or kirsch

Combine strawberries and sugar in work bowl of a food processor or blender; process or blend until smooth. Transfer mixture to a saucepan. Sprinkle cornstarch over brandy or liqueur; stir until smooth. Stir into strawberry mixture. Place over low heat and cook, stirring, until mixture thickens. Cool slightly before serving.

Fresh Peach Tarts with Peach Brandy Pastry Cream

Just like the ones you will find at a French bakery.

12 3-inch tart shells, baked and cooled
1 cup apricot preserves
2 Tbs. peach brandy
Peach Brandy Pastry Cream (recipe follows)
12 peach halves, canned or poached and well drained
1/2 cup dry macaroon or Amaretti (Italian cookie)
     crumbs

In a saucepan, combine apricot preserves and peach brandy; place over low heat and stir until preserves have melted. Remove from heat; let cool to room temperature. Preheat oven to 375°F. Lightly coat bottom of each tart shell with cooled apricot glaze. Place on a long, flat baking sheet in preheated oven for about 2 minutes, or until glaze has set. Remove from oven; cool to room temperature. Spoon pastry cream into each, dividing evenly. Cover each with a peach half, cut side down. Spoon macaroon or Amaretti cookie crumbs around peach halves, covering pastry cream completely. If necessary, reheat apricot glaze to liquefy; brush over each peach half. Refrigerate tarts until ready to serve. Makes 12 tarts.

Peach Brandy Pastry Cream

1 cup milk
1/3 cup Vanilla Sugar*, or 1/3 cup granulated sugar plus
    1/2 tsp. vanilla extract
2 Tbs. all-purpose flour
2 egg yolks
1 Tbs. butter
1 Tbs. peach brandy

In top half of a double boiler, scald milk to steamy hot. In a bowl, combine Vanilla Sugar and flour. Add egg yolks and beat until smooth. Slowly add hot milk, beating as added. Return mixture to double boiler. Place over simmering water and cook, stirring, to a smooth thick custard that will coat back of a spoon, about 15 minutes. Add butter and peach brandy, blending well. Cover custard directly with plastic wrap and refrigerate until cooked, or until ready to serve.

Note: These tarts are best if served the same day they are made.

Pastry Scallop Shells

Use in place of plain tart shells.

> *2 cups all-purpose flour*
> *1/4 tsp. salt*
> *1/2 tsp. sugar*
> *8 Tbs. (1 stick) butter, very cold*
> *2 Tbs. vegetable shortening*
> *Ice water (1/3 to 1/2 cup)*
> *1 egg, lightly beaten*
> *Confectioners' sugar, optional*

Processor Method: Combine flour, salt, and sugar in work bowl of a food processor. Cut butter into 1/4-inch cubes and add to flour mixture. Add shortening. Process mixture until it resembles coarse meal. Add water, about 2 tablespoons at a time, through feed tube and process until a ball of dough forms on top of blades, about 15 seconds (using from 1/3 to 1/2 cup). The dough should be damp but not sticky. If it is too soft, sprinkle with 1 or 2 tablespoons flour and process briefly or until combined. If it feels too dry, add 2 or 3 tablespoons of water and process to blend well.

Hand Method: Place the flour, salt, and sugar in a large mixing bowl. Cut butter into 1/4-inch cubes and add to the flour mixture. Add shortening. With your fingertips, quickly work butter, flour, and shortening together until mixture resembles coarse meal. Sprinkle evenly with about 1/3 cup water, toss with a fork to moisten evenly, then bring into a ball, adding the additional water if necessary.

Preheat oven to 375°F. Butter the outside of 6 or 8 small scallop shells or the outside of 6 or 8 fluted tart pans. Divide dough into 6 or 8 equal pieces. One at a time, slide a scallop shell or tart pan, buttered side up, under the dough; lift it up slightly, and use your fingers to "cut" off the edges. Holding the lined shell or tart pan in one hand, push the dough lightly around the edge of the shell or pan to anchor. Brush with beaten egg, and shake confectioners' sugar onto dough. Place prepared shells or pans, not touching, on a long, flat baking sheet. Bake in preheated oven for 15 to 16 minutes, or until lightly browned (if necessary, bake in batches). Transfer to a rack. Cool to room temperature before removing from shells or pans. Makes 6 or 8 pastry shells.

Christmas Cranberry Scallops

1 envelope unflavored gelatin
1/2 cup orange juice
3 cups fresh cranberries
3/4 cups granulated sugar
1/2 cup orange marmalade
2 Tbs. Cointreau or other orange liqueur
6 or 8 Cookie Scallop Shells*, cooled
Lightly sweetened whipped cream

In a 1-cup measure, sprinkle gelatin over orange juice. Set aside to soften. In a saucepan, combine cranberries, sugar, marmalade, and liqueur. Cook, stirring, over low heat until cranberry skins begin to burst open, about 15 minutes. Stir in softened gelatin. Remove pan from heat and stir until cooled slightly. Transfer to a storage bowl, cover, and refrigerate until chilled. Spoon mixture into shells, dividing evenly. Serve with lightly sweetened whipped cream. Serves 6 or 8.

Apricot Kissle Scallops

Both the kissle and the scallop cookie shells can be prepared ahead. The dessert is put together just before serving. Tart, sweet, and delicious.

1 1/2 cups water
8 ozs. dried apricots
1/2 cup granulated sugar
3 Tbs. cornstarch
1/2 cup apricot brandy
6 or 8 Pastry Scallop Shells*, cooled
Sweetened Whipped cream
Slivered, toasted almonds

Combine water and apricots in a saucepan over high heat. Bring to a boil, then lower heat and let simmer for about 20 minutes, or until apricots are tender. Transfer apricots and about 1/2 cup cooking liquid to work bowl of a food processor or blender. Process or blend until puréed. Mix sugar and cornstarch in a saucepan; stir in apricot purée and brandy. Cook, stirring, over medium heat until mixture thickens. Spoon into a storage bowl; refrigerate until chilled. When ready to serve, spoon kissle into shells, dividing evenly. Top each serving with sweetened whipped cream and slivered almonds. Serves 6 or 8.

Fresh Strawberry Scallops with Cassis Zabaglione

The tart shells can be prepared ahead and stored in freezer until about half an hour before using, and the zabaglione can be made at least one day ahead.

4 egg yolks, room temperature
2 Tbs. granulated sugar
1/3 cup Crème de Cassis, or Cassis (black currant) syrup
1/2 cup heavy (whipping) cream
1 pint fresh strawberries

1 Tbs. more sugar
6 or 8 Pastry Scallop Shells*, cooled
Slivered almonds

Combine yolks and sugar in a large, heat-proof bowl. Set bowl over, not in, a pan of simmering water. Beat with an electric hand mixer or whisk until sugar has dissolved. Slowly add Cassis liqueur or syrup, beating as added. Continue to beat until mixture is thick and about triple in volume. Remove bowl from water and beat until zabaglione is cooled. Cover surface with plastic wrap. Refrigerate until chilled. In a chilled bowl with chilled beaters, beat cream until stiff peaks form; fold into chilled zabaglione. Wash, hull, and slice strawberries into a storage bowl. Sprinkle with sugar; toss to blend. Refrigerate until ready to use. Just before serving, fold strawberries into zabaglione and spoon into shells. Serves 6 or 8.

Apple Scallops

Old-fashioned apple pie served in a new and elegant way.

3 lbs. tart, crisp cooking apples, peeled, cored, and thinly
*   sliced*
1/2 cup granulated sugar
Zest from 1 lemon, cut into julienne strips
1/2 cup (1 stick) butter
1/2 tsp. ground cinnamon
1/2 tsp. ground ginger
1/2 tsp. allspice
1/4 cup currant jelly
6 or 8 Pastry Scallop Shells*, cooled
6 or 8 small scoops vanilla ice cream, optional

Place apples in a heavy dutch oven or deep saucepan; add sugar, lemon zest, butter, and spices. Cook, stirring frequently, over low heat until apples are glazed and tender and almost all moisture has evaporated, 25 to 30 minutes. Remove from heat and allow to cool slightly. Spoon warm apple mixture into shells, dividing evenly. Top each, if desired, with vanilla ice cream. Serves 6 to 8.

Sweet Elegance: French Quiches

Pâté Sucre
(Sweet Quiche Pastry Shell)

A firm, slightly sweet, cookie-like crust that won't become soggy when baked under a quiche filling.

> *2 cups all-purpose flour*
> *2 Tbs. granulated sugar*
> *1/4 tsp. salt*
> *3/4 cup (1 1/2 sticks) very cold butter, cubed*
> *1 egg, lightly beaten and chilled*
> *2 to 4 Tbs. ice water*
> *Currant or other clear jelly, or lightly beaten egg white*

Processor Method: Place flour, sugar, and salt in work bowl of a food processor; process briefly to mix. Add butter cubes. Process, turning motor on and off at 1/2-second intervals 7 or 8 times, just to start breaking up butter. Continue to process, adding chilled beaten egg through feed tube, until dough begins to mass together. Turn out on a lightly floured work surface and sprinkle with sufficient ice water to form a dough that is pliable—neither dry and hard nor overly sticky. Knead briefly, then wrap in waxed paper or plastic wrap and refrigerate for 1 hour or until ready to roll out.

Hand Method: Place flour in a large mixing bowl. Make a well in center and add remaining ingredients. Gather dough together with fingers into a compact mass. Turn out onto a lightly floured work surface. Knead lightly into a soft dough, adding additional flour if too sticky or a few drops of water if too dry. Pinch off a walnut-size piece of dough and smear it away from you about 4 inches across work surface. Continue with remaining dough. Gather into a ball, flatten slightly, and wrap in waxed paper or plastic wrap. Refrigerate for 1 hour or until ready to use.

Place chilled, flattened dough on a lightly floured work surface and roll from center toward edge, turning the dough a quarter of a turn as you are rolling so that it forms an even circle about 14 inches in diameter. Roll dough back on rolling pin, lift it up, and unroll onto a 10-inch flan ring. With fingertips, push dough down into ring, very gently so that it does not become stretched. Press dough around inside of ring with thumb and forefinger. Trim off excess; crimp edges. Refrigerate until chilled.

Preheat oven to 400°F. Line chilled shell with waxed paper and weight it down with beans, rice, or pie weights. Bake in preheated oven for about 10 minutes. Remove weights and paper. Brush inside of shell with jelly or lightly beaten egg white. Return to oven for 5 to 8 minutes. Cool to room temperature before filling and baking. Makes one 10-inch shell.

Creamy Banana Quiche

As easy as pie and, some say, twice as delicious.

> 1 10-inch Sweet Quiche Pastry Shell*
> 2 tsp. currant jelly
> 2 eggs
> 1 cup light (or half-and-half) cream
> 4 or 5 large ripe bananas (about 1 pound)
> 1/2 cup brown sugar

1 3-oz. package slivered almonds, toasted
Confectioners' sugar

Preheat oven to 400°F. Place pastry shell in preheated oven until hot. Spread bottom of shell evenly with currant jelly and return to oven until jelly melts and forms a glaze. Set shell aside while preparing filling. Place eggs in a mixing bowl, preferably one with a pouring lip. Beat with a whisk until frothy, then beat in cream. Peel and slice bananas and arrange them in a circle in pastry shell. Sprinkle with brown sugar and almonds. Pour cream mixture over surface. Bake in preheated oven for 25 to 30 minutes, or until custard has set. Let quiche stand at room temperature until cooled to lukewarm, then sprinkle with confectioners' sugar and serve. Serves 6.

Tart-Sweet Apple Quiche

1/4 cup (1/2 stick) butter
3 cups peeled and thickly sliced apples (5 to 6 large tart,
*   crisp apples)*
1 10-inch Sweet Quiche Pastry Shell*
3 eggs
1/2 cup Vanilla Sugar*, or 1/2 cup granulated sugar plus
*   1/2 tsp. vanilla extract*
3/4 cup heavy (whipping) cream
1/4 cup Calvados, apple brandy, or apple juice
Brandy-Flavored Whipped Cream (recipe follows),
*   optional*

Preheat oven to 350°F. Melt butter in a heavy skillet over low heat. Add apple slices and cook, stirring occasionally, until tender but not falling apart. Cool slightly; with a slotted spoon, place in shell. Beat eggs and Vanilla Sugar until well blended. Stir in cream. Add Calvados or apple brandy. Place apple-filled shell on a flat baking sheet and pour egg mixture over apples. Bake in preheated oven for 30 to 35 minutes, or until custard has set and crust is golden. Serve warm with Brandy-Flavored Whipped Cream. Serves 6 to 8.

Brandy-Flavored Whipped Cream

1/2 cup heavy (whipping) cream
2 Tbs. confectioners' sugar
1 Tbs. Calvados or apple brandy

In a chilled bowl with chilled beaters, beat cream until soft peaks form. Fold in confectioners' sugar a little at a time, and continue to beat until stiff. Fold in Calvados or apple brandy. Refrigerate until ready to use.

Peachy Peach Quiche

This easy summer pie takes just a few minutes to prepare and is truly delicious.

4 Tbs. all-purpose flour
2 Tbs. light brown sugar, firmly packed
2 Tbs. granulated sugar
2 Tbs. unsalted butter
1 10-inch Sweet Quiche Pastry Shell*
4 large, ripe peaches (about 1 lb.)
1 egg
1/2 cup heavy (whipping) cream
Confectioners' sugar

Preheat oven to 375°F. In a bowl, combine flour, sugars, and butter; stir with a fork until mixture resembles fine meal. Sprinkle half of mixture over bottom of pastry shell. Slice peaches directly from pit and arrange segments in a circle in pastry shell. Complete circle, then place remaining peach slices in center in a decorative pattern. In a small bowl, beat egg with cream until well blended. Pour mixture on top of fruit. Sprinkle with remaining flour mixture. Bake in preheated oven for 35 to 40 minutes, or until crust is golden brown and peaches are slightly caramelized. Sprinkle pie with confectioners' sugar. Let cool to lukewarm before serving. Serves 6 or 8.

Banana Quiche

Use sliced bananas instead of peaches and add about 1 tablespoon dark rum to cream mixture before pouring over fruit.

Chocolate Quiche with Pecans

Rich, dense, and delicious.

1 cup pecan halves
1 10-inch Sweet Quiche Pastry Shell*
3 1-oz. squares semisweet chocolate
4 or 5 seedless white grapes, optional
1/4 cup water
1/4 cup light rum, or 1/4 cup more water
3 eggs
3/4 cup Vanilla Sugar*, or 3/4 cup granulated sugar plus
1 tsp. vanilla extract
1/2 cup light brown sugar, firmly packed
1/4 cup milk
4 Tbs. (1/2 stick) butter, melted
2 Tbs. cornstarch
1/2 cup heavy (whipping) cream

Preheat oven to 375°F. Sprinkle pecan halves evenly over pastry shell. Set aside. Melt chocolate in top half of a double boiler over hot, not boiling, water; remove from heat. If desired, spear each grape with a small fork and dip each halfway into melted chocolate; push from fork onto waxed paper. Let cool until ready to use. Stir water and rum or additional water into chocolate. Set aside. In a medium bowl, beat eggs until blended. Stir in sugars, chocolate mixture, milk, melted butter, and cornstarch, blending well. Pour over pecan halves in tart shell.

Bake in preheated oven for 10 minutes. Lower oven temperature to 325°F. Continue baking for 30 to 35 minutes, or until center is almost set but still soft; do not overbake. Cool on a wire rack. Remove tart from pan. Top center with mounds of whipped cream. If desired, garnish with chocolate-dipped grapes. Serves 8.

Sweet Pizza Pies

Jam-Filled Pizza Pie

2 2/3 cups all-purpose flour
1 1/3 cups granulated sugar
1 1/3 cups butter or margarine
1/2 tsp. salt
1 egg
3/4 cup jam
1/4 cup finely chopped or grated almonds

Preheat oven to 325°F. Butter a 10-inch pizza pan. In a large mixing bowl, combine flour, sugar, butter, salt, and egg. Blend at low speed of an electric mixer until dough forms. Divide dough in half. Press half in bottom of prepared pizza pan. Spread jam over dough to within 1/2 inch of edge. Press remaining half of dough between two sheets of waxed paper to form a 10-inch circle. Remove top layer of waxed paper. Place dough over jam; remove second sheet of waxed paper. Sprinkle almonds over top, then lightly press dough into place with fingertips. Bake in preheated oven for 45 to 55 minutes, or until light golden brown. Cut into wedges to serve. Serves 12.

Lemon-Lime Pizza

1 cup all-purpose flour
6 Tbs. granulated sugar
1 oz. walnuts, finely grated
1/4 cup (1/2 stick) butter, chilled and cut into cubes
1 egg
3 3-oz. packages lemon custard mix
Water (as directed in recipe)
1 Tbs. fresh lemon juice
1 tsp. grated lemon rind
1 pint blueberries, washed and blotted dry
1/2 cup more granulated sugar
1/2 cup water
1 Tbs. fresh lime juice
Lightly sweetened whipped cream, optional

In a large mixing bowl, combine flour, sugar, and grated nuts. Add butter cubes. Blend quickly with fingertips until mixture resembles coarse meal. Add egg; mix until dough comes away from sides of bowl and holds together. Gather dough into a ball; flatten into a disk. Wrap loosely in waxed paper. Refrigerate until chilled or ready to use. Preheat oven to 400°F. Place disk of dough in center of a 10-inch pizza pan; with fingertips, press out evenly to cover bottom and sides of pan. Bake until golden brown, for 12 to 14 minutes. Remove from oven and cool completely.

Prepare lemon custard according to package directions, substituting 1 tablespoon lemon juice for other liquid. Stir in grated lemon rind. Pour into cooled pizza shell. Smooth top with spatula; spread to edges. Cover evenly with blueberries. Combine water and sugar in a small saucepan over medium heat. Bring to a boil. Stir in lime juice and continue to cook until syrup registers 240°F. (soft ball stage) on a candy thermometer. Remove from heat and stir until slightly cooled.

Slowly pour over blueberries. Refrigerate pizza until thoroughly chilled. Just before serving, top with lightly sweetened whipped cream, if desired. Serves 8.

Glazed Fruit Pizza

1 1/2 cups all-purpose flour
1/2 tsp. baking powder
Pinch of salt
1/2 cup (1 stick) butter
6 Tbs. granulated sugar
3 egg yolks
1 8-oz. jar apricot preserves
2 Tbs. apricot or other brandy
2 16-oz. cans pitted dark sweet cherries, well drained
2 16-oz. cans apricot halves, well drained
1 pint fresh strawberries, hulled and sliced

Preheat oven to 350°F. Butter a 10-inch pizza pan; set aside. Sift flour with baking powder and salt onto paper. Set aside. In a large mixing bowl, beat butter with sugar until light and fluffy; beat in egg yolks and continue to beat until mixture is well blended. Stir in sifted flour. Pat dough evenly into prepared pizza pan. Bake in preheated oven until lightly browned, about 15 minutes. Cool on a rack in pan.

In a saucepan, combine preserves and brandy; place over low heat and stir until mixture simmers. Remove from heat and cool slightly. Pour about half of mixture over pizza crust; spread out evenly. Press remaining apricot mixture through sieve. Pour back into saucepan; set aside. Arrange cherries over apricot mixture in a ring around edge of crust; arrange apricots, cut side down, in a ring inside cherries. Place strawberries in center of pizza, spreading them out to cover completely. Reheat sieved apricot mixture; spoon evenly over fruit. Serves 8 to 10.

Sweet Pizza Extravaganza

These days, just about everyone knows how to make a Sicilian pizza, but here's pizza news: buttery sweet pizza crust topped with chocolate, almonds, marshmallows, and coconut.

1/2 cup (1 stick) cold butter, cut into small cubes
2 cups all-purpose flour (more if needed)
1/4 cup light brown sugar, firmly packed
1/2 cup granulated sugar
2 eggs, lightly beaten
1 8-oz. chocolate bar with almonds, chopped
2 cups miniature marshmallows
1/2 cup packed shredded coconut

Preheat oven to 350°F.

Processor Method: Place butter and flour in work bowl of a food processor; process until mixture resembles coarse meal. Add both sugars; process briefly to mix. Add beaten eggs and process briefly until mixture lumps together into several moist pieces. Turn out onto a lightly floured work surface and form into a soft, moist ball. Flatten ball into a disk.

Hand Method: In a large mixing bowl, combine butter and flour. Work mixture with fingers until it resembles coarse meal. Stir in both sugars; add beaten eggs and stir with a fork until mixture comes together in a soft ball. Turn out on a lightly floured work surface, flatten into a disk.

Place disk of dough in center of a lightly oiled 12- or 14-inch pizza pan. With floured hands, press out evenly, covering entire bottom of pan. Bring edges of dough up slightly to form a rim. Bake in preheated oven for 18 to 20 minutes, or until lightly browned. Remove from oven and immediately sprinkle with chopped chocolate. Cover chocolate with marshmallows. Place pizza about 3 inches under broiler heat, just until marshmallows are lightly browned. With a serrated knife, cut pizza, as soon as it comes from oven, into pie-shaped wedges. Sprinkle wedges with coconut. Serve immediately, or leave at room temperature until ready to serve, then wrap loosely in foil and reheat briefly. Serves 8 or 10.

Glazed Strawberry Pizza

1 1/2 cups all-purpose flour
1/2 tsp. baking powder
Pinch of salt
1/2 cup (1 stick) butter, softened
4 Tbs. granulated sugar
4 egg yolks, lightly beaten
1 cup currant jelly
2 Tbs. kirsch or orange liqueur
2 pints strawberries, hulled and cut into halves
Sweetened whipped cream

Preheat oven to 375°F. Lightly grease a 12-inch pizza pan with softened butter. Sift flour with baking powder and salt onto paper. Set aside. In a large mixing bowl, cream butter with sugar; add egg yolks, and beat at high speed of an electric mixer until light and fluffy. Fold in flour mixture; mix to a soft dough. Pat dough evenly into prepared pizza pan. Bake in preheated oven until lightly browned, about 15 minutes. Cool in pan for about 5 minutes, then carefully transfer to a wire rack. Cool completely, then transfer back to washed and dried pizza pan. In a small saucepan, combine jelly and kirsch; cook, stirring, over low heat only until jelly has melted. Brush pizza with about one-third of mixture. Top with halved strawberries. Brush with remaining glaze. Let pizza stand until glaze has set. When ready to serve, cut into wedges and top each with sweetened whipped cream. Serves 8 to 12.

A Medley of Custards and Creamy Desserts

*The simple mixture of eggs, sugar, and milk,
known in nursery parlance as custard, forms the base
of the most elaborate and sophisticated desserts
professional chefs and wickedly clever cooks have devised.
This collection admirably proves the point.*

Cookie Cups

1/2 cup sifted all-purpose flour
1/2 cup coarsely chopped walnuts or almonds
1/4 cup light corn syrup
1/4 cup granulated sugar
4 Tbs. (1/2 stick) butter
2 Tbs. water

Preheat oven to 350°F. Place flour and walnuts or almonds in work bowl of a food processor or blender. Process or blend until nuts are finely ground. Transfer to a mixing bowl. Set aside. Combine corn syrup, sugar, butter, and water in a saucepan. Cook, stirring constantly, until mixture comes to a full boil; remove from heat. Stir into flour mixture, blending well. Drop batter by tablespoonfuls onto an ungreased baking sheet. Use about 2 tablespoons of batter for each cookie and leave about a 1-inch space between each. Bake in preheated oven for 10 to 12 minutes, or until edges are lightly browned but center is still soft. Working quickly remove each cookie with a spatula and, using a pot holder, hold it over an orange to form cupped shape. Hold for about 30 seconds. If cookies cool too quickly and are too brittle to shape, return them to the warm oven briefly to soften. Makes 6 cookie cups.

Puff Pastry Dessert Cups

Crisp and delicious edible cups for any dessert.

1 sheet frozen puff pastry from 17 1/4-oz. package
1 egg, lightly beaten
2 Tbs. granulated sugar
1/2 tsp. cinnamon

Preheat oven to 400°F. Invert six 1-cup custard cups and butter bottoms and sides. Thaw puff pastry sheet for 20 minutes, then unfold. Cut lengthwise into three strips, using crease marks as a guide. Cut two strips across into three equal pieces. (Wrap remaining strip in foil; store in freezer for other use.) One at a time, roll each piece out to a 6- to 6 1/2-inch square; drape square over an inverted, buttered custard cup, pressing pastry onto cup. Trim overlapping pastry into a circle about 1/4 inch around cup. Place on a flat baking sheet. Crimp edges flat and pierce top and sides of pastry with tines of a fork. Use a pastry brush or fingers to brush pastry with beaten egg; sprinkle each with sugar and cinnamon.

Bake in preheated oven until deep golden brown, for about 20 minutes. Remove from oven and let stand on baking sheet until cooled to room temperature. Use point of a small knife to gently lift pastry cups from custard cups. Return pastry cups, hollow side up, to baking sheet. Place in warm oven until insides are dry, about 5 minutes. Makes 6 pastry cups.

Baked Custards and Elegant Pots de Crème

Tropical Flan

1 cup granulated sugar
2 cups light cream
1/3 cup more granulated sugar
1/4 cup dark rum
6 egg yolks
4 whole eggs

Preheat oven to 350°F. Place 1 cup sugar in a large, heavy skillet over medium heat, and stir until sugar has dissolved to a deep golden syrup. Immediately pour syrup into a 2-quart soufflé dish or other round, ovenproof dish. Quickly tilt and turn dish until syrup coats bottom and sides evenly. Continue to turn dish until syrup hardens to a smooth glaze. Set aside. Use remaining ingredients to prepare custard mixture following directions for Vanilla Custard*. Pour mixture into caramelized dish. Place dish into a larger pan and pour sufficient hot water around it to come about two-thirds up sides. Bake in preheated oven for 1 to 1 1/4 hours, or until a small knife inserted near center comes out clean. Remove dish from hot water and place it on a rack until cooled to room temperature. Refrigerate until chilled and very firm, 6 to 8 hours, or overnight.

When ready to serve, use a table knife to cut around upper edges of custard to release it from dish; cover dish with a large, round, rimmed dessert platter and carefully invert both platter and dish. Remove dish, letting caramelized syrup run over top of custard and onto dish. Refrigerate until ready to serve. Serves 6 to 8.

Baked Vanilla Custard

Understated elegance.

> *1 vanilla bean*
> *1/2 cup water*
> *2 1/4 cups light cream*
> *1/2 cup granulated sugar*
> *3 egg yolks*
> *2 whole eggs*

Preheat oven to 325°F. Place vanilla bean and water in a small saucepan over medium heat; let simmer until liquid has reduced to about half, 5 to 10 minutes. Remove bean and, holding it over water, split it open and scrape seeds back into water. (Blot vanilla pod dry; reserve for other use.) Set vanilla water aside. Place cream in a heavy saucepan over medium heat until scalding hot. Stir in sugar; remove pan from heat. In a large mixing bowl, beat yolks and whole eggs with a fork until mixed. Slowly add hot milk mixture, stirring as added. Strain through a fine sieve into a wide-mouth pitcher or a bowl with a pouring lip. Stir in vanilla water. Place six custard cups in a shallow baking pan no deeper than cups. Pour custard mixture into each, dividing equally. Stir mixture after filling each cup, so that vanilla seeds are evenly distributed. Pour hot water around cups into pan to about half the depth of cups. Cover with a baking sheet. Bake for 1 hour, or until a small knife inserted in center of custard comes out clean. Remove cups from hot water. Cool, uncovered, on a rack to room temperature. Refrigerate until chilled or until ready to serve. Serve in cups. Serves 6.

Crème Brûlé

Prepare Vanilla Custard as above; bake, cool, then refrigerate until thoroughly chilled, at least 4 hours. Sieve about 2 tablespoons light brown sugar over each chilled custard, making sure custard is covered completely. Place custard cups on a long, flat baking sheet. Preheat broiler oven. Place custards about 3 inches under high broiler heat just until sugar melts, 2 to 3 minutes. Cool on a rack, then refrigerate until very cold, about 1 hour or until ready to serve. Serves 6.

Crème de Cacao

2 1-oz. squares semisweet chocolate
2 cups light cream
1/4 cup granulated sugar

1/4 cup coffee liqueur
2 whole eggs
3 egg yolks

Preheat oven to 325°F. In a heavy saucepan, combine chocolate, cream, and coffee liqueur; stir over medium heat until chocolate has melted and mixture is smooth. Stir in sugar. Remove pan from heat. In a large mixing bowl, stir whole eggs and yolks with a fork until mixed. Slowly add hot milk mixture, stirring as added. Strain mixture through a fine sieve into a wide-mouth pitcher or a bowl with a pouring lip. Bake, following directions for Vanilla Custard*. Serves 6.

Chocolate Apricot Pots de Crème

A rich, dark, fudge-like custard with a contrast of tart, sweet apricots.

2 Tbs. finely chopped dried apricots†
6 Tbs. orange liqueur
1 6-oz. bar German sweet chocolate
6 Tbs. light cream
2 egg yolks, lightly beaten
3 egg whites
Lightly beaten whipped cream
Cocoa, optional

In a small bowl, combine apricots and orange liqueur; let stand about 30 minutes or until ready to use. Place chocolate in top half of a double boiler over hot water until partially melted. Remove pan from water; stir until smooth. Stir in cream and egg yolks; add apricots and any unabsorbed liqueur. In a separate bowl, beat egg whites until stiff peaks form. Stir about one-fourth of beaten whites into chocolate

† If apricots are extremely dry, let soak in hot water about 30 minutes. Drain and proceed with recipe.

mixture; fold mixture into remaining beaten whites. Spoon into pots de crème or demitasse cups, filling them about three-fourths full. Refrigerate until chilled. Just before serving, top with lightly beaten cream and, if desired, sprinkle with cocoa. Serves 8 to 10.

Mocha Pots de Crème

A dessert you can make a day ahead.

> 2 cups miniature marshmallows
> 3/4 cup freshly brewed strong coffee
> 2 3-oz. extra-bittersweet chocolate bars, such as Lindt or
>   Tobler, chopped or broken into small pieces
> 3 egg yolks
> 3 Tbs. rum
> 1/2 pint heavy (whipping) cream
> Sweetened whipped cream, optional

In a medium saucepan, combine marshmallows, coffee, and chocolate. Stir over low heat until mixture is smooth. Remove from heat. In a medium bowl, beat egg yolks with rum until blended. Stir in a small amount of marshmallow mixture. Stir this into remaining hot mixture. Cook, stirring, over low heat until mixture thickens slightly, 2 to 3 minutes. Pour into a storage bowl. Refrigerate until chilled. In a chilled bowl with chilled beaters, beat cream until stiff peaks form. Fold into chilled chocolate mixture. Spoon into pots de crème or demitasse cups. Refrigerate until firm, 4 to 6 hours, or overnight. Top each serving with slightly sweetened whipped cream, if desired. Makes 6 small servings.

First Choice: Mousse!

Chilling Gelatin

Chill until slightly thickened: Place the gelatin mixture in the refrigerator or in a bowl set over a larger bowl of ice cubes until it is the consistency of unbeaten egg whites.

Chill until thickened: Refrigerate or place over a bowl of ice cubes until mixture shows a definite impression when a spoon is drawn through it. At this consistency, when you add fruit or other solid ingredients they will not sink to the bottom, but remain suspended throughout the mixture.

Refrigerate until firm: Your mousse, bavarian, or other gelatin dessert is ready to be unmolded when you tilt the mold to one side and the mixture does not move. When touched, it will not stick to your fingers.

Unmolding Gelatin

To unmold a Bavarian, Mousse, or Other Gelatin or Frozen Dessert: Hold the mold by its upper rim and dip it quickly (no more than 1 or 2 seconds) into a larger bowl of hot water. Wipe the mold dry, then loosen the sides of the dessert with a table knife. With wet fingers, moisten both the serving platter you are going to use and the top of the dessert. The moist surface makes it easy to slide the dessert, when unmolded, onto the center of the platter. Place the platter upside down over the mold and, holding both, invert them. Rap the platter lightly on a work surface to loosen the dessert. If it does not slide out easily, wrap a damp, hot towel around the mold and leave it for a few seconds. This should do the trick. If not, again dip the mold briefly in hot water and repeat the entire process.

If you don't have a decorative mold, use a loaf pan and, to make unmolding extremely easy, cut a double thickness of waxed paper to line the bottom and short sides of the pan and extend about 1/2 inch over each end. When ready to unmold the dessert, use a table knife to release the sides; place a chilled serving platter over the pan, spreading the endpaper liner outward. Invert the mold and platter, and, holding the endpapers firmly on the platter, lift off the mold, then peel off the paper.

Classic Chocolate Mousse

12 1-oz. squares bittersweet or semisweet chocolate,
    chopped
1/2 cup (1 stick) butter, softened to room temperature
6 eggs, separated, plus two additional egg whites
1/4 cup brandy
1/2 cup heavy (whipping) cream
1 Tbs. confectioners' sugar
1 Tbs. light rum or brandy
Chocolate Curls*

In top half of a double boiler, combine chocolate and butter; stir over hot water until chocolate has partially melted. Remove pan from water and stir until mixture is smooth. Add yolks one at a time, beating well after each addition. Stir in brandy. In a large mixing bowl, beat whites until stiff, moist peaks form. Using a spatula or wire whisk, fold in chocolate mixture; continue to fold until no white streaks remain. Spoon into a 1-quart serving bowl. Refrigerate until chilled or until ready to serve. In a chilled bowl with chilled beaters, beat cream until soft peaks form. Fold in confectioners' sugar and rum. Refrigerate until ready to use. To serve, spoon mousse onto small dessert plates or bowls. Top each serving with sweetened whipped cream and garnish with Chocolate Curls. Serves 8.

Chocolate Cherry Mousse

Drain liquid from a 1-lb. can of pitted black bing cherries. Place in a bowl and cover with brandy. Cover bowl and refrigerate overnight.

Prepare Classic Chocolate Mousse as directed. Drain cherries and fold into mousse. Serve, if you like, with brandy marinade as a liqueur.

Mousse de Marron

Drain syrup from an 8-oz. jar of chopped marrons in heavy syrup. Prepare Classic Chocolate Mousse as directed, using drained syrup from marrons instead of brandy. Fold chopped marrons into prepared mousse.

Classic White Chocolate Mousse

Prepare Classic Chocolate Mousse as directed, substituting white chocolate for bittersweet or semisweet chocolate.

Chocolate Mousse Loaf with Whipped Cream Frosting

This very rich chocolate loaf cuts into elegant dessert slices.

16 1-oz. squares semisweet chocolate, chopped
6 eggs, separated
1 cup (2 sticks) butter
2 Tbs. unsweetened cocoa
1 tsp. instant espresso
1/4 cup granulated sugar
1 cup heavy (whipping) cream
1 cup more heavy cream

2 Tbs. confectioners' sugar
1 Tbs. Crème de Cacao or other chocolate-flavored
liqueur, optional
Grated bittersweet chocolate, optional

Grease a 9-inch loaf pan with butter; line bottom and both ends of pan with parchment or waxed paper, extending paper 1/2 inch beyond ends. Butter paper. Place chocolate in top half of a double boiler over simmering water until partially melted; remove pan from water and stir until chocolate is smooth. Add egg yolks one at a time, beating well after each addition. Add butter, cocoa, and instant espresso and beat until mixture is thoroughly blended. Use a rubber spatula to scrape mixture into a large mixing bowl.

In a chilled bowl with chilled beaters, beat cream until soft peaks form; fold into chocolate mixture. In another bowl, beat egg whites until stiff; fold into chocolate mixture. Spoon mixture into prepared loaf pan. Cover pan and refrigerate until well chilled and firm, several hours or overnight. About 1 hour before serving, turn loaf out onto a serving platter. Whip remaining cream until stiff peaks form; fold in confectioners' sugar and, if desired, Crème de Cacao; spread on top and sides of loaf. If desired, sprinkle with grated chocolate. Return loaf to refrigerator until ready to serve. Serves 8 to 10.

Chocolate Soufflé Glace
(Cold Chocolate Mousse Soufflé)

This cool and sumptuous creation can be whipped up in less time than the telling.

2 envelopes unflavored gelatin
1/4 cup water
4 eggs, separated
1 cup granulated sugar

3/4 cup light cream
4 1-oz. squares semisweet chocolate, finely chopped or
  grated
1/4 cup brandy
1/2 cup more granulated sugar
1 1/2 cups heavy (whipping) cream
1/4 cup confectioners' sugar
Chocolate Curls*, optional

Tear off a piece of aluminum foil sufficiently long to wrap around a 1-quart soufflé dish. Fold foil into thirds lengthwise. Brush half of one side with tasteless salad oil. Wrap foil around soufflé dish, oiled side up and facing in. Pull tightly together and fasten with string or adhesive tape. In a small saucepan, sprinkle gelatin over water. Stir over low heat until gelatin has dissolved. Set aside. In top half of a double boiler, combine egg yolks and sugar. Place over simmering water. Beat mixture until it is about double in volume. Fold in cream, add dissolved gelatin, and stir until thoroughly combined. Add chocolate and brandy, and stir from bottom and sides of pan to a smooth custard. Remove pan from water and place in a large bowl of ice water. Let stand, stirring occasionally, until custard thickens and mounds when dropped from spoon.

In a large bowl, beat egg whites at high speed of an electric mixer until soft peaks form when beaters are lifted. Add remaining 1/2 cup sugar about 2 tablespoons at a time, beating well after each addition. Beat until stiff peaks form; fold in chocolate custard mixture. In a chilled bowl with chilled beaters, beat cream with confectioners' sugar until stiff. Remove about one-fourth of whipped cream to a small bowl and refrigerate until ready to use for topping. Fold remaining whipped cream into chocolate custard mixture. Spoon into prepared soufflé dish. Refrigerate until set, about 3 hours. To serve, remove collar from soufflé dish, mound reserved whipped cream over surface of soufflé, and, if desired, garnish with Chocolate Curls. Serves 8.

Chocolate Mousse Soufflé with Strawberry Whipped Cream

A dessert lover's fantasy come true.

1 envelope unflavored gelatin
1/2 cup brandy
6 egg yolks
1 cup confectioners' sugar
6 1-oz. squares bittersweet chocolate, chopped
1 pint heavy (whipping) cream
1 3-oz. bar Lindt or Tobler dark chocolate with hazelnuts
or almonds, chopped
1 tsp. more unflavored gelatin
1/4 cup water
1/2 pint more heavy cream
1/2 tsp. almond extract
1/2 pint strawberries, hulled and chopped
2 Tbs. slivered almonds

Prepare a collar for a 1 1/2-quart soufflé dish following directions for Chocolate Soufflé Glace. In a small skillet, sprinkle gelatin over brandy; let stand until softened, then stir over low heat until gelatin has dissolved. Set aside. In top half of a double boiler, combine egg yolks and sugar. Place over simmering water and beat with a whisk or electric hand mixer until about double in volume. Fold in dissolved gelatin and bittersweet chocolate. Remove pan from water, and beat until mixture has cooled to room temperature. In a chilled bowl with chilled beaters, beat cream until soft peaks form; fold into yolk mixture, then fold in chopped chocolate with hazelnuts or almonds. Spoon into prepared soufflé dish. Refrigerate until mixture is firm.

Sprinkle remaining gelatin over water in a small saucepan. Let soften, then stir over low heat until gelatin has dissolved and mixture is clear. In a chilled bowl with chilled beaters, beat remaining cream until soft peaks form; fold in dissolved gelatin, almond extract, and strawberries. Mound over firm chocolate soufflé mixture and sprinkle with almonds. Refrigerate until topping is firm or until ready to serve. Just before serving, carefully remove foil collar. Serves 10 to 12.

Party-Perfect Orange Chocolate Mousse

A 10-minutes-to-make recipe, but so flavorful they'll never know.

> *2 8-oz. bittersweet chocolate bars*
> *2 Tbs. orange liqueur*
> *2 Tbs. finely chopped Candied Orange Rind**
> *1 pint heavy (whipping) cream*
> *Slivered Candied Orange or Lemon Rind**

Place chocolate bars in top half of a double boiler over hot, not boiling, water until partially melted. Remove from heat; stir until smooth. Stir in chopped Candied Orange Rind. Cool to room temperature, stirring occasionally. In a chilled bowl with chilled beaters, beat cream until stiff peaks form. Fold in chocolate mixture. Spoon into eight shallow dessert bowls or stemmed glasses. Refrigerate until ready to serve. Just before serving, sprinkle with slivered Candied Orange or Lemon Rind. Serves 8.

Apricot Mousse

Light and lovely to look at—*and* to eat.

> *2 envelopes unflavored gelatin*
> *1/4 cup cold water*
> *1/4 cup lemon juice*

5 eggs
1/2 cup granulated sugar
1/4 tsp. almond extract
2 Tbs. apricot brandy
1 12-oz. can (Solo brand) apricot filling
1/2 pint heavy (whipping) cream
Sweetened whipped cream, optional

In a small saucepan, sprinkle gelatin over cold water; let stand until softened, 2 to 3 minutes. Add lemon juice and stir over low heat until gelatin has completely dissolved and mixture is clear. Set aside. In a large mixing bowl, combine eggs and sugar; beat at high speed of an electric mixer until very pale, thick, and about triple in volume. Add dissolved gelatin, beating at high speed as added. Fold in apricot filling, blending well. In a chilled bowl with chilled beaters, beat cream until soft peaks form. Fold in about 1 cup of apricot mixture, then fold this into remaining apricot mixture. Spoon into eight dessert bowls or wine glasses, dividing evenly. Refrigerate until chilled. Garnish each serving with sweetened whipped cream, if desired. Serves 8.

Very Berry Mousse

Cassis syrup ups the flavor of this very pretty strawberry mousse.

1 10-oz. package frozen strawberries in heavy syrup
1 envelope unflavored gelatin
1/4 cup Cassis syrup
2 tsp. lemon juice
2 egg whites
2 Tbs. granulated sugar
1/2 pint heavy (whipping) cream
Fresh raspberries or strawberries

Place frozen block of strawberries in a sieve set over a bowl until thawed. Pour syrup from berries into a saucepan; reserve berries. Sprinkle gelatin over syrup. Add Cassis and lemon juice; stir to mix. Place over low heat and stir until gelatin has completely dissolved. Place reserved strawberries in work bowl of a food processor or blender. Process or blend until smooth; add to gelatin mixture. Cover and refrigerate until mixture mounds slightly when dropped from a spoon, about 20 minutes. In a large bowl, beat egg whites until soft peaks form; add sugar and beat until dissolved. Fold in strawberry mixture.

In a chilled bowl with chilled beaters, beat cream until soft peaks form; fold about 2 tablespoons into strawberry mixture, then fold mixture into remaining whipped cream. Refrigerate until chilled. When ready to serve, spoon mousse into individual dessert bowls or stemmed wine glasses; garnish each serving with fresh raspberries or strawberries. Serves 6.

Lemon Chiffon Mousse

Light and airy, with a tart, sweet taste that is especially enjoyable after a hearty meal.

> *3 eggs*
> *1/3 cup strained fresh lemon juice (from 3 small*
> *lemons)*
> *1 package unflavored gelatin*
> *1/2 cup granulated sugar*
> *Pinch of salt*
> *1/3 cup orange liqueur or light rum*
> *1/4 cup more granulated sugar*
> *1 cup heavy (whipping) cream*
> *Bittersweet Chocolate Sauce*, optional*

Separate eggs; set egg whites aside. Place lemon juice in top half of a double boiler. Sprinkle gelatin over surface; let stand until softened. Add 1/2 cup sugar, salt, and egg yolks; stir to blend. Cook over simmering water, stirring constantly from bottom and sides of pan, until gelatin dissolves and mixture thickens slightly. Remove from heat; stir in liqueur or rum. Transfer to a cool bowl and refrigerate until custard begins to thicken, about 5 minutes. In a separate large bowl, beat egg whites until foamy. Continue to beat, adding remaining sugar in four parts, until stiff peaks form when beater is lifted from bowl. In a separate bowl, beat cream until soft peaks form. Fold beaten egg whites into chilled custard, then fold in whipped cream. Spoon into stemmed glasses, individual dessert dishes, or one large, decorative serving bowl. Drizzle with chocolate sauce, if desired. Refrigerate until ready to serve. Serves 6 to 8.

Mocha Mousse

Brown sugar and coffee liqueur give special flavor to this light and lovely mousse.

1/4 cup light brown sugar, packed
3 Tbs. freshly brewed strong coffee
3 Tbs. coffee liqueur
6 1-oz. squares semisweet chocolate
1/2 pint heavy (whipping) cream, chilled
4 egg whites
4 Tbs. confectioners' sugar

In a saucepan, combine brown sugar and coffee. Place over low heat until sugar has dissolved. Stir in liqueur. Set aside. Place chocolate in top half of a double boiler over simmering water until melted. Stir in 4 tablespoons cream. Add coffee mixture. Remove pan from water, place in a large pan of ice water, and stir until cooled to room temperature. In a chilled bowl with chilled beaters, beat remaining cream until soft peaks form. Fold in confectioners' sugar a little at a time, and continue to beat until stiff. In a second bowl, beat egg whites until stiff peaks form; gently stir in about one-fourth of chocolate mixture. Fold this mixture into remaining beaten whites. Fold in whipped cream. Spoon into stemmed glasses, individual dessert dishes, or one large, decorative serving bowl. Refrigerate until chilled or until ready to serve. Serves 8.

Nesselrode Mousse

As rich as a Rockefeller or Rothschild.

> 2 envelopes unflavored gelatin
> 1/4 cup cold water
> 2 cups light cream
> 1/2 cup granulated sugar
> 2 eggs, separated
> 1/4 cup light rum
> 1 8-oz. bottle Nesselrode sauce
> 1/2 pint heavy (whipping) cream
> 2 Tbs. confectioners' sugar
> 1 1-oz. square semisweet chocolate

In a small saucepan, sprinkle gelatin over cold water; let stand until softened, 2 to 3 minutes. Pour light cream into top half of a double boiler; place over medium heat until steamy hot. Do not allow to boil. Add sugar and stir in softened gelatin. Cook, stirring, until gelatin has dissolved. Remove pan from heat. In a mixing bowl, beat egg yolks until light and lemony yellow. Stir in about half of hot cream mixture, blending well; stir into remaining cream. Place pan over simmering water and cook, stirring, to a smooth custard sufficiently thick to coat spoon. Remove pan from water and place it in a large bowl of ice water. Let stand, stirring often, until custard mounds slightly, 15 to 20 minutes. Stir in rum and Nesselrode sauce. Remove pan from water.

In a large chilled bowl with chilled beaters, whip cream until soft peaks form. Fold in confectioners' sugar. Spoon about one-fourth into a storage bowl; cover and refrigerate until ready to use. Fold remainder into Nesselrode custard mixture. In another bowl, beat whites until stiff peaks form; fold into custard mixture. Spoon into eight stemmed wine glasses or dessert bowls. Just before serving, top with remaining whipped cream. Use a vegetable parer or sharp knife to shave chocolate over top. Serves 8.

Picture-Perfect Bavarians

Classic Bavarian

2 envelopes unflavored gelatin
1/2 cup brandy, rum, kirsch, or other liqueur
5 eggs, separated, plus one additional egg yolk
1/2 cup granulated sugar
2 cups light cream
1/2 pint heavy (whipping) cream
1 cup puréed fresh fruit (strawberries, peaches, apricots,
*   nectarines, bananas, etc.)*
Additional fresh fruit or fruit sauce, optional

In a small saucepan, sprinkle gelatin over brandy, rum, or liqueur. Let stand until softened. In a large mixing bowl, combine egg yolks and sugar. Beat with a whisk or electric beater until about triple in volume. Place light cream in a saucepan over medium heat until scalding hot. Add to yolk mixture in a thin, steady stream, beating as added. Pour mixture back into saucepan. Cook, stirring, over medium heat to a smooth custard sufficiently thick to coat spoon. Stir in softened gelatin. Remove from heat and transfer to a storage bowl. Cover custard surface with plastic wrap; refrigerate until chilled.

In another bowl, beat egg whites until soft peaks form. Fold into chilled mixture. In a chilled bowl with chilled beaters, beat heavy cream until soft peaks form. Fold into custard mixture until no streaks of white remain. Fold in desired puréed fruit. Spoon into a 2-quart mold. Cover mold and seal with aluminum foil. Refrigerate until very firm, 6 to 8 hours or overnight. Unmold just before serving. Garnish with additional fresh fruit or fruit sauce, if desired. Serves 8.

Sherry Macaroon Bavarian

Substitute semisweet sherry for brandy, rum, or liqueur. Fold 1 cup crumbled macaroons into prepared Bavarian before spooning it into mold.

Coffee Bavarian

Substitute freshly brewed strong coffee for brandy, rum, or liqueur. Fold about 1/2 cup crushed candy coffee beans into Bavarian before spooning it into mold.

Orange Bavarian

Substitute fresh orange juice for brandy, rum, or liqueur. Fold about 1/2 cup orange marmalade into Bavarian before spooning it into mold.

Chocolate Satin Bavarian

Sumptuous, densely chocolate Bavarian afloat in a luxurious tart, sweet lemon custard.

> *12 1-oz. squares semisweet chocolate*
> *1 Tbs. instant coffee*
> *1/4 cup (1/2 stick) butter*
> *1/4 cup milk*
> *2 large eggs, separated, plus 2 additional egg whites*
> *1/4 cup coffee liqueur*
> *1/2 cup heavy (whipping) cream*
> *1/2 cup granulated sugar*
> *Lemon Custard Sauce (recipe follows)*

Combine chocolate, instant coffee, butter, and milk in top half of a double boiler. Place over hot water and stir until chocolate has melted and mixture is steamy hot. Remove pan from water. Stir in beaten egg yolks and coffee liqueur. Place pan in a large bowl of ice water and beat until cooled to room temperature. In a chilled bowl with chilled beaters, beat cream until stiff peaks form. In another bowl, beat egg whites at high speed until soft peaks form. Add sugar about 1 tablespoon at a time, beating constantly until mixture is very stiff and glossy; fold in chocolate mixture and whipped cream. Pour mousse into a long, shallow baking dish. Cover mousse directly with plastic wrap, cover pan with foil, and seal. Refrigerate for 6 to 8 hours or overnight. To serve, pour Lemon Custard Sauce into rimmed dessert plates; tilt plates to coat evenly with sauce. Place scoops of cold mousse over each. Serve at once. Serves 8 to 10.

Lemon Custard Sauce

> *1/2 cup fresh lemon juice*
> *1 tsp. grated lemon zest*
> *1 cup granulated sugar*

1/2 cup (1 stick) butter, cut into 8 slices
3 eggs
1 Tbs. kirsch

In top half of a double boiler, combine lemon juice, lemon zest, sugar, and butter. Cook over simmering water, stirring frequently, until butter is melted and sugar dissolved. In a mixing bowl, beat eggs until blended. Stir this mixture into remaining lemon mixture. Add kirsch and cook, stirring, over simmering water until smooth and slightly thickened. Serve warm or at room temperature.

Chocolate-Glazed Raspberry Bavarian

1 4 3/4-oz. package vanilla pudding mix
2 1/2 cups milk
1/4 cup Framboise liqueur, raspberry brandy, or kirsch
1 3-oz. package raspberry gelatin
1 envelope unflavored gelatin
1 1/2 cups boiling water
1 10-oz. package frozen raspberries in heavy syrup
1/2 pint heavy (whipping) cream
6 1-oz. squares bittersweet or semisweet chocolate,
*   chopped*
2 tsp. flavorless salad oil

Prepare vanilla pudding with milk and liqueur, following package directions. Transfer to a storage bowl, and cover custard surface with plastic wrap. Refrigerate until ready to use. In another bowl, combine raspberry and unflavored gelatins; pour in boiling water. Stir until gelatins have dissolved. Break frozen block of raspberries and syrup into small chunks; add to gelatin mixture and stir until raspberries thaw and separate. Refrigerate until chilled and slightly thickened.

Fold into vanilla pudding and continue to fold until no streaks of raspberry gelatin remain. In a chilled bowl with chilled beaters, beat cream until soft peaks form. Fold into pudding mixture, blending well. Pour mixture into a 9 1/4- × 5 1/4- × 2 3/4-inch metal loaf pan. Cover pan and seal with foil. Refrigerate until very firm, 6 to 8 hours or overnight.

Several hours before serving, unmold Bavarian onto an oblong serving platter and return to refrigerator. Place chopped chocolate and oil in a small saucepan over low heat until chocolate has partially melted; remove pan from heat and stir until mixture is smooth. Let stand at room temperature, stirring occasionally, until cooled to room temperature. Pour over top of unmolded Bavarian, and quickly use a metal spatula or table knife to smooth top, letting excess spill onto sides. Refrigerate until ready to serve. To serve, cut Bavarian across into thick slices. Serves 8 to 10.

Grand Marnier Bavarian with Caramelized Orange Slices

2 envelopes unflavored gelatin
1/2 cup Grand Marnier or other orange liqueur
5 large eggs, separated, plus 1 additional egg yolk
1 cup granulated sugar
2 cups milk
2 Tbs. confectioners' sugar
1/2 pint heavy (whipping) cream
3 large navel oranges
1 more Tbs. orange liqueur
1/2 cup more confectioners' sugar

In a small bowl, sprinkle gelatin over liqueur; set aside. In a mixing bowl, combine egg yolks and granulated sugar, beating until mixture is about double in volume. Pour milk into a saucepan; place over low heat until scalded. Add to beaten yolk mixture in a slow, steady stream, beating as added. Return this mixture to saucepan and cook over low heat, stirring constantly, to a thick, smooth custard. Stir in gelatin and liqueur. Transfer to a large mixing bowl. Place bowl in a larger bowl of ice water; beat until cooled to room temperature. Allow to stand, stirring occasionally, until mixture mounds slightly. In a separate bowl, beat egg whites until soft peaks form. Fold in 2 tablespoons confectioners' sugar and beat until stiff but not dry.

In a chilled bowl with chilled beaters, beat cream until soft peaks form. Fold in beaten whites, then chilled custard mixture, and continue to fold until cream, egg whites, and custard are thoroughly incorporated. Spoon into a 2-quart mold; cover and seal mold with plastic wrap or aluminum foil. Refrigerate until firm or until ready to serve. Several hours before serving, peel and cut oranges into thick slices. Cut each slice in half. Arrange halves, slightly overlapping, in a long, shallow baking dish. Sprinkle with remaining liqueur and sugar. Place about 4 inches under a preheated broiler; broil until sugar has dissolved and caramelized over slices. Cool to room temperature, then refrigerate until ready to serve. To serve, unmold Bavarian onto a decorative platter and surround with caramelized oranges. Serves 8.

Quick-Mix Lemon Bavarian

1 3-oz. package lemon gelatin
1 envelope unflavored gelatin
1 cup boiling water
3/4 cup cold water
1/4 cup lemon juice
1 4 3/4 oz. package lemon pudding mix
1 tsp. grated lemon rind
1/2 pint heavy (whipping) cream
Raspberry or chocolate sauce (see sauce chapter)

Place lemon gelatin and unflavored gelatin in a large mixing bowl; pour in boiling water and stir until gelatins have completely dissolved. Add cold water and lemon juice, stirring to blend. Refrigerate until gelatin has thickened slightly. Prepare lemon pudding with milk, following package directions. Fold in lemon rind; transfer to a storage bowl and cover surface with plastic wrap. Refrigerate until chilled. Fold chilled gelatin into pudding, blending well. In a chilled bowl with chilled beaters, beat cream until soft peaks form; fold into pudding mixture, blending well. Pour into a 1 1/2-quart mold. Cover mold and seal with foil. Refrigerate until very firm, 6 to 8 hours or overnight. When ready to serve, unmold onto a serving platter. Spoon a little raspberry or chocolate sauce over surface. Serve any remaining sauce separately. Serves 8 to 10.

Berries and Cream

Pineapple-Raspberry Parfait

1 6-oz. package strawberry gelatin
1 1/2 cups boiling water
2 10-oz. packages frozen raspberries in heavy syrup
1 8-oz. can crushed pineapple in syrup
1/2 pint sour cream
2 Tbs. Framboise or other liqueur, optional
1/2 pint heavy (whipping) cream
Slightly sweetened whipped cream, optional

Place gelatin in a large bowl. Add boiling water and stir to dissolve. Break frozen raspberries into small chunks; add to gelatin mixture and stir until berries separate. Stir in crushed pineapple, pineapple syrup, sour cream, and, if desired, liqueur. In a separate chilled bowl with chilled beaters, beat cream until soft peaks form. Fold into gelatin mixture. Spoon into stemmed glasses, individual dessert dishes, or one large, decorative serving bowl. Refrigerate until ready to serve. Just before serving, top with slightly sweetened whipped cream, if desired. Serves 10 to 12.

Strawberry Cream à la Russe

1 pint light (or half-and-half) cream
3/4 cup granulated sugar
2 envelopes unflavored gelatin
1/4 cup grenadine or Hero brand Swiss strawberry syrup
1 pint sour cream, chilled
1 tsp. lemon flavoring or 1 tsp. grated lemon zest
1 pint fresh strawberries, hulled and cut into halves or
*   quarters*

Place cream and sugar in a saucepan over low heat; stir until sugar has dissolved and mixture is hot. Sprinkle gelatin over grenadine; let stand until softened, about 1 minute. Add to hot cream and sugar mixture and stir until dissolved. Pour into a large mixing bowl, preferably one with a pouring lip. Refrigerate until cold. Fold in chilled sour cream and lemon flavoring or zest. Return mixture to refrigerator until it begins to thicken. Pour or spoon into six 1-cup molds, or one 6-cup ring mold. Refrigerate several hours or until ready to serve. Unmold individual servings onto chilled dessert plates and surround each with chopped strawberries, or unmold ring onto a chilled platter and fill center with strawberries. Serves 6.

Berries with Crème Anglaise and Tipsy Whipped Cream

A beautiful combination of fresh berries, classic custard, and whipped cream just slightly inebriated with a heady liqueur.

> *1 cup milk*
> *4 egg yolks*
> *1/2 cup granulated sugar*
> *1 cup heavy (whipping) cream*
> *2 Tbs. confectioners' sugar*
> *1 to 2 Tbs. liqueur: Fraise de Bois (for strawberries),*
> *Framboise (for raspberries), Maraschino (for*
> *cherries), or kirsch (for any combination of berries)*
> *1 quart berries: strawberries, raspberries, blueberries,*
> *cherries, or any combination of berries*

Pour milk into top half of a double boiler. Place over low heat until steamy hot. In a bowl, beat egg yolks with sugar until well blended, then whisk them into hot milk. Place over simmering water and stir constantly until mixture is thick and smooth. Remove from heat and continue to stir, scraping mixture from bottom and sides of pot, until cooled to room temperature. Cover custard surface with plastic wrap and refrigerate until chilled. In a chilled bowl with chilled beaters, beat cream until soft peaks form; fold in sugar, liqueur, and chilled custard. Add berries; fold to distribute evenly. Spoon into one large, decorative glass serving bowl or into stemmed wine or parfait glasses. Serves 8 to 12.

Zabaglione Berry Parfait

Elegant and completely irresistible.

Zabaglione Sauce (recipe follows)
1 pint fresh strawberries, raspberries, or blackberries
2 cups bite-sized cake cubes, from Génoise, sponge,
*   soufflé, or angel food cake*

Spoon about 2 tablespoons chilled Zabaglione Sauce into each of 6 to 8 stemmed wine or parfait glasses. Top sauce with a sprinkling of fruit and a few cake cubes. Repeat until glasses are filled, ending with sauce and reserving enough berries for garnish. Refrigerate until sauce has been partially absorbed by cake, about 30 minutes, or until ready to serve. Just before serving, sprinkle each parfait with a few more berries. Serves 6 to 8.

Zabaglione Sauce

4 large egg yolks
1/2 cup granulated sugar
3 Tbs. Marsala wine

Combine ingredients in top half of a double boiler. Cook over simmering water, beating constantly with an electric hand beater or whisk, until mixture is very thick, pale, and about triple in volume. Remove from heat and beat a final minute. Pour into a storage bowl; cover with plastic wrap. Refrigerate until chilled or ready to use.

Elegant Fruit Creations

*There are those who believe that fresh fruit should be
eaten "out of hand" and that it is sacrilegious
to try to improve on nature. Here, however, is proof
that gilding can improve the lily.*

Fruit Desserts
for Special Occasions

Sparkling Fresh Fruit Compote

Serve this dramatically beautiful blend of the summer's bounty in one large, straight-sided glass bowl, or in eight stemmed bubble-shaped wine glasses.

>   1 large navel orange
>   4 to 6 fresh peaches
>   1 Tbs. lemon juice
>   1 Tbs. granulated sugar
>   1 pint strawberries, hulled and halved
>   1 pint blueberries
>   3 or 4 kiwis, peeled and cut into rounds
>   1 cup champagne or other sparkling white wine
>   Lemon Ice Cream*
>   Mint sprigs

Cut orange in half; cut each half into six wedges. One at a time, hold each wedge over a large bowl and, with a small, sharp knife, cut fruit from peel, dropping fruit into a separate bowl. Pour juice into a 2-cup measure; set aside. Peel, pit, and chop peaches; add to bowl with oranges. Sprinkle with lemon juice and sugar. Toss to blend. Spoon half of fruit mixture into bottom of one large bowl or eight large wine glasses. Place strawberry halves, cut side out, around sides. Fill center with blueberries. Arrange kiwi rounds around sides above strawberry halves. Fill with remaining oranges and peaches. Refrigerate until chilled or ready to serve. Just before serving, mix champagne with orange juice; stir, and pour over prepared fruits. Top with scoops of lemon ice cream. Sprinkle with mint sprigs, if desired. Serves 8.

Croute des Fruits

A super-easy dessert to make on short notice. If you like, serve hot from the oven with chilled sour cream.

>*4 1/2-inch slices Pound Cake**
>*1 Tbs. butter, softened*
>*Peeled and sliced ripe fruit: peaches, strawberries,*
>   *plums, bananas, or oranges—or a combination of*
>   *any of these fruits*
>*Granulated sugar*
>*1 Tbs. more cold butter, cut into slivers*
>*Sour cream, optional*

Place broiler rack about 4 inches under source of heat. Preheat broiler. Arrange pound cake slices in a single layer on a long, flat baking sheet. Place under high broiler heat until lightly toasted on both sides. Cool to room temperature. Spread slices with soft butter. Cover completely with sliced fruit. Sprinkle fruit generously with sugar. Dot with butter slivers. Broil under high heat until sugar is lightly caramelized. Serve warm from oven. Top each serving with sour cream, if desired. Serves 4.

Amaretto Cream—Filled Fruit

Perfect for a summer evening buffet.

>*6 Amaretti cookies* or medium-size, dry macaroons*
>*6 ozs. Petit-Suisse cheese, or top-quality cream cheese*
>   *without preservatives*
>*1 Tbs. Amaretto liqueur*
>*2 Tbs. heavy (whipping) cream*

6 to 8 ripe purple plums
6 to 8 ripe small apricots
Lemon juice
Slivered almonds, optional
Fresh mint leaves
1/2 lb. fresh sweet cherries with stems

Place Amaretti cookies or macaroons in work bowl of a food processor; process until crumbled. (Or place cookies between sheets of waxed paper and pound with a rolling pin to crumble.) In a bowl, beat cream cheese with liqueur and cream until light and fluffy. Fold in crumbled cookies. Cut plums and apricots in half and remove pits. Brush cut sides with lemon juice; stuff with cream cheese mixture, mounding it high. Swirl with tines of a fork. If desired, top each stuffed fruit with an almond sliver. To serve, arrange mint leaves in an overlapping fish-scale pattern on a serving platter; place fruit over leaves. Scatter cherries around fruit. Serves 12 to 16.

Tropical Fruit Flambé

The "pièce de résistance" for even the most elegant party meal.

1/4 cup (1/2 stick) butter
1/4 cup granulated sugar
1/2 cup orange juice
1/4 cup orange liqueur
1 pint strawberries, hulled and thickly sliced
1 kiwi, peeled and sliced
1 medium mango, peeled and sliced or diced
6 thin wedges ripe honeydew melon
Small bunch seedless green grapes, stemmed
6 fresh or canned pineapple cubes
2 Tbs. more granulated sugar
1/4 cup light rum or brandy
1 pint vanilla ice cream

Melt butter in a chafing dish or electric skillet at table; add sugar. Stir over low heat until sugar has dissolved. Combine orange juice with orange liqueur; stir into butter mixture. Bring to boil; boil until reduced to about half, 3 to 4 minutes. Add fruits and stir until heated. Sprinkle fruits evenly with remaining sugar. Cook, without stirring, until liquid comes to a boil.† Pour warm rum or brandy over fruit (do not stir). Immediately ignite, using a long wooden match. Spoon flaming sauce over fruits. When flames subside, ladle fruit over ice cream and serve at once. Serves 6.

Fresh Fruit in
Crème Grand Marnier

Serve this beautiful dessert in a clear-glass bowl.

> 1 cup milk
> 4 egg yolks
> 1/2 cup Vanilla Sugar*, or 1/2 cup granulated sugar plus
>   1 tsp. vanilla extract
> 1/4 cup sifted cake flour
> 1/4 cup Grand Marnier liqueur, other orange liqueur,
>   brandy, or light rum
> 1/2 pint heavy (whipping) cream
> 3 cups mixed fresh fruit cut into bite-sized cubes or
>   slices
> Praline Powder*, toasted flaked coconut, or slivered
>   almonds, optional

Pour milk into a saucepan; place over medium heat until scalded. Remove from heat; set aside. In a large mixing bowl, combine egg yolks and Vanilla Sugar; beat at high speed of an electric mixer or

† To warm rum or brandy, pour into a 1-cup measure or small silver or silver-plated pitcher, and place in a pan of very hot water over very low heat until warm.

with a whisk until very light, smooth, and about triple in volume. Fold in flour. Slowly pour in half of hot milk, beating as added. Add this mixture to remaining hot milk. Place over medium heat and cook, stirring from bottom and around sides of pan, until mixture comes to a boil. Reduce heat and continue to cook, stirring, to a smooth sauce sufficiently thick to coat spoon. Remove from heat and place pan in a larger pan of cold water and ice cubes. Beat until cooled slightly, then stir in Grand Marnier or other liqueur. Transfer to a storage bowl; cover sauce surface with plastic wrap to keep a film from forming. Refrigerate until chilled. In a chilled bowl with chilled beaters, beat cream until stiff peaks form; fold in chilled custard mixture. Blend thoroughly, then fold in fruit mixture. Spoon into a serving bowl. Refrigerate until ready to serve. Just before serving, sprinkle top of custard with Praline Powder, toasted flaked coconut, or slivered almonds, if desired. Serves 8 to 10.

Winter Fruit Compote

1 large navel orange
1 8-oz. package mixed dried fruit
1/4 cup dark rum
1/4 cup water
2 Tbs. light or dark brown sugar
2 more large navel oranges
Sour cream, optional

Squeeze juice from one orange. Set juice aside. With a sharp knife, cut zest from rind; cut into julienne strips. Place zest in a small saucepan; cover with water and bring to a boil over high heat. Lower heat and let simmer for about 15 minutes. Drain; blot dry. Place dried fruit in a medium, non-corrodible saucepan; add orange strips and rum. Let stand for about 30 minutes. Add orange juice, water, and sugar. Bring to a simmer, stirring occasionally. Cover, and cook over low heat until fruit is tender but not too soft, about 20 minutes. Transfer to a storage bowl; refrigerate until chilled. About 1 hour before serving cut each orange into eight or twelve wedges. With a sharp knife, cut fruit from peel and add to dried fruit in bowl. Stir to blend, then return mixture to refrigerator until ready to serve. Spoon fruit and some of sauce into individual dessert bowls, stemmed glasses, or one large, decorative serving bowl. Top each serving with a bit of sour cream, if desired. Serves 6.

Poached Fruit

Light and beautiful, a sophisticated dessert to serve after any meal. It can be prepared ahead and kept in the refrigerator 2 to 3 days before serving.

> *2 cups granulated sugar*
> *1/2 vanilla bean*
> *Zest of 1 lemon, cut into julienne strips*
> *4 cups poaching liquid (see Notes)*
> *1 lb. fruit of your choice, peeled, cored, and halved:*
> *pears, tart sweet apples, peaches, or whole*
> *unpeeled apricots*

Combine sugar, vanilla bean, lemon zest, water, and poaching liquid in a large saucepan. Cover, and place over low heat until sugar has dissolved. Uncover, and let simmer for about 10 minutes. Add prepared fruit. Bring syrup back to a simmer and cook until fruit is tender but not mushy—10 to 12 minutes, depending on fruit used. Remove pan from heat and let fruit cool in syrup. Transfer to a storage bowl and refrigerate until ready to serve. Place fruit in shallow dessert bowls and spoon a little syrup on top. Serves 4.

Notes: Poach pears in 3 cups of fruity red wine such as Beaujolais plus 1 cup water. Top each serving with a dollop of fine French double-crème or other soft dessert cheese, whipped with just enough cream to make it light and fluffy. To complete the picture, sprinkle with crumbed Amaretti cookies or slivered almonds.

Poach apples in 3 cups apple cider plus 1 cup dark rum. Add 1/2 cup raisins to the syrup. Serve with very lightly sweetened whipped cream spiked with a little more dark rum.

Poach peaches in 3 cups dry white wine plus 1 cup water. To remove skins easily from peaches, plunge each into a large pan of rapidly boiling water, then hold under cold running water and slip off skins.

Poach apricots in 3 cups dry white wine plus 1 cup water. Let the apricots cool in the syrup, then remove skins. Cut each in half and remove pits. Return the apricots to the syrup to mellow and chill.

A Fruit Dessert for Every Season

Glazed Apples with Armagnac

The taste and aroma of this simple dessert are unforgettable.

> *6 large, crisp, tart-sweet apples*
> *1 cup water*
> *1 cup granulated sugar*
> *1/4 cup Armagnac*
> *1/2 cup more Armagnac*
> *6 small scoops vanilla ice cream, optional*

Core apples and peel top third of each. Combine peel and water in a deep, heavy skillet. Place over medium heat and let simmer for about

10 minutes. Stir in sugar and cook, stirring, until dissolved. Add apples, stem end up, in a single layer to skillet; baste each with simmering syrup. Cover and cook over low heat, basting often, until apples are fork tender but not falling apart. Using a slotted spoon, transfer them to a shallow dish. Set aside. Cook liquid in skillet over medium heat until reduced to about half; stir in 1/4 cup Armagnac. Pour over apples in dish. Cover and refrigerate until chilled. When ready to serve, place each apple in an individual glass dessert bowl. Spoon chilled liquid around each, dividing evenly. Fill center of each with Armagnac and, if desired, top with ice cream. Serves 6.

Normandy Apples

1/2 cup sifted all-purpose flour
1/2 cup granulated sugar
1/4 tsp. ground cinnamon
1/4 tsp. ground ginger
1/4 tsp. ground allspice
1/2 cup (1 stick) cold butter, cut into small cubes
1 cup chopped walnuts
5 or 6 large Granny Smith or other tart-sweet apples
3 Tbs. more butter
2 Tbs. Calvados or brandy
Sweetened whipped cream or vanilla ice cream, optional

Preheat oven to 400°F. Combine flour, sugar, spices, butter cubes, and walnuts in a large mixing bowl; mix well, and set aside. Peel, core, and cut apples into thick slices. Arrange, slightly overlapping, in a long, shallow baking dish. Dot with butter and sprinkle with Calvados or brandy. Cover evenly with flour mixture. Bake in preheated oven for 25 to 30 minutes, or until topping is lightly browned. Serve warm or at room temperature with, if you like, sweetened whipped cream or vanilla ice cream. Serves 6.

Blueberry-Lemon Parfait

A light and lovely dessert.

1 pint blueberries, washed and blotted dry
1 8-oz. jar commercially prepared lemon curd
1 pint heavy (whipping) cream
1/4 cup confectioners' sugar
1 Tbs. blanched, slivered almonds
1 tsp. grated lemon zest

Place blueberries in bottom of an attractive glass serving bowl or into four to six individual bowls or stemmed glasses. Spoon lemon curd over each, dividing evenly. In a chilled bowl with chilled beaters, beat cream until stiff peaks form. Fold in confectioners' sugar. Spoon over blueberries and lemon curd. Sprinkle with slivered almonds and grated lemon zest. Refrigerate until chilled or until ready to serve. Serves 4 to 6.

Grapefruit Cups with Crème de Menthe

2 medium grapefruits
Crème de Menthe liqueur
Fresh mint leaves

Cut each grapefruit in half. With a small, sharp knife, remove sections from each. Cut and pull out membranes, leaving empty shells. If necessary, cut a very thin slice from bottom of each half so it will be flat. Pile grapefruit sections back into each shell, dividing evenly. Refrigerate until ready to serve. Just before serving, place each filled grapefruit cup on a small dessert plate and pour Crème de Menthe generously over each. Garnish with fresh mint leaves and serve at once. Serves 4.

Nectarines in Asti Spumante

2 cups water
1 cup granulated sugar
6 large, ripe nectarines
1/4 cup brandy
Asti Spumante or other sparkling wine

Combine water and sugar in a deep, heavy skillet. Place over medium heat; simmer until sugar has dissolved and mixture is reduced to a thin syrup. Plunge each nectarine into a large pan of rapidly boiling water, then hold under cold running water and slip off skin. Cut each in half and remove pits. Add nectarine halves to simmering syrup; cover and let simmer until halves are tender but not falling apart. Remove skillet from heat; cool fruit in syrup. Refrigerate until chilled. When ready to serve, place three nectarine halves in each of four stemmed champagne glasses. Top each with about 1/4 cup of chilled syrup. Bring to dining table, along with a bottle of chilled Asti Spumante. Fill each glass to rim. Serves 4.

Oranges Oriental

6 large navel oranges
Water
4 cups more water

1 cup granulated sugar
1/4 cup brandy
1 3-oz. package slivered almonds

Peel and cut oranges into thick slices; cut slices in half. Cut peel from half an orange into julienne strips. Place strips in a saucepan, cover with water, and bring to a boil. To eliminate bitterness, let boil for about 20 minutes. Drain, and rinse peel under cold water. Return peel to saucepan; add 4 cups water and sugar. Cover, and bring to a boil over high heat. Uncover, and let simmer gently for about 30 minutes. Add orange slices, and continue to simmer for about 10 minutes. Remove from heat, and cool to room temperature. Cover, and refrigerate until chilled. Stir in brandy. When ready to serve, spoon oranges and some of sauce into shallow dessert bowls. Sprinkle each serving with almonds. Serves 6.

Oranges in Champagne Gelatin

4 large navel oranges
2 envelopes unflavored gelatin
1/2 cup water
Additional fresh orange juice
2 cups champagne
1/2 pint heavy (whipping) cream
1/4 cup confectioners' sugar
1 Tbs. kirsch
1 tsp. grated orange rind

Using a small, serrated knife, cut peel and pith from oranges. Working over a bowl, cut oranges one at a time between membranes into segments, letting segments and any juice fall into bowl. Drain juice from fruit; if necessary, add sufficient water to measure 1 cup; reserve. Set orange sections aside. In a small saucepan, sprinkle gelatin over water; let stand until softened. Place over low heat and stir until gelatin has dissolved and mixture is clear. Stir in reserved juice. Pour mixture into a mixing bowl; add champagne. Refrigerate until thickened to consistency of egg whites. Fold in half of orange sections. Rinse a 1 1/2-quart mold with cold water; shake out excess water. Pour in gelatin mixture. Cover and refrigerate until firm.

In a chilled bowl with chilled beaters, beat cream until stiff peaks form. Fold in confectioners' sugar, kirsch, and orange rind. Refrigerate until ready to serve. When ready to serve, unmold gelatin ring onto a decorative platter and fill center with remaining orange sections. Top with chilled whipped cream mixture. Serves 6 to 8.

Brandied Plums

Serve these heady plums and their sauce over vanilla ice cream, or, for a dramatic finale, flambé them in a chafing dish at the table before serving.

> *1 1/2 cups brandy*
> *1/2 cup granulated sugar*
> *1 3-inch piece cinnamon stick, broken into several pieces*
> *1 whole clove*
> *6 to 8 firm, ripe red or purple plums, or combination of*
> *   both, unpeeled, halved, and pitted*
> *2 Tbs. butter*
> *Vanilla ice cream*
> *2 more Tbs. granulated sugar, optional*
> *1/3 cup more brandy, warmed, optional*

Combine brandy and 1/2 cup sugar, cinnamon stick, and clove in a deep, heavy skillet. Place over high heat and bring to a boil. Cook, stirring, until sugar has dissolved. Reduce heat. Add plums and let simmer until slightly softened, about 5 minutes; do not overcook. With a slotted spoon, transfer plums to a large bowl. Remove and discard seasoning from cooking liquid. Simmer until reduced to half.

Stir in butter; pour over plums in bowl. Cool slightly. Serve warm over scoops of vanilla ice cream, or, if preferred, pour warm plums and liquid into a chafing dish and bring to serving table. Bring to a full boil over a high flame; sprinkle evenly with sugar. Pour warmed brandy into a large ladle and ignite with a match; pour, flaming, over plums. Stir until flame subsides, then ladle over scoops of ice cream and serve at once. Serves 6.

Poires à la Belle Hélène

A classic.

3 cups water
1 cup granulated sugar
Rind from 1 orange cut into julienne (1- × 1/4-inch)
strips
6 firm, ripe pears
4 Tbs. Eau de Vie de Poire (pear liqueur) or pear brandy
4 1-oz. squares unsweetened chocolate, chopped
4 oz. sweet German chocolate, chopped
6 scoops of vanilla ice cream

Place water, sugar, and orange strips in a deep, heavy skillet; simmer over low heat until sugar has dissolved and mixture is reduced to a thin syrup. Peel pears, cut in half lengthwise and remove cores. Add to simmering syrup. Cover and simmer over low heat until pears are tender, about 15 minutes. Stir in liqueur; remove from heat. Let stand at room temperature until cool. Cover and refrigerate several hours or overnight. Remove pears from syrup and blot dry. Refrigerate syrup until ready to use. Place chocolate in top half of a double boiler over hot water until partially melted. Remove pan from water; stir until chocolate is smooth.

Spear cored side of each pear half with a fork and dip it, rounded side down, into melted chocolate. Hold over chocolate until dripping stops. Place rounded side up on aluminum foil. Refrigerate until chocolate is firm. To serve, pour about 1/4 cup of chilled pear liquid into each serving dish. Add a scoop of vanilla ice cream, top with two pear halves, and serve at once. Serves 6.

Note: Though whole poached pears are traditional for this dessert, we have substituted pear halves because they are much easier to cut and eat with a dessert spoon, yet equally beautiful.

Heavenly Berry Fool

2 pints fresh raspberries or blackberries (or frozen,
*   unsweetened blackberries, thawed)*
1/2 cup confectioners' sugar
3 Tbs. Framboise or blackberry brandy
1/2 pint heavy (whipping) cream

Reserve about 1/2 cup berries for garnish. In a bowl, crush remaining berries with sugar; stir in liqueur. In a chilled bowl with chilled beaters, beat cream until stiff peaks form; fold in mashed berries. Spoon into stemmed glasses, parfait glasses, or one large, decorative serving bowl. Sprinkle with reserved whole berries. Serves 4 to 6.

Pink and White Ambrosia

A Southern favorite with a new look and taste.

1 grapefruit
4 large navel oranges
1 1 lb., 4 oz. can pineapple chunks in juice

3 Tbs. Cassis syrup or Cassis liqueur
4 Tbs. confectioners' sugar
1 3-oz. can flaked coconut

Peel grapefruit; section and remove fruit by cutting between membranes. Peel and section oranges. Reserve rind from half an orange and cut zest into julienne strips. Blanch strips in enough boiling water to cover for about 2 minutes. Drain and rinse under cold water. Drain pineapple; combine juice with Cassis. In an attractive serving bowl layer half of grapefruit and orange sections; sprinkle with half of confectioners' sugar. Cover with half of pineapple chunks; sprinkle with half of coconut. Repeat layers of fruit and sugar. Pour Cassis mixture over fruit. Sprinkle with remaining coconut and julienned orange rind. Refrigerate until chilled or until ready to serve. Serves 8 to 10.

Caramelized Grapefruit Cups

Picture-pretty and festive.

> 3 grapefruits
> 2 large navel oranges
> 1 1 lb., 4 oz. can pineapple chunks in juice
> 1/2 cup granulated sugar
> 2 Tbs. kirsch, peach brandy, or rum
> 1/2 cup light brown sugar

Slice grapefruits in half. Section and remove fruit by cutting between membranes. Remove and discard membranes from each grapefruit shell and reserve shells. Peel and section oranges. Drain pineapple chunks, reserving juice for other use. In a bowl, combine grapefruit, oranges, and pineapple. Add granulated sugar and liqueur; toss to blend. Spoon mixture into reserved grapefruit shells. Sprinkle each with brown sugar. Place filled cups 3 to 4 inches under a preheated broiler; broil just until brown sugar caramelizes, about 3 minutes. Serves 6.

Peach Melba Cream

Luxurious.

> 6 to 8 large, ripe peaches
> 1 Tbs. lemon juice
> 1/2 cup black or red currant jelly
> 2 Tbs. peach brandy or kirsch
> 1/2 pint heavy (whipping) cream
> 8 thin, crisp cookies, optional

Peel, pit, and coarsely chop peaches; place in work bowl of a food processor or blender. Add lemon juice; process or blend until puréed. Transfer to a storage bowl; set aside. Melt currant jelly and brandy or kirsch in a small saucepan over low heat. Pour into a storage bowl. Add peach purée, and stir to blend. Refrigerate until chilled. In a chilled bowl with chilled beaters, beat cream until soft peaks form. Fold in chilled peach mixture. Refrigerate until ready to serve. Spoon into parfait glasses or stemmed wine glasses. Serve each with a crisp cookie, if desired. Serves 8.

Butterscotch Peaches

> 4 large, ripe peaches
> 2 Tbs. lemon juice
> 2 Tbs. granulated sugar

2 Tbs. butter, slivered
3 Tbs. more butter
1/2 cup light corn syrup
3/4 cup light brown sugar
1/2 cup heavy (whipping) cream
8 small scoops vanilla ice cream

Preheat oven to 400°F. Plunge each peach into a large pan of rapidly boiling water, then hold under cold running water and slip off skin. Cut each in half and remove pit. Place peach halves in a single layer in a long, shallow dish; sprinkle each with lemon juice, granulated sugar, and 2 tablespoons butter. Bake in preheated oven for 10 to 15 minutes, or until softened but not falling apart. In a deep, heavy skillet, combine remaining butter, corn syrup, and brown sugar. Bring to a full boil; boil, stirring, for about 5 minutes. Stir in heavy cream, and again bring to a full boil. Remove sauce from heat; cool to room temperature. When ready to serve, arrange peach halves in individual dessert bowls. Spoon sauce over each, dividing evenly. Top each with a small scoop of ice cream. Serves 8.

Dody's Easy Bananas Foster

A classic recipe—easy, yet elegant.

6 large, ripe bananas
1/4 cup lemon juice
1/2 cup light brown sugar, firmly packed
4 Tbs. butter, chilled and cut into slivers
1/4 cup light or dark rum
12 scoops vanilla ice cream

About 1/2 hour before serving dinner, peel and cut each banana lengthwise in half. Place halves in a single layer in a long, flat baking dish. Brush each with lemon juice, then sprinkle evenly with sugar.

Dot with butter slivers and drizzle with rum. Just before serving first course of meal, preheat oven to 350°F. and place pan of bananas on middle rack. Remove ice cream from freezer and spoon two scoops into each of six long "banana split" dishes or other dessert bowls. Place in refrigerator to soften. When ready to serve dessert, remove dishes with ice cream from refrigerator. Add two banana halves to each. Spoon hot and bubbly banana cooking liquid over each and serve at once. Serves 6.

Strawberries in
Pink Champagne Ice

Très bon!

> *1/2 cup water*
> *1/2 cup granulated sugar*
> *2 pints ripe red strawberries, hulled*
> *2 Tbs. more granulated sugar*
> *Water*
> *1 cup pink champagne*
> *1 Tbs. kirsch*

Place water and 1/2 cup sugar in a small saucepan; cover, and place over medium heat until sugar has dissolved. Uncover, and let mixture simmer to a thin syrup. Remove from heat; cool to room temperature. Set aside. Place 1 pint of strawberries in work bowl of a food processor or blender; process or blend until puréed. Place remaining whole berries in a storage bowl; add half of strawberry purée and 2 tablespoons sugar. Stir to blend. Refrigerate until ready to use.

Combine remaining strawberry purée with sufficient water to make 3/4 cup. Add cooled sugar syrup, champagne, and kirsch; pour into a long, shallow metal pan. Place in freezer until firm around edges but still mushy in center. Transfer to a chilled bowl; beat with a whisk until frothy. (Or place in work bowl of a food processor or blender; process or blend only until frothy.) Return mixture to pan; freeze until firm. Spoon whole strawberries and strawberry purée into individual glass dessert bowls or stemmed glasses. Remove frozen champagne mixture from freezer. Beat to a frothy ice. Spoon over strawberries and serve. Serves 6.

Strawberries and Cream Deluxe

A five-minutes-to-make sensation.

> *2 pints fresh strawberries, hulled and sliced*
> *6 to 8 Tbs. brandy*
> *3 1-oz. squares bittersweet chocolate*
> *1/2 pint heavy (whipping) cream*
> *2 Tbs. confectioners' sugar*
> *Gaufrettes, or crisp rolled cookies*

Place strawberries in six to eight shallow dessert bowls, dividing evenly. Spoon 1 tablespoon brandy over each. Coarsely chop or grate chocolate. Set aside. In a chilled bowl with chilled beaters, beat cream until soft peaks form. Fold in confectioners' sugar and choco- late. Spoon over each bowl of berries and garnish with a Gaufrette or crisp rolled cookie. Serve immediately. Serves 6 to 8.

Tropical Fruit Creams

You are going to love these frozen fruit desserts. They are as smooth and rich as fine custard ice cream, but you don't need an ice cream machine to make them.

Raspberry Banana Cream

1 banana
3 to 4 large, ripe peaches (sufficient to make about 2
*   cups sliced)*
1/2 pint raspberries
2 Tbs. lemon juice
2 to 3 Tbs. granulated sugar
2 Tbs. Framboise liqueur

Peel and thinly slice banana. Peel peaches, remove pits, and cut into thin slices. Place fruits in a single layer in one or more long, shallow, nonmetal baking dishes. Sprinkle evenly with lemon juice and sugar. Turn slices to coat evenly. Freeze until firm. Follow method used for Tropical Frozen Fruit Cream*, adding liqueur before processing or blending as directed. Serves 4 to 6.

Strawberry Cream

1 pint strawberries
1 large banana
3 Tbs. lime juice
2 to 3 Tbs. granulated sugar
2 Tbs. kirsch or other liqueur

Cut strawberries into thin slices. Peel and slice banana. Place fruits in a single layer in one or more long, shallow, nonmetal baking dishes. Sprinkle evenly with lime juice and sugar. Turn slices to coat evenly. Freeze until firm. Follow method used for Tropical Frozen Fruit Cream*, adding liqueur before processing or blending as directed. Serves 4 to 6.

Tahini Banana Cream

4 large bananas (about 1 lb.)
2 Tbs. lemon juice
2 to 3 Tbs. granulated sugar
Tahini (sesame seed paste)
2 Tbs. honey

Peel and thinly slice bananas. Place in a single layer in one or more long, shallow, nonmetal baking dishes. Sprinkle evenly with lemon juice and sugar. Turn slices to coat evenly. Freeze until firm. Follow method used for Tropical Frozen Fruit Cream*, adding tahini and honey before processing or blending as directed. Serves 4 to 6.

Tropical Frozen Fruit Cream

2 to 3 ozs. crystallized ginger
1 large, ripe mango
4 to 6 ripe peaches (sufficient to make about 2 cups sliced)
1 large banana
3 Tbs. lime juice
3 Tbs. granulated sugar
2 Tbs. white Crème de Menthe
Mint sprigs, optional

With kitchen shears, cut crystallized ginger into very thin slivers. Set aside. Peel, pit, and thinly slice mango and peaches. Peel and thinly slice banana. Place fruits in one or more long, shallow, nonmetal baking dishes. Sprinkle evenly with lime juice and sugar. Turn fruits to coat evenly. Freeze until firm. Place frozen fruit in work bowl of a food processor or blender; add Crème de Menthe and slivered ginger. Process or blend until smooth. (If using a blender, blend in four parts.) Spoon into stemmed glasses or dessert bowls and serve at once; or spoon into an airtight container and store in freezer. Transfer container to refrigerator for 2 to 3 hours, or until sufficiently softened to serve; or break frozen mixture into chunks, then reprocess or blend until smooth. If desired, garnish each serving with a sprig of mint. Serves 4 to 6.

Frozen Passions

*Ice cream, sherbets, and frozen creations.
Subtle addictions that prove ice can be just as passionate as fire.*

About Ice Cream and Sherbet

If you chill the ice cream mixture thoroughly before it is frozen, it will not only freeze quickly but taste even better.

If you use a metal bowl to mix or chill even a slightly acid fruit it will discolor the fruit and alter the taste of the ice cream.

If you use too much brandy, rum, liqueur, or other alcoholic ingredients in an ice cream base, it will not freeze. Use no more than 3 tablespoons per 1 quart ice cream base, adding it to the ice cream just before it has frozen firm.

Almond extract will slow down the freezing process; use sparingly.

Ice cream will be sticky if too much sugar is used.

Chopped nuts, chocolate chips, and other such ingredients should be finely chopped before adding to ice cream mixture; large pieces become rock hard with freezing. Fresh fruit should be puréed.

For best flavor, transfer ice cream from freezer to refrigerator to soften for about 30 minutes before serving.

When buying an ice cream maker, select one that is capable of freezing the cream in less than 30 minutes. There are a number of inexpensive electric machines on the market today that will make ice cream the easiest of all desserts to prepare.

To soften firmly frozen ice cream, transfer it from freezer to refrigerator for 1 to 2 hours. If softened at room temperature it will melt on the outside but remain hard in the center. If time is of the essence, cut firmly frozen ice cream into small cubes and place in the work bowl of a food processor or blender; quickly process or blend, part at a time, using on and off method and stopping to push the cubes down as necessary.

Unbuyable
Homemade Ice Creams

Chocolate Scallop Shells

To hold scoops of your best homemade ice cream. Simply beautiful!

8 1-oz. squares semisweet chocolate, chopped
1 Tbs. vegetable shortening

One at a time, cover six natural scallop shells with plastic wrap, smoothing wrap into each indentation and keeping it wrinkle-free and taut. Cut wrap to extend about 1 1/2 inches around shell; bring together under shell and twist into a ball. Place as prepared on a flat baking sheet in refrigerator until ready to use. Place chocolate in top half of a double boiler over simmering water until partially melted. Remove pan from water; add vegetable shortening and stir until mixture is smooth. One at a time, hold each shell up by ball of twisted plastic wrap. Using a pastry brush, spread a thin, even layer of chocolate on outside of each shell. Chocolate should just reach edges of shell. Let first layer set, then cover it with a second layer of chocolate. Refrigerate coated shells until chocolate is firm, about 5 minutes. Repeat with two more coatings of chocolate. Refrigerate until chocolate is very firm.

To unmold: Working one at a time, untwist ball of plastic wrap carefully from underside of each shell, then gently loosen chocolate scallop on plastic wrap from natural shell. Carefully peel plastic wrap from chocolate shell. If shell cracks, it can be mended by brushing cracks together with additional melted chocolate. Store shells on a baking sheet, rounded side down, in refrigerator until ready to use. Makes six chocolate shells.

Cappuccino Ice Cream

As a gourmet friend remarked, "This ice cream tastes just like the fragrant aroma of freshly brewed coffee." It is so sensational, I like to serve it on its own, accompanied only by a thin, crisp cookie.

1/2 cup finely ground dark roast coffee
3 cups light cream
1 cup granulated sugar
6 egg yolks
1/4 tsp. salt
1/2 cup Kahlua or dark Jamaican rum
Candied coffee beans, optional

Place ground coffee in a large mixing bowl. In a saucepan, bring cream to just below boiling point. Pour over ground coffee, cover, and let stand for about 1 hour. Strain mixture through a fine sieve lined with cheesecloth into a clean saucepan. Stir in sugar. Bring nearly to a simmer over moderate heat, stirring occasionally. In a mixing bowl, beat yolks with salt until very frothy. Slowly add strained coffee mixture, stirring as added. Pour back into saucepan and stir over medium heat until mixture thickens to a soft custard that will coat spoon. Stir in liqueur. Cover, and refrigerate until chilled. Freeze in an ice cream freezer, following manufacturer's directions. Spoon into shallow dessert bowls or parfait glasses. Garnish with candied coffee beans, if desired. Makes about 1 1/2 quarts.

Cherry Ice Cream

1 1-lb. can black bing cherries
1/2 cup granulated sugar
4 egg yolks

1/2 pint heavy (whipping) cream
1/4 cup maraschino syrup
2 Tbs. maraschino liqueur, optional

Drain cherries through a colander set over a bowl. Reserve cherries. Place 1/2 cup of cherry liquid and sugar in a heavy saucepan. Cover, and simmer over low heat until sugar has dissolved. Uncover, increase heat to high, and bring mixture to a full boil. Remove from heat. In a large bowl, beat egg yolks until very pale and about triple in volume. Slowly add hot sugar mixture in a thin, steady stream, beating constantly as it is added. Return mixture to saucepan. Place over low heat and cook, stirring constantly from bottom and sides of pan, until mixture thickens to a smooth custard that will coat spoon. Transfer to a storage bowl; cover surface with plastic wrap. Refrigerate until chilled.

In a chilled bowl with chilled beaters, beat cream until stiff peaks form; fold in maraschino syrup, chilled yolk mixture, and reserved cherries. Refrigerate until thoroughly chilled, about 1 hour. Freeze in an ice cream freezer, following manufacturer's directions. If desired, add maraschino liqueur when ice cream is almost firm. Makes about 1 quart.

Brandied Apricot Ice Cream

Pale apricot color, intense apricot flavor.

1 1-lb. can apricot halves in heavy syrup
1/4 cup granulated sugar
4 egg yolks
1/2 pint heavy (whipping) cream
3 Tbs. apricot brandy

Pour apricot halves into a colander set over a bowl. Place apricots and about 2 tablespoons of syrup in work bowl of a food processor or blender; process or blend until puréed. Set aside. Combine 1/2 cup of apricot syrup and sugar in a heavy saucepan. Place over medium heat and cook, stirring constantly, until sugar has dissolved. Increase heat to high and bring mixture to a boil. Remove from heat. In a mixing bowl, beat yolks until very pale and about triple in volume. Slowly pour in hot apricot mixture, beating constantly as it is added. Return mixture to saucepan. Place over low heat. Cook, stirring constantly from bottom and sides of pan, to a smooth custard sufficiently thick to coat spoon. Transfer to a bowl and stir in puréed apricots. Cool to room temperature, stirring occasionally.

In a chilled bowl with chilled beaters, beat cream until stiff peaks form; fold in cooled apricot mixture. Refrigerate until thoroughly chilled, about 1 hour. Freeze in an ice cream freezer, following manufacturer's directions. Add apricot brandy when ice cream is almost firm. Makes about 1 quart.

Bittersweet Chocolate Ice Cream

1 cup water
1/2 cup granulated sugar
3 4-oz. bars German sweet chocolate, chopped
6 egg yolks
1/2 pint heavy (whipping) cream

Combine water and sugar in a heavy saucepan. Cover, and cook over medium heat until sugar has dissolved. Uncover, increase heat to high, and bring mixture to a full boil. Stir in chopped chocolate; remove pan from heat and continue to stir until chocolate has dissolved. In a large mixing bowl, beat yolks at high speed of an electric mixer until about triple in volume. Add hot chocolate mixture in a thin, steady stream, beating constantly. Return mixture to saucepan. Place over low heat and cook, stirring constantly from bottom and sides of pan, until mixture thickens to a soft custard that will coat spoon. Remove from heat and cool to room temperature, stirring occasionally. In a chilled bowl with chilled beaters, beat cream until stiff peaks form; fold in chocolate mixture. Refrigerate until chilled. Freeze in an ice cream freezer, following manufacturer's directions. Makes 1 quart.

Peachy Peach Ice Cream with Raspberries

Prepare this summertime treat at the height of peach season.

1 lb. ripe peaches
2 Tbs. fresh lemon juice
3/4 cup granulated sugar
1 pint heavy (whipping) cream
1 Tbs. Southern Comfort or peach brandy
3 or 4 additional large, ripe peaches
1 to 2 Tbs. lemon juice
1/4 cup more granulated sugar
1 cup water
1/4 cup more Southern Comfort or peach brandy
1/2 pint fresh raspberries

Bring a large pot of water to a full boil. Add peaches. Boil for about 45 seconds, then immediately remove peaches with slotted spoon and plunge them into a pan of cold water. Place lemon juice in a bowl large enough to hold sliced peaches. Peel each peach and slice it from pit into bowl with lemon juice. Toss to coat thoroughly. Add sugar, and stir until slices are thoroughly coated. Cover and refrigerate for 1 to 2 hours, or until well chilled. Transfer to work bowl of a food processor or blender and process or blend until puréed, or put peaches and sugar through a sieve or food mill. Combine puréed mixture with cream. Stir in 1 tablespoon Southern Comfort or brandy. Freeze in an ice cream freezer, following manufacturer's directions.

Remove skins from remaining peaches, cut in half, and discard pits. Sprinkle with lemon juice. In a saucepan, combine sugar and water. Cover, bring to boil over high heat, and boil until sugar has dissolved. Uncover, lower heat, add peach halves, and let simmer until tender but not too soft. Transfer with a slotted spoon to a bowl. Let syrup boil until reduced to about half. Remove from heat, cool slightly, and add remaining Southern Comfort or brandy. Pour over peach halves; refrigerate until chilled. To serve: Arrange peach halves in individual dessert bowls, spoon about 1 tablespoon of syrup over each, top each serving with a scoop of ice cream, and sprinkle with raspberries. Serves 6 to 8.

Crème de Marron
(Chestnut Ice Cream)

1 cup water
3/4 cup granulated sugar
8 egg yolks
1/2 pint heavy (whipping) cream
1 8-oz. jar chopped marrons in heavy syrup

Combine water and sugar in a heavy saucepan. Cover, place over medium heat, and simmer until sugar has dissolved. Remove cover, increase heat to high, and bring to a full boil. Remove from heat. In a large mixing bowl, beat egg yolks until very light and about triple in volume. Slowly pour in hot syrup, beating constantly as it is added. Return mixture to saucepan. Place over low heat and cook, stirring constantly from bottom and sides of pan, until mixture thickens to a smooth custard that will coat back of spoon. Transfer to a storage bowl. Cover custard surface with plastic wrap; refrigerate until chilled. In a chilled bowl with chilled beaters, beat cream until stiff peaks form; fold in chilled custard. When smooth, fold in chopped marrons and their syrup. Refrigerate until thoroughly chilled, about 1 hour. Freeze in an ice cream freezer, following manufacturer's directions. Makes about 1 quart.

French Vanilla Custard Ice Cream

It's not necessary to cook a custard first for this rich, satiny smooth ice cream.

> *1 vanilla bean*
> *1/2 cup water*
> *1/2 cup granulated sugar*
> *5 egg yolks, room temperature*
> *1 pint heavy (whipping) cream*

Place vanilla bean and water in a saucepan over low heat. Let simmer for 4 to 5 minutes. Remove bean from water and, with a sharp knife, cut it lengthwise in half; then scrape seeds back into water. (Blot pod dry and reserve for other use.) Add sugar and return saucepan to high heat. Cover, and let boil until sugar has dissolved. Uncover, and continue to boil until mixture reaches 239°F. on a candy thermometer. In a large bowl of an electric mixer, beat egg yolks until very thick and light. Add hot vanilla syrup in a slow, steady stream, beating at low speed and scraping down sides of bowl as necessary. Increase speed to high, and beat until mixture is very thick and cool. In a separate, chilled bowl with chilled beaters, beat cream until soft peaks form; fold into yolk mixture. Freeze in an ice cream freezer following manufacturer's directions. Makes about 1 quart.

Fresh Fruit Ice Creams

Omit vanilla bean, and add 1 to 2 cups puréed fresh, thawed, or canned fruit to ice cream base just before freezing. If desired, add 1 to 2 tablespoons compatible fruit-flavored liqueur just before ice cream becomes firm.

Spicy à la Mode Ice Cream

Serve scoops of this fragrant and extremely flavorful ice cream over pumpkin or any fresh fruit pie, warm from the oven; use it to top plain chocolate cake squares, steamed chocolate pudding, or homemade pound cake; or just serve it "solo," with or without crisp cookies.

> *1 cup granulated sugar*
> *1 cup water*
> *1 pint heavy (whipping) cream*
> *1 tsp. ground cinnamon*
> *1/4 tsp. ground ginger*
> *Dash ground cloves*
> *Dash ground nutmeg*

In a saucepan, combine sugar and water; cover, and bring to a full boil. Reduce heat, and let simmer for 2 to 3 minutes. Transfer to a storage bowl and refrigerate until chilled. Add remaining ingredients and stir to blend. Freeze in an ice cream freezer, following manufacturer's directions. Makes about 1 quart.

A Small Collection of Incredibly Easy to Make, Incredibly Delicious Ice Creams

Light, luscious, and positively sensational!

For a number of years, the following recipes were top secret in my house. I guess I just didn't want people to know how ridiculously easy these ice creams were to prepare. But, because they really do belong in this book, it's time I confessed.

Sensational Lemon Ice Cream

1/4 cup granulated sugar
1/4 cup water
1 cup lemon curd (commercially prepared lemon custard jelly)
1 pint heavy (whipping) cream
1 tsp. lemon extract

In a saucepan, combine sugar and water; cover, and bring to boil over medium heat. Uncover, and let simmer for 2 to 3 minutes. Pour into a mixing bowl and stir in lemon curd. Refrigerate until chilled. Add cream and lemon extract; beat with a whisk until thoroughly blended. Freeze in an ice cream freezer, following manufacturer's directions. Makes 1 quart.

Crème de Menthe Parfait Ice Cream

This pale green, creamy smooth ice cream is the perfect ending to a hearty meal.

> *1/2 cup granulated sugar*
> *1/4 cup water*
> *1/4 cup Crème de Menthe Parfait (nonalcoholic Crème*
> *   de Menthe sauce)*
> *1 pint heavy (whipping) cream*
> *1 tsp. vanilla extract*
> *1/2 tsp. lemon extract*

Place sugar and water in a saucepan. Cover, place over medium heat, and bring to a boil. Uncover, and let simmer for about 3 minutes. Pour into a mixing bowl; add Crème de Menthe Parfait. Stir mixture until thoroughly blended. Refrigerate until chilled. Add cream, vanilla, and lemon extract. Freeze in an ice cream freezer, following manufacturer's directions. Makes 1 pint.

Orange Chocolate Ice Cream

A tart-sweet flavor and sunny orange color is counterbalanced by rich chocolate in every bite.

> *3 1-oz. squares sweet or bittersweet chocolate*
> *1 6-oz. container frozen orange juice concentrate*
> *1 pint light (or half-and-half) cream*

Place chocolate in work bowl of a food processor or blender; process or blend until finely chopped. (Or grate chocolate on coarse side of a hand grater.) Thaw frozen orange juice until liquid, but still very cold.

Combine grated chocolate, thawed orange juice, and cream; blend well. Pour into an ice cream freezer and freeze, following manufacturer's directions. Makes about 1 quart.

Peach Melba Ice Cream

A classic combination of ingredients makes this ice cream extra special.

> *4 large, ripe peaches*
> *Juice from 1/2 small lemon (about 1 Tbs.)*
> *1 cup commercially prepared melba sauce*
> *1 pint heavy (whipping) cream*

One at a time, plunge each peach into a large pan of rapidly boiling water, then hold under cold running water and slip off skin. Cut each peach in half and remove pit; slice into a mixing bowl. Add lemon juice and toss to blend. Place in work bowl of a food processor or blender and process or blend to a smooth purée. In a bowl, combine melba sauce and cream; stir until thoroughly mixed. Stir in peach purée. Freeze in an ice cream freezer, following manufacturer's directions. Makes 1 quart.

Crème Cassis Ice Cream

> *1 cup Cassis (black currant) syrup*
> *1 pint heavy (whipping) cream*

In a bowl, stir Cassis into cream; blend thoroughly. Freeze in an ice cream freezer, following manufacturer's directions. Makes 1 pint.

Quick-Fix
Ice Cream Desserts

Mocha Rum Parfait

1 pint vanilla ice cream, softened
2 Tbs. dark rum
4 to 6 chocolate wafers, crumbled
4 Tbs. more dark rum
1 tsp. instant coffee
1 tsp. unsweetened cocoa

Transfer frozen ice cream to refrigerator until softened. Fold in 1 tablespoon rum and crumbled cookies. Spoon into parfait glasses. Pour a tablespoon of rum over each serving and sprinkle each with instant coffee and cocoa. Serves 4.

Pousse-Café Parfait

Vanilla ice cream, slightly softened
Curaçao or other orange liqueur
Green Crème de Menthe
Brandy
Finely chopped hazelnuts, walnuts, almonds, or
*   pistachios*

Layer small scoops of ice cream alternately with liqueurs in order listed in stemmed parfait glasses. Top with a final small scoop of ice cream; sprinkle with nuts. Serve at once.

Saturday Night Sundae

1/2 cup finely chopped pecans or walnuts
4 scoops chocolate ice cream
1/2 cup chocolate sprinkles
4 scoops coffee ice cream
4 scoops strawberry ice cream
1/2 cup chopped fresh strawberries
1/2 cup Amaretto liqueur
Crisp cookies

Spread nuts out on waxed paper. Roll each scoop of chocolate ice cream in nuts and place in a single layer on a flat surface in freezer. Spread out chocolate sprinkles on a second sheet of waxed paper. Roll scoops of coffee ice cream in sprinkles. Place with nut-rolled chocolate scoops in a single layer on flat surface in freezer. Add scoops of strawberry ice cream. When ready to serve, arrange one of each scoop of ice cream in each of four chilled saucer champagne glasses or banana split dishes. Top strawberry ice cream with chopped fresh strawberries. Drizzle Amaretto liqueur over all. Serve with crisp cookies. Serves 4.

Crème de Menthe Parfait
with Meringues

1 pint vanilla ice cream
1 Tbs. Crème de Menthe liqueur
1 3-oz. bar bittersweet chocolate
4 Tbs. heavy cream
1 Tbs. Crème de Cacao
24 Miniature Meringues*

Break firmly frozen ice cream into chunks. Place in work bowl of a food processor. Add Crème de Menthe; process only until mixture is blended. Spoon into freezer storage container, cover, and place in freezer until mixture is refrozen. (Crème de Menthe will keep ice cream from freezing solid, but in an hour or so, it will freeze to a soft, custardlike consistency.) Place chocolate and cream in top half of a double boiler over simmering water; stir until chocolate has partially melted. Stir in Crème de Cacao. Remove from heat; stir until mixture is smooth. Place over hot water until ready to use. Put 4 meringues in each of 4 small glass dessert bowls or parfait glasses. Top each with some ice cream. Cover with 2 more meringues and top with remaining ice cream, dividing evenly. Pour chocolate sauce over each serving. Serve at once. Serves 4.

Frozen Irish Coffee

Coffee ice cream
Irish whiskey
Thin chocolate wafer cookies or small squares of
  sponge cake
Lightly sweetened whipped cream
Instant coffee, optional

Use your best, most elegant small coffee cups. Fill each to about 1 inch from rim with softened ice cream; place in freezer until firm. With a small spoon, scoop out a deep, but not too wide, hollow in center of each. Return cups to freezer until ice cream is ready to serve. Place cups of frozen ice cream on saucers. Working quickly, fill each hollow with Irish whiskey, then top with a chocolate wafer or small cake square. Sprinkle cookie or cake with a few drops of whiskey. Top each cup with sweetened whipped cream. Sprinkle lightly with instant coffee, if desired. Serve at once.

Splendid
Short-Cut Ice Creams

Colonel Foster's
Apple Bourbon Ice Cream

1 pint vanilla ice cream
1 cup unsweetened applesauce
1/4 cup bourbon whiskey
Pound cake slices or crisp cookies, optional

Let ice cream stand at room temperature until slightly softened. Place in a chilled bowl; add applesauce and bourbon. Blend well. Spoon into ice cube trays or a metal baking dish. Cover with plastic wrap and seal. Place mixture in freezer until ready to serve. If desired, serve over slices of pound cake or with crisp cookies. Serves 4 to 6.

Gingerman Ice Cream

1 quart vanilla ice cream
1/2 cup preserved stem ginger in heavy syrup, drained
*   and coarsely chopped*
2 Tbs. syrup from preserved ginger

Place softened ice cream in a chilled bowl; add chopped ginger and syrup. Blend quickly, but thoroughly, using a cold spoon or whisk. Spoon into a metal baking dish. Cover with plastic wrap and seal.

Place mixture in freezer for several hours to allow flavors to mellow, or until ready to serve. Makes 1 quart.

Strawberry Ice Cream with Strawberry Sauce

The flavor of the fruit comes through in every spoonful.

> *1 pint fresh strawberries, hulled*
> *1/2 cup granulated sugar*
> *2 tsp. cornstarch*
> *Water*
> *1 Tbs. kirsch or Framboise liqueur*
> *1 pint vanilla ice cream*

Reserve 4 to 6 large, perfect berries. Place remaining berries in a bowl and crush lightly with back of a wooden spoon; add sugar and stir to blend. Refrigerate several hours or overnight. Pour accumulated juices into a 1-cup measure, and stir in cornstarch. Add sufficient water to make 1 cup liquid. Pour into a small saucepan and cook, stirring, over low heat until sauce thickens slightly; stir in liqueur. Refrigerate until chilled. Fold drained berries into softened ice cream. Spoon into freezer container; refreeze until firm. About 30 minutes before serving, transfer ice cream to refrigerator to soften slightly. Spoon into parfait glasses or shallow dessert bowls and pour a little dessert sauce over each serving. Serves 4 to 6.

Short-Cut Raspberry Ice Cream

Substitute frozen raspberries in heavy syrup for strawberries and sugar. Place frozen block of berries in a colander set over a bowl until thawed. Pour thawed raspberry syrup into a 1-cup measure, and stir in cornstarch. Pour into a small saucepan; cook, stirring, over low heat until sauce thickens slightly. Pour into a storage bowl and refrigerate until chilled. Just before serving, fold thawed, drained raspberries into softened ice cream. Spoon into parfait glasses. Serve sauce separately. Serves 4 to 6.

Note: You can do the same trick with any flavored ice cream and any fruit, fresh or frozen.

Vanilla Ice Cream with Coffee Ice

A marvelous mix.

> 1 cup water
> 2 Tbs. granulated sugar
> 2 Tbs. instant coffee
> 2 Tbs. brandy or rum
> 1 quart rich vanilla ice cream, softened

Combine water and sugar in a small saucepan over high heat, and bring to a full boil. Remove pan from heat; add coffee and stir until dissolved. Stir in brandy or rum. Pour into a shallow metal pan and place in freezer until mixture is firm around outside and mushy in middle. Stir with a fork, mixing well. Stir again every 15 or 20 minutes until mixture has frozen to a soft sherbet, about 1 hour. Fold sherbet into softened ice cream. Spoon into stemmed wine glasses or shallow glass dessert bowls, and serve at once. Serves 6.

Special
Ice Cream Creations

Black Hole Bombe

An ice cream bombe with fudge sauce in the middle rather than on the outside. With Raspberry Peach Sauce* spooned over each serving, it looks and tastes sensational.

> *1 pint rich vanilla ice cream, slightly softened*
> *1/2 cup sifted cocoa*
> *1 1/2 cups sifted confectioners' sugar*
> *1/4 cup (1/2 stick) butter*
> *3/4 cup heavy (whipping) cream*
> *1/2 pint more vanilla ice cream, slightly softened*
> *Raspberry Peach Sauce (recipe follows)*

Rinse a 6-cup mold and place in freezer for about 15 minutes. Spoon softened ice cream into bowl; using back of a spoon dipped in hot water, spread it evenly to coat interior. Freeze for about an hour or overnight. In a heavy saucepan, combine cocoa, confectioners' sugar, butter, and cream. Bring to a full boil, stirring constantly. Lower heat and simmer for about 5 minutes, stirring occasionally. Remove from heat and stir until bottom of saucepan is no longer hot. Set aside until cool. Pour into ice cream–lined mold. Tap mold lightly on counter to settle filling. Cover with plastic wrap and return mold to freezer until center is firm. Cover with remaining ice cream and spread it out evenly. Cover mold with plastic wrap and return it to freezer until ready to serve. An hour before serving, wrap bottom and sides of mold in a hot towel or dip it into hot water; unmold bombe onto serving platter. Cut bombe into wedges with a sharp knife dipped in hot water. Place a wedge in center of each serving plate; surround with Raspberry Peach Sauce. Serves 8 to 10.

Raspberry Peach Sauce

1/2 pint fresh raspberries
1/4 cup peach brandy or kirsch
1/4 cup granulated sugar
Juice of 1/2 lemon
4 large ripe peaches, peeled and pitted

Combine raspberries, liqueur, and sugar in work bowl of a food processor or blender; process or blend until puréed. Spoon lemon juice into a medium bowl. Slice peaches into thin crescents; add to bowl, and toss to coat with lemon juice. Pour in puréed raspberry mixture. Stir to blend. Cover and chill for several hours or until ready to serve.

Biscuit Tortoni

6 Amaretti cookies or 6 crisp macaroons
1 egg white
1/4 cup confectioners' sugar
1 Tbs. sherry
1 pint vanilla ice cream, softened

Place Amaretti or macaroons in work bowl of a food processor or blender; process or blend to fine crumbs. In a mixing bowl, beat egg whites until frothy. Add sugar a little at a time, and continue beating until soft peaks form. Fold in half of cookie crumbs. Add sherry and softened ice cream; blend quickly but thoroughly. Pour mixture into twelve individual foil cupcake liners. Sprinkle each with remaining cookie crumbs. Place in cupcake pans. Freeze until firm or until ready to serve. Serve in cupcake liners. Serves 12.

Peach Melba Bombe

A delicate pink and creamy white creation.

1 pint peach ice cream, softened
1 10-oz. package frozen raspberries in heavy syrup
Water
1 cup granulated sugar
2 egg yolks
1/4 tsp. almond extract
1 tsp. Framboise (raspberry brandy) liqueur, optional
1/2 pint heavy (whipping) cream
Peach Melba Sauce (recipe follows)

Rinse a 6-cup ring mold and place it in freezer for about 15 minutes. Spoon in softened ice cream, using back of a spoon dipped in hot water; spread it evenly to coat interior of mold. Cover and freeze for about 1 hour or overnight. Place frozen block of raspberries in a colander set over a bowl until thawed and syrup has drained into bowl. Set berries aside. Pour syrup into a 2-cup measure and add sufficient water to make 1 1/2 cups liquid; pour into a saucepan and add sugar. Place pan over medium heat, cover, and let mixture simmer until sugar has dissolved. Uncover, increase heat to high; let boil until syrup reaches 242°F. on a candy thermometer.

While syrup boils, place yolks in a large mixing bowl and beat with an electric mixer at medium speed until about triple in volume. Increase speed to high and add syrup in a thin, steady stream, beating constantly. Continue to beat until mixture has cooled to room temperature. Stir in raspberries, almond extract, and, if desired, Framboise liqueur. Chill thoroughly. In a chilled bowl with chilled beaters, beat cream until soft peaks form; fold into chilled raspberry mixture. Pour into ice cream–lined mold. Cover mold with plastic wrap and freeze bombe until firm. About an hour before serving, dip mold briefly in hot water and unmold bombe onto serving platter. Return it to freezer until ready to serve. Just before serving, fill center with Peach Melba Sauce. Serves 8.

Peach Melba Sauce

4 large, ripe peaches
2 Tbs. lemon juice
1/2 cup commercially prepared melba sauce
2 Tbs. Framboise liqueur, optional

Peel, pit, and slice peaches into a mixing bowl; add lemon juice and toss to coat. Stir in Melba Sauce and, if desired, Framboise liqueur. Refrigerate until ready to serve.

Angel Ice Cream Cake

1 Angel Food Cake*, cooled
4 Tbs. Cassis syrup or maraschino cherry syrup
1 quart pink ice cream (strawberry, raspberry, Cassis)
1 quart vanilla or lemon ice cream
1/2 pint heavy (whipping) cream
Chocolate Curls*

Tear Angel Food Cake into bite-sized pieces. Place one-third of cake pieces in a layer on bottom of a chilled 10-inch tube pan. Sprinkle with about 2 tablespoons of Cassis or maraschino syrup. Cover with a layer of alternating scoops of two ice creams, using 1 pint of each. Press firmly into cake. Add a second layer of cake pieces; sprinkle with remaining syrup. Cover with remaining ice cream, and top with remaining cake pieces. Press top layer down firmly on level cake. Cover pan with plastic wrap and place in freezer until cake is firm, about 6 hours, or until about 30 minutes before serving. To serve, remove cake from freezer and let stand at room temperature for about 5 minutes. Run a metal spatula around edge of pan. Using center post, lift out cake. Turn upside down on a serving plate and ease off bottom of pan. Return cake on serving plate to freezer to firm. In a chilled bowl with chilled beaters, beat cream until soft peaks form. Spread on top and onto sides of firmly frozen cake. Garnish with Chocolate Curls. Serves 10 to 12.

Frozen Cheese Italian-Style

From Italy with love.

> *1/4 cup orange liqueur*
> *1/2 cup raisins*
> *1 cup granulated sugar*
> *1/2 cup water*
> *Zest from 1 small lemon, finely chopped*
> *1 pint skim milk or whole milk ricotta cheese*
> *1 pint light cream*
> *1/4 cup ginger root from jar of ginger root in heavy*
> *   syrup, drained and chopped*
> *1 3-oz. bar bittersweet chocolate, broken into very small*
> *   pieces*

In a small bowl, mix liqueur with raisins. Let stand at room temperature for 1 to 2 hours, or refrigerate overnight. In a saucepan, combine sugar, water, and lemon zest; cover, place over high heat, and bring to a full boil. Uncover, let boil for 2 to 3 minutes, and remove from heat. Transfer to a storage bowl and refrigerate until cold. In a large mixing bowl, combine ricotta and cream. Beat at low speed of an electric mixer until mixture is blended. Stir in cold sugar syrup with zest. Stir in ginger, chocolate, raisins, and any unabsorbed liqueur. Freeze in an ice cream freezer, following manufacturer's directions. Makes 1 quart.

Multi-Layered Ice Cream Cake

Easy to make and impressive to serve.

3 quarts ice cream, each a different color
1 1/2 cups chocolate wafer cookie crumbs
1/2 pint heavy (whipping) cream
1/3 cup confectioners' sugar
2 Tbs. kirsch or Amaretto liqueur
Chocolate Curls*
Strawberry Sauce*, optional
Warm Fudge Sauce*, optional

About half an hour before assembling cake, transfer ice cream from freezer to refrigerator to soften. Place a 9-inch springform pan in freezer until chilled. Sprinkle 1/2 cup of crumbs over bottom of pan. Add 1 quart of softened ice cream and spread it out evenly. Cover with another 1/2 cup cookie crumbs, then another layer of softened ice cream and remaining crumbs. Top with third quart of ice cream. Cover pan with plastic wrap and freeze until very firm, 4 to 6 hours, or until ready to serve.

In a chilled bowl with chilled beaters, beat cream until soft peaks form; fold in confectioners' sugar and kirsch or Amaretto liqueur. To serve, release sides of pan, dislodge frozen cake from pan's bottom disk, and set it on a chilled platter. Top with swirls of whipped cream, and garnish with Chocolate Curls. Or store in freezer; let soften for 15 to 20 minutes in refrigerator before serving.

If you like, surround cake with fresh Strawberry Sauce or Warm Fudge Sauce. Serves 8 to 12.

Frozen Mississippi Mud Pie

1 9-inch Chocolate Cookie Crumb Pie Crust*, baked
  and cooled
1 quart coffee ice cream, softened
1/4 cup bourbon whiskey
1/2 cup heavy (whipping) cream
1/4 cup confectioners' sugar
1 Tbs. more bourbon whiskey
2 1-oz. squares bittersweet chocolate

Place crust in freezer until chilled. In a chilled bowl with chilled beaters, beat softened ice cream with bourbon until well blended; spoon into chilled crust. Freeze until firm. In a chilled bowl with chilled beaters, beat cream until stiff peaks form; fold in confectioners' sugar and remaining bourbon; spoon over frozen pie filling and smooth out evenly with back of a spoon. Return pie to freezer until cream is firmly frozen. Place chopped chocolate in a small saucepan over low heat. Stir until partially melted. Remove from heat and stir until smooth. Drizzle over top of frozen pie. Return pie to freezer until ready to serve. Serves 6 to 8.

Soufflé Glace Grand Marnier

Frozen elegance.

6 egg yolks
3/4 cup granulated sugar
1/2 cup Grand Marnier or other orange liqueur
1 pint heavy (whipping) cream
1 pint vanilla ice cream, softened

Butter a 6-cup soufflé dish and sprinkle with sugar. Fold a 28-inch strip of foil lengthwise into thirds to form a 28- × 4-inch strip. Lightly butter 2 inches of one side of strip and sprinkle with sugar. Wrap around soufflé dish with butter side extending 2 inches above rim of the dish; secure with tape or string. Place dish in freezer until ready to use. Combine egg yolks and sugar in top half of a double boiler; place over simmering water and beat with a whisk or electric hand beater until about triple in volume. Remove from heat. Transfer to bowl and stir in Grand Marnier or other liqueur. In a chilled bowl with chilled beaters, beat cream until stiff peaks form. Fold in egg mixture. Refrigerate until chilled. Remove from refrigerator and fold in softened ice cream. Pour into prepared soufflé dish. Place filled dish in freezer until soufflé is very firm, about 4 hours, or until ready to serve. Remove foil collar just before serving. Serves 6 to 8.

Pink Satin Ice Cream Pie

1 envelope unflavored gelatin
1/4 cup water
1/2 cup Cassis syrup
1/2 pint heavy (whipping) cream
1 pint vanilla ice cream, softened
1 8-oz. jar maraschino cherries, drained and chopped
1 9-inch Cookie Crumb Pie Crust*

In a small saucepan, sprinkle gelatin over water and let stand for 2 to 3 minutes to soften. Stir over low heat until gelatin has dissolved and mixture is clear. Remove from heat; stir in Cassis syrup. Set aside until cooled to room temperature. In a chilled bowl with chilled beaters, beat cream until stiff peaks form; stir in gelatin mixture. Add chopped cherries. Fold this mixture into softened ice cream. Spoon into prepared crumb crust, mounding mixture high in center. Freeze until firm or until ready to serve. Serves 6 to 8.

Sorbet

Most American food writers now label sherbet as sorbet—perhaps because the French pronunciation more aptly describes this elegant dessert. Certainly there is no more delightful way to end a fine French meal, or any good meal for that matter.

Still-Freeze Method for Sherbet

Even if you don't own an ice cream machine, you can still prepare satiny smooth sherbet in your freezer or the freezing compartment of your refrigerator. All it takes is time and a bit of vigilance on your part.

When the sherbet mixture is ready to freeze, pour it into either metal ice cube trays with dividers removed, or a shallow metal pan. Place in freezer until the mixture is firm around the edges but still slushy in the center, 1 to 2 hours. Remove from the freezer, scrape into a chilled, preferably metal bowl, and beat with a whisk until frothy. (Or scrape the mixture into the work bowl of a food processor or blender, and process or blend very briefly.) If the recipe calls for egg whites, beat them separately until soft peaks form, and fold them into the mixture after the first partial freezing. Repeat the freezing and whipping process 2 or 3 more times for optimum smoothness.

Brandied Apple Sorbet

For a festive ending to a special meal.

> *3 large winesap or other crisp, tart apples*
> *2 cups bottled apple juice*
> *3/4 cup granulated sugar*
> *1/4 cup fresh lemon juice*
> *3 Tbs. apple brandy or applejack*
> *Pinch of nutmeg, preferably freshly ground*

Pinch of ground ginger
Candied ginger, finely chopped
Additional apple brandy

Peel and core apples and cut into thin slices; place in saucepan. Add apple juice, sugar, and lemon juice. Let simmer over low heat for 10 to 15 minutes, or until apples are soft. Drain through a colander set over a bowl. Refrigerate bowl of drained liquid until chilled. Place apple slices in work bowl of a food processor or blender; process or blend to a purée. Combine with chilled syrup; stir in apple brandy, nutmeg, and ground ginger. Freeze in an ice cream freezer, following manufacturer's directions, or use still-freeze method. Just before serving, sprinkle individual sorbets with finely chopped candied ginger and pour a jigger of apple brandy over each. Makes about 1 quart.

Peach Sorbet

1 cup granulated sugar
1/2 cup water
4 cups peaches (10 to 12 ripe, medium-size, fresh
*   peaches, diced*
2 Tbs. lemon juice
2 Tbs. peach or apricot brandy
1 egg white

In a saucepan, combine sugar and water. Bring to a boil, reduce heat, and let simmer for 3 to 4 minutes. Set aside to cool. Combine diced peaches and lemon juice in work bowl of a food processor or blender; process or blend until smooth. Add to syrup; stir in brandy. Bring to a boil and cook, stirring, about 5 minutes. Remove from heat. Transfer to a bowl. Refrigerate until chilled. In a mixing bowl, beat egg white until stiff peaks form. Fold into cooled peach mixture. Freeze in an ice cream freezer according to manufacturer's directions, or freeze by still-freeze method. Makes 1 quart.

Fresh Strawberry Sorbet

It's unbelievable that something so simple could be so superb.

> *1 quart fresh strawberries, hulled*
> *2 cups granulated sugar*
> *2 Tbs. lemon juice*
> *Candied Lemon Rind**

Place strawberries in work bowl of a food processor or blender; process or blend to a smooth purée. Strain into a large bowl and add sugar. Stir until sugar has dissolved; stir in lemon juice. Refrigerate until chilled. Freeze in an ice cream freezer, following manufacturer's directions, or use still-freeze method. Garnish with Candied Lemon Rind, if desired. Serves 6 to 8.

Pineapple Sorbet

As beautiful to look at as it is to eat.

> *1 1-lb. can crushed unsweetened pineapple*
> *Water*
> *1 cup granulated sugar*
> *2 Tbs. fresh lemon juice*
> *1 Tbs. rum*
> *1 fresh, ripe pineapple*
> *1/4 cup more granulated sugar*
> *1/2 cup more rum*
> *Fresh mint leaves, optional*

Drain canned pineapple through a fine sieve set over a bowl; add sufficient water to juice to make 1 cup liquid. Place juice and sugar in a saucepan over low heat until sugar has dissolved. Transfer to a storage bowl, and refrigerate until chilled. Combine chilled syrup with crushed pineapple, lemon juice, and rum. Freeze in an ice cream freezer, following manufacturer's directions, or use still-freeze method. Peel and core pineapple. Cut into bite-sized cubes; place in a nonmetal storage bowl. Sprinkle cubes with sugar and rum. Cover, and refrigerate several hours or overnight. Drain pineapple cubes; arrange in circles on individual dessert plates, dividing evenly. Place a scoop of sherbet in center of each. Garnish with fresh mint leaves, if desired. Serves 6 to 8.

Strawberry Champagne

A beautiful, festive, bubbly soft sorbet.

> *1 1/2 quarts strawberries, washed and hulled*
> *1 cup granulated sugar*
> *2 Tbs. lemon juice*
> *1 1/2 cups champagne*

Place strawberries and sugar in work bowl of a food processor or blender; process or blend until puréed. Stir in lemon juice and champagne. Pour into ice cream freezer and freeze according to manufacturer's directions, or use still-freeze method. Makes 1 quart.

Miraculous Meringues

A gourmet collection of elegant, ethereal, pretty-as-a-picture meringue creations.

Tips for Perfect Meringues

If past disasters—such as lemon meringue pie with a topping that was far less than perfect, or meringue shells that were crumbly and dry—have turned you away from any dessert involving meringue, don't be discouraged from trying the following recipes. They have been tested and retested for guaranteed success.

To make perfect meringues: Start with an absolutely clean, dry, and nongreasy bowl. Even a smidgen of butter inadvertently smeared on it with greased fingers or an infinitesimally small bit of egg yolk will prevent you from making a high and airy meringue. To avoid these disasters, first wash and dry your hands, then wash the bowl, rinse it in very hot water, and dry it thoroughly. Separate the eggs while they are still cold; the yolks will be firm and won't dare separate into the whites. Then, to achieve the highest possible volume in the shortest amount of time, let the whites come to room temperature before you begin.

For best results, remember to preheat the oven and prepare the pans or baking sheet(s) before you begin; once the meringue batter is prepared, it should be baked immediately. If held too long, it can become grainy, lose volume, or become weepy while baking.

Egg Arithmetic

1 whole large egg = 3 Tbs.	5 whole eggs = about 1 cup
1 large egg yolk = 1 Tbs.	14 egg yolks = about 1 cup
1 large egg white = 2 Tbs.	8 egg whites = about 1 cup

Meringue Batter

1/3 cup granulated sugar
1/2 cup confectioners' sugar
3 large egg whites
Generous pinch of cream of tartar
2 tsp. more granulated sugar

Combine 1/3 cup granulated sugar with confectioners' sugar. Set aside. In a large bowl, beat egg whites at medium speed of an electric mixer until frothy; add cream of tartar. Increase beating speed to high; when whites begin to hold soft peaks, sprinkle with 2 teaspoons granulated sugar. Continue to beat, gradually adding 3/4 of remaining mixture of granulated and confectioners' sugars, until meringue is very stiff and shiny. Fold in remaining sugar mixture. (Adding this last part of the sugars at the end makes for a tender meringue, crisp on the outside but creamy within.) Makes six to eight individual shells, one 9-inch pie shell, or about three dozen meringue kisses.

Variations

Chocolate Meringue: Fold 1 tablespoon Dutch-process cocoa into basic meringue batter.

Nutty Meringue: Fold in 1/3 cup finely chopped pecans, walnuts, or almonds.

Pale Pink Meringue: Fold in 1 tablespoon maraschino syrup.

Pristine White Meringue: Add a single drop of blue food coloring.

Spiked Meringue: Fold in 1 tablespoon liqueur, brandy, or rum.

Coconut Meringue: Fold in 1 cup toasted, flaked coconut.

Jewel Meringue: Fold in 1/2 cup finely diced mixed candied fruit.

Individual Meringue Shells

Preheat oven to 200°F. Line a long, flat baking sheet with aluminum foil cut to fit. To hold foil in place, place a dot of meringue under foil in each corner of sheet. To form marvelously irregular, free-form shells: Use a large spoon and spatula to place mounds of meringue about 1/2 inch apart on prepared baking sheet; with spoon, press centers of each up sides, leaving shallow indentations. To form "bakery-shop perfect" 3-inch meringue shells: Spoon meringue into a large pastry bag with a 1 1/2-inch tube and form a small shell by squeezing out 3-inch flat rounds, then piping a circle on outer rim of each.

Bake in preheated oven for 1 hour. Turn off oven; leave meringues in oven with door closed for about 1 1/2 hours, or until dry and cooled to room temperature. Pack in single layers or an airtight container with waxed paper between layers. Store in a cool, dry place or in freezer until ready to use. Thawing is not necessary.

Meringue Pie Shell

Preheat oven to 200°F. Spread a 9-inch glass pie plate evenly with butter and dust with flour. Spread prepared meringue batter over bottom and up sides, mounding high around rim of plate. Place on a baking sheet and bake in preheated oven for 1 to 1 1/2 hours, or until crisp to the touch and just slightly colored. Cool in pan on a rack. Fill as desired (see following recipes), or place in an airtight container and store at room temperature or in freezer until ready to use.

Chocolate Mousse Meringue Pie

You can prepare the meringue pie shell several days ahead if you like. It only takes about 20 minutes to prepare the mousse, and that can be made early in the day; then the pie can be refrigerated until ready to serve. Easy, elegant, and so delicious.

4 1-oz. squares unsweetened chocolate
4 Tbs. (1/4 stick) butter
1 egg yolk
1/2 pint heavy (whipping) cream
1/4 cup granulated sugar
1 9-inch Meringue Pie Shell*

In a saucepan, combine chocolate and butter; place over low heat until partially melted, stirring occasionally. Remove pan from heat and stir until mixture is smooth. Scrape into a mixing bowl and beat until slightly cooled. Add egg yolk and beat until blended. In a chilled bowl with chilled beaters, beat cream until soft peaks form. Fold in sugar and beat until stiff. Fold in chocolate mixture, blending well but quickly. Spoon into meringue pie shell, mounding it high. Refrigerate until ready to serve. Serves 8.

Chocolate Chip Meringue Kisses

1 cup superfine granulated sugar
2 Tbs. cocoa
4 egg whites
1/4 tsp. cream of tartar
1/2 tsp. almond extract
3 1-oz. squares bittersweet or sweet chocolate, finely
    chopped

Preheat oven to 275°F. Line a long, flat baking sheet with aluminum foil cut to fit. To hold foil in place, place a dot of meringue under foil in each corner sheet. Sift sugar with cocoa onto paper; set aside. In a large bowl, beat egg whites with cream of tartar until frothy. Add almond extract. Continue to beat, adding sugar mixture about 1 tablespoon at a time, beating well after each addition. Carefully fold in chocolate. Don't overfold, just be sure chocolate is evenly incorporated. Drop meringue by heaping teaspoonfuls onto prepared sheet. Bake in preheated oven for 1 hour. Turn off oven and leave meringue kisses in oven, with door closed, about 1 1/2 hours, or until they are very dry. Store at room temperature in an airtight container until ready to serve. Makes about three dozen kisses.

Peach Melba Meringue

8 Individual Meringue Shells*
8 scoops vanilla ice cream
8 Fresh Poached Peaches (recipe follows)
Easy Melba Sauce (recipe follows)

Place each meringue shell in a shallow glass dessert bowl. Fill each with a scoop of ice cream and top with a poached peach half. Spoon Easy Melba Sauce over top. Serves 8.

Fresh Poached Peaches

1 cup granulated sugar
1 cup water
1/2 vanilla bean, broken into small pieces
4 large, ripe peaches
1/4 cup peach brandy or liqueur of your choice

Combine sugar, water, and vanilla bean in a large saucepan over medium heat. Cover, and let come to a boil. Reduce heat, uncover, and let simmer for about 10 minutes. Bring a large pot of water to a full boil. Add peaches and let boil for about 30 seconds; drain into a colander and hold under cold running water. When cool enough to handle, rub off skins. Cut each peach in half and remove pit. Drop peach halves into simmering syrup; simmer until fork tender (time depends on ripeness of peaches). Transfer peach halves and syrup to a storage bowl and add peach or other brandy. Cover and refrigerate until chilled or until ready to use. Drain just before using. Reserve syrup for poaching other fruit or for a marvelous pancake topping.

Easy Melba Sauce

1 10-oz. package frozen raspberries in heavy syrup
2 Tbs. Framboise liqueur, raspberry brandy, or water
1 Tbs. cornstarch

Place frozen block of raspberries in a colander set over a bowl until completely thawed and syrup has drained into bowl. In a small saucepan, combine liqueur and cornstarch; stir until smooth. Add raspberry syrup and cook, stirring, over low heat until thickened. Pour into a storage bowl and add thawed berries. Cover, and refrigerate until chilled or until ready to use. Makes about 1 cup sauce.

Meringue Shells with Fresh Peach Sabayon

Peach brandy spikes a creamy sabayon custard sauce spooned over luscious mounds of fresh peach slices in snowy white meringue shells.

4 large, ripe peaches
1 Tbs. lemon juice
2 egg yolks
2 Tbs. Vanilla Sugar*, or 2 Tbs. granulated sugar plus
    1/2 tsp. vanilla extract

2 Tbs. peach brandy
1/2 pint heavy (whipping) cream
8 Individual Meringue Shells*
Caramel Gold Dust* or chopped pecans, optional

Plunge each peach into a large pan of rapidly boiling water; hold under cold running water and peel off skins. Cut into halves and remove pits; cut halves into slices, and drop them into a bowl. Sprinkle with lemon juice; toss to coat. Refrigerate until ready to use. In a large, heat-proof bowl with electric hand beater at high speed, beat yolks until thick. Place bowl over, not in, a pan of simmering water and add Vanilla Sugar; beat until peaks form when beater is slowly raised. Add brandy, and continue to beat to a thick custard, about 5 minutes. Remove bowl from simmering water and place in a larger bowl of ice water. Beat until cool.

In another chilled bowl with chilled beaters, beat cream until stiff peaks form; fold into custard mixture. Cover bowl and refrigerate sauce until ready to use. Place meringue shells onto individual serving plates. Fill with peach slices. Whip chilled sauce to reblend; spoon over peach slices. If desired, sprinkle with Caramel Gold Dust or chopped pecans. Serves 8.

Meringue Shell with Strawberry Mousse

1/2 pint fresh strawberries, hulled
Water
1 envelope unflavored gelatin
1/2 cup granulated sugar
2 egg yolks
1/4 cup Crème de Cassis or other liqueur
1/2 pint heavy (whipping) cream
8 Individual Meringue Shells*

Cut four large strawberries in half; reserve for garnish. Place remaining strawberries in a large bowl and crush slightly; pour juices into a 1-cup measure. Add sufficient water to make 1/2 cup liquid; transfer to a large, heat-proof bowl. Sprinkle with gelatin and let stand until softened. Add sugar and egg yolks; stir to blend. Place bowl over, not in, simmering water and stir until gelatin and sugar have dissolved and mixture has thickened sufficiently to coat spoon. Transfer bowl from simmering water to a large bowl of ice cubes and water; beat with a whisk until cooled to room temperature. Stir in liqueur. Refrigerate until mixture mounds slightly, about 30 minutes. In a chilled bowl with chilled beaters, beat cream until soft peaks form. Fold into gelatin mixture and stir in crushed strawberries. Spoon into individual meringue shells, dividing evenly. Use reserved strawberry halves to garnish each serving. Serves 8.

Chocolate Strawberry Mousse

Prepare strawberry mousse following directions above. After folding in the strawberries, fold in 2 ounces finely chopped semisweet chocolate.

Fresh Strawberry Meringue Pie

With a baked meringue pie shell on hand in your freezer, this festive dessert can be prepared in a matter of minutes.

1 pint strawberries, hulled
2 Tbs. confectioners' sugar
1/2 cup currant jelly
1 Tbs. kirsch or other liqueur
1 9-inch Meringue Pie Shell*

In a bowl, combine strawberries and confectioners' sugar; toss to blend. Combine currant jelly and liqueur in a small saucepan. Place over low heat and stir until jelly has dissolved and mixture has turned into a clear glaze. Fill meringue pie shell with strawberries and spoon glaze over surface. Serves 8.

Almond Meringue Cake

This delectable, cloudlike dessert is both easy to prepare and elegant. It glistens seductively, and delights the senses.

> *1/2 cup finely diced candied apricots or pineapple or*
> *   mixed candied fruit*
> *1/2 cup apricot or other brandy*
> *1 Tbs. butter, room temperature (for baking pan)*
> *1 Tbs. granulated sugar (for baking pan)*
> *1/2 tsp. unflavored gelatin*
> *4 Tbs. water*
> *9 egg whites, room temperature*
> *1 cup granulated sugar*

Place a large, round, 12-inch or 14- × 2-inch pan or oblong roasting pan on a rack one-third up from bottom of oven. Pour in sufficient water to come up about 2 inches on sides of pan. Preheat oven to 325°F. In a small bowl, combine candied fruit and brandy. Let stand at room temperature 1 to 2 hours, or overnight if you like. Generously butter a 10- × 4-inch tube or Bundt pan. Sprinkle with about 3/4 tablespoon sugar; tilt pan to distribute it evenly. With your fingers, sprinkle tube evenly with remaining 1/4 tablespoon sugar. In a small saucepan, sprinkle gelatin over water. Let stand about 5 minutes to soften. Place over low heat and stir until clear. Cool to room temperature.

In a large bowl, combine egg whites, gelatin mixture, and one teaspoon of brandy from fruit. Beat with an electric mixer on high speed until frothy. Add sugar about 2 tablespoons at a time, beating well after each addition. Continue to beat until mixture forms stiff, glossy peaks. Drain fruit, reserving brandy for Almond Glaze. Gently fold fruit into egg-white mixture. Spoon into prepared pan. Place in a pan of water in preheated oven. Bake for 25 to 30 minutes, or until top feels dry when touched with fingertips and can be gently pulled away from sides of pan. Let stand on a rack for about 5 minutes. Place a large platter over pan, center it carefully, and, holding pan and platter firmly together, turn them both over. Remove pan. Cool to room temperature.

Almond Glaze

1/2 cup slivered almonds
1/2 cup granulated sugar
Reserved apricot or other brandy

Sprinkle top of cake evenly with slivered almonds. In a small saucepan, combine 1/2 cup sugar and reserved brandy. Stir constantly over medium heat until mixture becomes a pale, golden syrup. Spoon immediately over top and down sides of cake. Serve as soon as glaze has hardened, about 20 minutes, or let stand several hours at room temperature before serving. Serves 8.

Lemon Meringue Pie

In this version, the baked meringue shell makes a delightful change in taste and texture from the usual pastry crust. Filled with a rich but light lemony custard, it becomes a very elegant dessert.

4 egg yolks
1/2 cup granulated sugar
3 Tbs. lemon juice
2 Tbs. orange liqueur

1 tsp. grated lemon rind
1 9-inch Meringue Pie Shell*
1/2 pint heavy (whipping) cream
Candied Lemon Peel*

Place egg yolks in a large, heat-proof bowl. Beat until frothy. Add sugar and place bowl over, not in, a pan of simmering water. Beat with a wire whisk or electric hand mixer until sugar has dissolved. Add remaining ingredients and continue to beat until mixture is very thick and about triple in volume. Remove bowl from simmering water and beat until mixture cools to room temperature. Spoon into meringue pie shell. In a chilled bowl with chilled beaters, beat cream until soft peaks form. Spread over lemon filling. Sprinkle with candied lemon peel. Makes one 9-inch lemon meringue pie.

Frozen Meringue Cake with Grand Marnier Sauce

A simply fabulous dessert. Slice the cake at the table and spoon sauce over each serving, or serve it Nouvelle Cuisine style. Spoon a thin layer of the sauce onto small, chilled dessert plates and place a slice of cake in the center. For added flavor and visual excitement, sprinkle a few whole raspberries or sliced strawberries on top of the sauce.

1 Tbs. butter, room temperature
1 Tbs. granulated sugar
8 egg whites
1 tsp. strawberry, raspberry or lime gelatin
1/2 tsp. vanilla or almond extract
1 cup more granulated sugar
Grand Marnier Sauce*
Whole, fresh raspberries or sliced strawberries, optional

Place a large, round pan or an oblong roasting pan on a rack one-third up from bottom of oven. Pour in sufficient water to come about 2 inches up sides of pan. Preheat oven to 325°F. Spread butter inside a 12-cup Bundt pan or angel food cake pan. Sprinkle with about 3/4 tablespoon sugar. Tilt pan to distribute sugar evenly. With fingers, sprinkle tube evenly with remaining 1/4 tablespoon sugar. In a large bowl, beat egg whites until frothy. Sprinkle gelatin evenly over surface. Add vanilla or almond extract. Beat at high speed of an electric mixer until whites hold soft peaks. Reduce speed to moderate and add sugar about 2 tablespoons at a time, beating thoroughly after each addition. Continue to beat until mixture is very thick, marshmallowlike, and holds a stiff shape when beaters are raised or some of meringue is lifted on a rubber spatula. Spoon into prepared pan, pushing it into pan to avoid air holes. Smooth surface. Place in pan of water in preheated oven. Bake for 25 to 30 minutes, or until top feels dry when touched with fingertips and meringue pulls slightly away from sides of pan.

Let stand on a rack for about 5 minutes. Place platter over pan, centering it carefully; holding pan and platter firmly together, turn both over. Remove pan. Cool to room temperature. Meringue will shrink a bit as it cools, but this is as it should be. Place meringue in freezer until very firm, at least 3 hours, or until ready to serve. To serve, cut meringue with a serrated knife into pie-shaped wedges and transfer wedges to flat dessert plates. Top each serving with ice-cold sauce and, if desired, sprinkle with whole raspberries or sliced strawberries. Or, if preferred, spoon ice-cold sauce onto cold dessert plates and top each with a slice of frozen cake, sprinkle with berries, and serve. Serves 8 to 10.

Note: The flavored gelatin in this recipe turns the cake either a beautifully soft pink or pale green that looks simply divine with creamy white custard sauce. However, if you prefer, you may reverse this color scheme by using an unflavored plain gelatin instead of the flavored variety, which will give you a glistening white cake. Then use either Crème de Cassis (black currant liqueur) or Cassis (nonalcoholic black currant syrup) instead of the Grand Marnier for the sauce. Or, for an entirely different color scheme, such as for a St. Patrick's Day party, use green Crème de Menthe liqueur in the sauce. It's sensational any way you slice it.

Pink Cloud Angel Ring

Cold as ice cream but with a soft and fluffy texture. No cooking required!

> *1/2 cup granulated sugar*
> *3 Tbs. maraschino syrup*
> *4 egg whites*
> *1/2 pint heavy (whipping) cream*
> *1 pint fresh strawberries, hulled, or 2 cups any sliced or*
>   *diced fresh fruit*

Combine sugar and maraschino syrup in a small saucepan over medium heat; cover and bring to a full boil. Reduce heat; let simmer uncovered for 3 to 4 minutes. Beat egg whites in a large bowl until stiff. Slowly add simmering syrup, beating as added. In a separate chilled bowl with chilled beaters, beat cream until soft peaks form. Fold in egg white mixture. Spoon into a 6-cup ring mold, cover, and seal. Freeze until firm. Dip bottom of mold briefly in hot water, and unmold ring onto serving platter. Fill center with fresh strawberries or other fruit. Serves 8.

Walnut Dacquoise

An easy-to-make, particularly luscious rum custard filling makes this dacquoise extra delicious.

> *1 1/2 cups ground walnuts*
> *3/4 cup granulated sugar*
> *3/4 cup sifted cake flour*
> *9 egg whites*

1/2 tsp. cream of tartar
1/4 tsp. salt
1 1/2 cups more granulated sugar
1 tsp. vanilla extract
Easy Rum Custard Filling (recipe follows)
Chopped walnut halves

Preheat oven to 325°F. Butter three 8-inch layer cake pans and line bottoms with waxed paper or parchment paper cut to fit. Combine walnuts, 3/4 cup sugar, and cake flour. Set aside.

In a large mixing bowl, beat egg whites with cream of tartar and salt until very soft peaks form. Continue to beat, adding sugar a little at a time, until meringue forms stiff peaks when beater is lifted from bowl. Fold in vanilla, then walnut mixture, only until blended. Spoon batter into prepared pans, spreading evenly. Bake in preheated oven for 35 to 40 minutes, or until tops are firm to touch. Cool in pans on racks for about 30 minutes. Loosen sides with a small spatula and remove layers carefully. Peel off paper. Put layers together on an attractive serving plate with Easy Rum Custard Filling between each layer and on top. Garnish top with walnuts or walnut halves if desired. Serves 8.

Easy Rum Custard Filling

1 3-oz. package vanilla pudding mix
1 1/2 cups milk
1/4 cup light or dark rum
2 egg yolks, lightly beaten
1/2 pint heavy (whipping) cream

Empty package of vanilla pudding mix into a saucepan. Stir in milk, rum, and egg yolks. Place over medium heat, stirring constantly, until mixture reaches a full boil. Transfer to a storage bowl. Cover custard surface with plastic wrap. Refrigerate until chilled. Just before serving, beat until smooth, light, and fluffy. In a chilled bowl with chilled beaters, beat cream until soft peaks form; fold in chilled custard. Refrigerate until ready to use.

Chocolate Meringue Cake with Whipped Cream Filling and Frosting

This beautiful cake tastes best when made a day ahead.

> *1 cup granulated sugar*
> *1/2 cup confectioners' sugar*
> *6 egg whites*
> *1 tsp. white vinegar*
> *1/2 tsp. vanilla*
> *1 1/2 cups ground walnuts*
> *Whipped Cream Filling and Frosting (recipe follows)*
> *Chocolate Glaze (recipe follows)*

Butter two 8-inch round cake pans; line with parchment or waxed paper cut to fit. Butter paper and flour pans. Sift granulated sugar with confectioners' sugar onto paper. Set aside.

In a large mixing bowl, beat egg whites until soft peaks form. Add sugars in four parts, beating well after each addition. Fold in vinegar and vanilla; continue to beat until mixture holds stiff peaks when beater is lifted from bowl. Fold in nuts. Spoon batter into prepared pan, dividing evenly. Bake in preheated oven for 35 to 40 minutes. Run a knife around edge of each layer and invert onto a rack; remove pans and peel off paper. Cool on racks. Place one layer on a decorative serving plate. Cover with filling. Top with second layer and cover with frosting. Drizzle top of assembled cake with glaze. Refrigerate until ready to serve.

Whipped Cream Filling and Frosting

1/2 pint heavy (whipping) cream
1/4 cup confectioners' sugar
1 Tbs. cocoa

In a chilled bowl with chilled beaters, beat cream until soft peaks form. Fold in confectioners' sugar. Spoon half of mixture into a second bowl, fold cocoa into this half, and blend well. Use as filling for cake. Use remaining whipped cream as topping.

Chocolate Glaze

4 Tbs. (1/2 stick) butter
1/4 cup cocoa
2 Tbs. confectioners' sugar

In a small saucepan, melt butter over low heat. Stir in cocoa and confectioners' sugar. Remove from heat and let stand until tepid before using.

Small Temptations

*Elegant truffles, adult cookies, pastry creations,
and old-fashioned candy.*

It has been said you can't please all the people all of the time, but you can. When I am not quite certain what dessert my guests will like, I serve several. I find that a small selection of sweet temptations, attractively arranged on my best silver tray, accompanied by a pretty basket filled with clusters of green grapes or juicy ripe strawberries, and a pot of fragrant, freshly brewed coffee, can't help but satisfy even the most varied group.

The following Potpourri of recipes includes everything from elegantly rich chocolate truffles to satiny smooth, melt-in-your-mouth Creole pralines; from crisp, not-too-sweet cookies to chewy macaroons. Among them, I think you will find something to please everyone—including yourself, because each one can be made ahead of time.

A Richness of Truffles

Classic Chocolate Truffles with Walnuts

These creamy, double-rich chocolate truffles are surprisingly easy to make. Rolled in chopped walnuts and presented in paper candy cups, they look and taste irresistible.

> *8 1-oz. squares sweet chocolate, broken into small*
>   *pieces*
> *3 Tbs. unsalted butter, cut into small cubes*
> *1/2 cup heavy (whipping) cream*
> *1 Tbs. brandy*
> *Confectioners' sugar*
> *6 ozs. walnuts, finely chopped*

Place chocolate and butter in a heat-proof mixing bowl. Place bowl over a large pan of simmering water. Stir until chocolate is three-fourths melted. Remove from water; stir until chocolate is completely melted and mixture is smooth. Place cream in a small saucepan over medium heat until scalded. Slowly add hot cream to chocolate mixture, beating with a whisk or at low speed of an electric mixer until cream is absorbed. Stir in brandy. Cover bowl and refrigerate until chocolate mixture is firm, or until ready to use. Line a baking sheet with waxed paper. Spoon 1-inch mounds of chilled chocolate mixture onto paper. Refrigerate until chocolate mixture is again firm, about 30 minutes. Dip palms of hands into powdered sugar. Working quickly, roll each chocolate mound between palms into a smooth ball. Spread chopped nuts out onto a sheet of waxed paper; roll each truffle in nuts, coating completely. Place, not touching, on a flat baking sheet in freezer until firm. Transfer each truffle to a paper candy cup. Store in refrigerator until ready to serve. Makes about 20 truffles.

Marron Chocolate Truffles

Outrageously rich, smooth, and intensely flavorful.

> 8 1-oz. squares bittersweet chocolate, chopped
> 1 7- or 8-oz. can sweetened marron (chestnut) purée
> 2 Tbs. light corn syrup
> Pinch of salt
> 2 Tbs. unsweetened cocoa
> 2 Tbs. brandy
> Additional unsweetened cocoa

Processor Method: Place chopped chocolate in work bowl of a food processor; process until finely ground. Add remaining ingredients; process until mixture is smooth. Transfer to a storage bowl and refrigerate until chilled.

Hand Method: Finely grate chocolate into a large mixing bowl. Add chestnut purée and corn syrup, and salt. Knead with fingers until mixture is smooth. Stir in 2 tablespoons unsweetened cocoa and brandy. Transfer to a storage bowl and refrigerate until chilled.

Form chilled truffle mixture into small, bite-sized balls. Roll each ball in unsweetened cocoa powder. Place, not touching, on a flat surface in refrigerator until ready to serve. If desired, place each truffle in a small paper candy cup. Makes 30 truffles.

Chocolate Almond Truffles

So easy to make, you won't believe it; so rich and densely delicious, they won't believe that you did.

> *8 1-oz. squares extra bittersweet, bittersweet, or*
> *semisweet chocolate, chopped*
> *1 7-oz. roll soft almond paste, cut into small pieces*
> *2 Tbs. freshly brewed strong, hot, black coffee*
> *2 Tbs. rum or brandy*
> *Cocoa powder*

Processor Method: Place chopped chocolate in work bowl of a food processor; process until finely ground. Add almond paste, and process until mixture is smooth. With motor running, pour coffee and rum or brandy through feed tube of processor, then continue to process until mixture forms a soft ball.

Hand Method: Finely grate chocolate into a large mixing bowl. Add almond paste and knead with fingers until well blended and smooth. Stir in coffee and rum or brandy, blending well.

Shape mixture into small, bite-sized balls. Roll each ball in unsweetened cocoa powder, coating well. Place prepared balls, not touching, on a flat surface in refrigerator until ready to serve. If desired, place each truffle in a small paper candy cup. Makes 24 to 30 truffles.

Chocolate Rum Truffles

A Deep South specialty.

1 8 1/2-oz. box chocolate wafer cookies
1 cup chopped pecans
1 cup confectioners' sugar
3 Tbs. dark corn syrup
1/4 cup rum
1 cup more confectioners' sugar

Break chocolate wafers into large pieces. Place in work bowl of a food processor or blender, and process or blend to fine crumbs. Transfer to a large mixing bowl. Add pecans, 1 cup confectioners' sugar, corn syrup, and rum. Knead until mixture holds together, adding additional rum if necessary. Roll mixture, 1 tablespoon at a time, into balls. Roll in remaining confectioners' sugar to coat. Place in paper candy cups. Refrigerate several days for flavors to intensify. Makes 24 truffles.

Apricot Almond Truffles

6 ozs. dried apricots
1/4 to 1/2 cup confectioners' sugar
3 Tbs. rum or brandy
1 cup more confectioners' sugar for coating
Toasted slivered almonds

Processor Method: Place apricots in work bowl of a food processor; process until finely ground. Add about 1/4 cup confectioners' sugar. Process until mixture comes to a ball, adding additional sugar if necessary. Place in a large mixing bowl.

Blender Method: Grind apricots a few at a time in blender, and place in a large mixing bowl. Stir in about 1/4 cup sugar.

Add additional sugar a little at a time, kneading with hands until mixture is fairly stiff. Add enough rum or brandy to make it sufficiently moist to shape into small balls. Roll balls as prepared in additional confectioners' sugar and place a sliver of almond in center of each. Let stand at room temperature for several hours to dry. Store in airtight containers. To serve, place each truffle in a decorative paper cup. Makes 24 truffles.

Truffled Fruit

These elegant sweets are at their best when made with top-quality dried fruit.

> *10 large, dried pitted prunes*
> *10 large, dried apricot halves*
> *10 large, dried pear halves*
> *Armagnac or brandy*
> *3 1-oz. squares semisweet chocolate*
> *5 Tbs. butter*
> *1 egg yolk*
> *2/3 cup sifted confectioners' sugar*
> *1 tsp. more Armagnac or other brandy*
> *Unsweetened cocoa*

Place fruit in a 1-quart screw-top jar. Add sufficient brandy to cover it completely. Cover jar, shake well, and put in a cool place (not in refrigerator) for 2 to 3 days. Drain fruit well, reserving brandy. Place chocolate in a saucepan over low heat until partially melted; remove from heat and stir until smooth. Cool to room temperature. In a bowl, cream butter until light and fluffy. Fold in egg yolk. Add sugar a little at a time, beating well after each addition. Fold in cooled, melted chocolate and brandy. Refrigerate until firm enough to handle. Shape into small balls. Pry prunes open and insert a truffled ball into each. Press balls of truffle mixture onto cut side of each apricot and pear half, bringing fruit up around ball to hold it in place. Roll filled fruit in cocoa to coat lightly. Place each in a small, foil candy cup. Refrigerate until ready to serve. Makes 30 truffles.

Note: Use reserved marinade as a sauce for ice cream, or serve as a liqueur with the truffled fruit.

The Adult's Cookie Jar

Rolled Lace Cookies

These delicate cookie cylinders are the perfect accompaniment for ice cream or sorbet.

> *1/2 cup sifted all-purpose flour*
> *1/2 cup finely ground walnuts*
> *1/4 cup light corn syrup*
> *1/4 cup granulated sugar*
> *4 Tbs. (1/2 stick) butter*
> *1 Tbs. water*

Preheat oven to 325°F. In a small bowl, combine flour and walnuts. Combine corn syrup, sugar, butter, and water in a saucepan. Cook, stirring constantly, until mixture comes to a full boil; remove from heat. Stir in flour mixture in four parts, blending well after each addition. Drop mixture by rounded teaspoonfuls about 3 inches apart onto an ungreased baking sheet; bake no more than six at a time. Bake in preheated oven for 8 minutes, or until edges are lightly browned; do not overbake. (If first batch of cookies is too thick, stir 1 to 2 tablespoons more water into the batter before baking second batch. Let cookies remain on baking sheet for about 30 seconds. Scoop up warm cookies with large metal spatula; quickly roll around a wooden spoon handle (about 1/2 inch in diameter). Hold a few seconds until cookie stiffens. If cookies cool too quickly and are too brittle to roll, return to warm oven briefly to soften. Slide cookies off handles onto rack; cool completely. Makes about 2 dozen cookies.

Hazelnut Cookies

Make these cookies in advance; they improve with aging.

> *1 1/2 cups cake flour*
> *1 tsp. baking powder*
> *3/4 cup hazelnut meal†*
> *1 cup (2 sticks) butter, softened*
> *1/2 cup confectioners' sugar*
> *1 egg yolk*
> *1 Tbs. brandy*
> *1/2 tsp. vanilla extract*
> *Additional confectioners' sugar*

Sift flour with baking powder into a mixing bowl; stir in hazelnut meal. Set aside. In a large mixing bowl, beat butter at medium speed of an electric mixer until very light and fluffy. Gradually beat in confectioners' sugar about 1 tablespoon at a time, and continue to beat for another 1 to 2 minutes. Add egg yolk and beat a final minute. Fold in brandy and vanilla extract. Carefully fold in flour mixture. Cover bowl with plastic wrap and refrigerate until firm enough to shape, about 30 minutes.

---

† Available in gourmet food shops and the gourmet food section in some supermarkets.

Preheat oven to 350°F. Shape chilled dough into small balls; place about 1/2 inch apart on an ungreased baking sheet. Dip bottom of a glass in confectioners' sugar and use it to flatten each ball into a small round, about 1 inch in diameter and about 1/2 inch high. Bake in preheated oven for 12 to 15 minutes; cookies should be pale golden, not brown. Place baking sheet with cookies on a wire rack; immediately sift confectioners' sugar over each. Let stand for 5 minutes before removing from sheet. Roll in additional confectioners' sugar to coat. Place cookies in an airtight container, with waxed paper between layers. Store for 2 days or up to several weeks before serving. Makes about 3 dozen cookies.

Tahinis

1/2 cup butter (1 stick), softened to room temperature
1/2 cup Tahini (sesame seed paste)
3/4 cup granulated sugar
1 egg
1 1/4 cups all-purpose flour
1/4 tsp. baking powder
1/4 tsp. salt
1/2 cup slivered almonds

Preheat oven to 350°F. Lightly grease two square, 8-inch baking pans or one jelly-roll pan. In a mixing bowl, cream butter with Tahini until fluffy and light. Beat in sugar and egg. Add flour, baking powder, and salt. Blend thoroughly. Spoon dough into prepared pan or pans; press down evenly with fingertips. Sprinkle with almonds; press them down lightly into dough. Bake in preheated oven for 20 to 22 minutes, or until lightly browned. Place pan or pans on rack and cool to room temperature. Cut into finger-shaped pieces about 1 inch wide. Remove pieces with spatula. If desired, freeze on a flat surface until firm; store in airtight plastic containers in freezer until about 10 minutes before serving. Makes about 4 dozen cookies.

Pecan Crescents

These delicate cookies are a favorite with ice cream or sorbet.

> *4 ozs. pecans, finely ground*
> *2 1/4 cups sifted all-purpose flour*
> *1/2 cup Vanilla Sugar*, or 1/2 cup granulated sugar plus*
> * 1/2 tsp. vanilla extract*
> *1 cup (2 sticks) butter, room temperature*
> *Confectioners' sugar*

In a large bowl, combine pecans, flour, Vanilla Sugar, and butter. Mix together with hands to form a soft ball. Wrap in waxed paper and place in refrigerator until chilled, about 20 minutes. Preheat oven to 325°F. Shape chilled dough into a roll; cut across into slices about 1/4 inch thick. Roll each slice into a small sausage shape about 2 inches long; curve into plump crescents. Place on an ungreased baking sheet about 1 inch apart. Bake for 20 to 25 minutes, or until just barely colored. Remove from oven and let stand until cool; dust each with confectioners' sugar. Pack in an airtight container with waxed paper between layers. These cookies stay fresh for 2 to 3 weeks. Makes about 3 dozen cookies.

Black Walnut Bars

Rich with walnuts.

> *1/4 lb. (1 stick) unsalted butter*
> *1 Tbs. granulated sugar*
> *1 cup all-purpose flour*
> *1/4 tsp. salt*
> *1 cup dark brown sugar, firmly packed*

3 eggs
1 Tbs. dark rum
1 1/2 tsp. more flour
1 tsp. baking powder
2 cups finely chopped shelled black walnuts

Preheat oven to 350°F. In a large mixing bowl, cream butter and sugar until light and fluffy. Fold in flour and salt. Form dough into a ball and pat it smoothly into a 9- × 12-inch baking pan. Combine remaining ingredients and blend well. Spread over dough in pan. Bake in preheated oven for 30 to 35 minutes. Cool on a rack in pan. Cover and refrigerate several hours or overnight. Cut into bars. Makes about 4 dozen bars.

Chocolate Walnut Fingers

6 eggs
1 cup (2 sticks) butter, softened
1 1/2 cups granulated sugar
1 1/2 cups all-purpose flour
1/2 tsp. salt
1 cup chopped walnuts
3/4 cup more granulated sugar
1 1/2 cups more chopped walnuts
4 1-oz. squares semisweet chocolate, finely chopped

Preheat oven to 300°F. Break 3 eggs into a bowl. Separate remaining eggs, adding 3 yolks to whole eggs, and putting remaining whites in a separate bowl. Set aside. In a large mixing bowl, cream butter with 1 1/2 cups sugar. Beat in whole eggs and egg yolks. Add flour and salt; blend thoroughly. Stir in 1 cup chopped walnuts. Spoon batter evenly into an 11- × 16-inch jelly-roll pan. Bake in preheated oven for 35 minutes; let cool for 10 minutes. Beat remaining egg whites until stiff. Gradually beat in remaining sugar until mixture is glossy and holds soft peaks when beater is lifted from bowl. Stir in remaining walnuts and chocolate. Spread this mixture evenly over baked layer. Bake for 15 more minutes. Transfer pan to a rack to cool. Cut into finger-length bars. Makes about 4 dozen 2-inch bars.

Macaroons

Crisp on the outside and chewy on the inside—with just the right amount of sweetness.

1 7-oz. package soft almond paste
2 egg whites
3/4 cup granulated sugar
1 Tbs. grated lemon zest
1/2 tsp. vanilla extract
1 Tbs. dark or light rum, or 1/2 tsp. rum flavoring or
  almond extract

Processor Method: Cut almond paste into small cubes; set aside. Place remaining ingredients in work bowl of a food processor; process until well mixed and frothy. With motor running, add cubes of almond paste a few at a time until all are added and mixture is smooth.

Hand method: Break almond paste into small cubes. Place in a large mixing bowl and beat until softened. Add remaining ingredients and stir until well blended.

Let mixture stand at room temperature for about 30 minutes. Preheat oven to 325°F. Butter and flour a long, flat baking sheet. Use about 2 teaspoons of mixture to form small balls. Place, not touching, on prepared baking sheet; flatten. Bake in preheated oven for 20 to 25 minutes. Transfer to racks to cool. To store, place macaroons in a single layer, with waxed paper between each, in an airtight container. Makes about 3 dozen cookies.

Coconut Macaroons

An astonishing flavor!

> *1/2 cup granulated sugar*
> *1 7-oz. package soft almond paste*
> *1/2 tsp. vanilla extract*
> *3 egg whites*
> *1 cup coconut, shredded*

Preheat oven to 350°F. Line a long baking sheet with foil or parchment paper. In a mixing bowl, combine sugar, almond paste, and vanilla extract. Knead until blended. Add egg whites one at a time, beating after each addition. Fold in coconut. Let mixture stand about 30 minutes at room temperature. Drop by spoonfuls onto lined baking sheet. Bake in preheated oven for 25 to 30 minutes or until tops are dry. Cool on rack in pan for about 5 minutes. Remove from paper and let stand, covered, for 6 to 8 hours at room temperature. To store, place in layers with waxed paper between each layer in airtight container. Makes about 2 dozen macaroons.

Brandy Snaps

Crisp, thin, and buttery.

> *1/2 lb. (2 sticks) unsalted butter*
> *1 cup granulated sugar*
> *1 egg, lightly beaten*
> *1/4 tsp. salt*
> *1/2 tsp. ground ginger*

1/2 tsp. mace
1/4 cup brandy
2 1/2 cups all-purpose flour

In a large mixing bowl, cream butter with sugar until light and fluffy. Beat in egg. Stir in salt, ginger, mace, and brandy. Fold in flour. Form dough into a ball and wrap in waxed paper; chill for 1 to 2 hours. Divide dough into six pieces; roll each between hands to form a cylinder about 4 inches long and 1 1/2 inches wide. Preheat oven to 350°F. With a sharp knife, slice each cylinder into thin rounds. Place on ungreased baking sheet. Bake in preheated oven for 10 to 12 minutes, or until edges are very lightly browned. Immediately transfer from baking sheet to wire rack. Cool to room temperature. These cookies will become crisp as they cool. Makes about 10 dozen cookies.

Note: If desired, cylinders of dough can be wrapped in waxed paper and stored in refrigerator for 3 to 4 days. Or, they may be placed on a flat surface in freezer until firm, then individually wrapped in foil, and stored in freezer. Thaw frozen cylinders of dough at room temperature until sufficiently softened to slice and bake.

Pastry Shop Magic

Truffle Pastry Puffs

1 17 1/4-oz. package frozen puff pastry
32 Chocolate Almond Truffles*

Thaw puff pastry for about 20 minutes. One at a time, unfold each sheet. Roll out on a lightly floured work surface to an 11-inch square. Cut each square into 16 small squares. Place a truffle in center. Brush edges of pastry with water. Fold over to form a triangle. Press edges together with tines of a fork. Place as prepared on a flat surface in freezer until very firm. Preheat oven to 425°F. Place pastries, not touching, on a flat baking sheet. Bake for 10 to 12 minutes, or until golden brown. Cool to room temperature before serving. Makes 32 puffs.

Strawberry Pastry Puffs

1 17 1/4-oz. package frozen puff pastry
32 large, ripe strawberries, hulled
Granulated sugar

Thaw and cut frozen puff pastry sheets as for Truffle Pastry Puffs*. Roll each berry in sugar, coating completely, then place on a pastry square. Brush edges of square with water. Fold over to form a triangle and press edges together with tines of a fork. Prick top of pastry with fork. Place as prepared, not touching, on a flat surface in freezer until pastry is very firm. Preheat oven to 450°F. Place puffs on a flat baking sheet. Bake for 12 to 15 minutes, or until lightly browned. Makes 32 puffs.

Note: For variety, banana slices or peach chunks (rolled first in lemon juice) can be substituted for strawberries.

Middle-Eastern Date-Nut Squares

1 1-lb. package frozen Phyllo pastry leaves
1/4 cup chopped dates
1/4 cup chopped pecans

1/2 cup miniature chocolate morsels
1/4 cup shredded coconut
1 1/2 cups honey
1 cup (2 sticks) butter

Place unwrapped package of Phyllo leaves in refrigerator until thawed, 6 to 8 hours or overnight. In a mixing bowl, combine dates, pecans, chocolate morsels, and coconut. Bring honey to room temperature. Preheat oven to 350°F. Open thawed package of Phyllo leaves and unfold; cover with plastic wrap, then cover wrap with a dampened cloth to keep leaves from drying out. Place butter in a small saucepan over low heat until melted. Remove pan from heat; cool to room temperature.

Cut entire stack of Phyllo leaves across into 6 equal strips. Cut each strip across into 3 equal squares. Working with one stack at a time, place four layers on work surface and brush with melted butter. Cover with four more squares, brush with butter, and top with another four layers. Brush top layer with butter. Place about 1 1/2 teaspoons filling in center. Fold each point of square toward center, pressing lightly into filling; leave center of filling uncovered. Brush top of pastry with additional butter, then spoon about 1 1/2 teaspoons honey onto exposed filling. Place as prepared on a flat baking sheet. When all are prepared, bake in preheated oven for 12 to 15 minutes, or until pastry is lightly browned. Transfer with a spatula to a wire rack; cool to room temperature before serving. Makes 36 squares.

Chocolate Godiva Puffs

Fantastic! So easy to prepare, you won't believe it.

1 sheet frozen puff pastry from a 17 1/4-oz. package
9 strawberry cream or other soft-centered Godiva chocolates

Thaw sheet of puff pastry for 20 minutes, then unfold. Cut lengthwise into three strips, using crease marks as a guide. Cut strips across into three equal pieces. One at a time, place each piece of pastry on a lightly floured board and roll out to a 5-inch square. Place a Godiva chocolate in center. With a pastry brush or fingers, moisten edges of pastry with cold water. Bring pastry up over chocolate, then pinch together just above chocolate so that top of pastry spreads out in petal shapes. Make sure chocolate is completely encased and sealed in pastry. As each is prepared, place, not touching, on flat surface in freezer until very firm.

Preheat oven to 425°F. Place pastries, not touching, on a flat baking sheet. Bake in preheated oven for 12 to 15 minutes, or until golden brown. Cool to room temperature before serving, or let stand at room temperature until ready to serve. Makes 9 pastry puffs.

Baklava

For those who think a day without chocolate is a day lost.

> *1 1-lb. package frozen Phyllo pastry leaves*
> *1/2 cup (1 stick) butter*
> *1 6-oz. package miniature chocolate morsels*
> *1/2 cup (1 stick) more butter*
> *3 cups (approximately 1 lb.) finely chopped or coarsely*
>   *ground walnuts, hazelnuts, or pecans*
> *Maple Sugar Syrup (recipe follows)*

Place frozen package of Phyllo leaves in refrigerator until completely thawed—several hours or overnight. Preheat oven to 350°F. Open thawed package of Phyllo leaves and unfold them into a neat stack on work surface. Invert a 13- × 9-inch baking pan over stack, placing it along one side and edge. With a sharp knife, cut through stack to shape of pan. Cover stack and cut portion of leaves with plastic wrap and cover plastic wrap with a moistened cloth. (Plastic wrap will keep leaves from becoming soggy, but dampened cloth will keep them from drying out as you work.) Place 1/2 cup butter and chocolate in a small saucepan over low heat until chocolate has partially melted; remove pan from heat and stir until mixture is smooth. Let stand until cooled to room temperature.

In another saucepan over low heat, melt remaining butter. Remove from heat and let stand until cooled. With a pastry brush, coat bottom and sides of pan with a little of melted butter. Carefully peel and lift first leaf from stack and place it on bottom of buttered pan. Cover with three more leaves and brush again with butter. Add four more leaves, brushing each with butter, before adding next. Sprinkle evenly with half of nuts. Cover nuts with one more leaf and brush with butter. Cover with cut strips of leaves and one more uncut leaf. Brush with half the melted chocolate mixture. Add four more leaves, brush with butter, and top with remaining nuts. Build four more layers, brush with remaining chocolate, and finish with remaining leaves, buttering each. Push sides of leaves down into sides of pan. With a sharp knife, cut through pastry to bottom of pan into 6 lengthwise strips. Cut 2-inch diagonal slices across strips. Bake Baklava in preheated oven until golden brown, 1 to 1 1/4 hours. Place pan on a wire rack; pour Maple Sugar Syrup over top. Cool to room temperature before serving. Makes 36 pieces.

Maple Sugar Syrup

2 cups granulated sugar
1 cup water
1 cup maple syrup
1 Tbs. fresh lemon juice
1 tsp. lemon rind, grated

In a saucepan, combine sugar, water, and maple syrup. Place over low heat and stir until sugar has dissolved. Bring to a boil, lower heat, and let simmer for about 10 minutes. Remove from heat and stir in lemon juice and rind. Cool slightly, then pour over pan of baklava when it comes from oven.

Almond Pastry Tarts

These rich, bite-sized tarts are surprisingly easy to make.

> *1/2 cup (1 stick) butter*
> *3/4 cup all-purpose flour*
> *1/4 cup confectioners' sugar*
> *1/4 cup finely ground almonds*
> *1 to 2 Tbs. water*
> *Raspberry preserves, orange marmalade, or lemon curd*
> *Sweetened whipped cream or sour cream*
> *Slivered almonds, optional*

Place butter in a large mixing bowl and let stand at room temperature until very soft. Preheat oven to 350°F. Add flour, confectioners' sugar, and almonds to softened butter, and mix to a soft dough. If necessary, add 1 to 2 tablespoons cold water. Pinch off small pieces of dough and press them against bottom and sides of ungreased tartlet pans or 1 3/4- × 1-inch muffin cups. (Place miniature tartlet pans on a baking sheet.) Bake tarts in preheated oven until lightly browned, 15 to 20 minutes. Use tip of a knife to remove them from the pans or cups; cool on a wire rack.

Just before serving, fill each tartlet with preserves, marmalade, or lemon curd, and top each with a dollop of sweetened whipped cream or sour cream. Garnish with slivered almonds, if desired.

Makes about 24 tarts.

Newly Fashionable
Old-Fashioned Candy

Candy Temperatures

At 234°F. to 240°F., a small amount of mixture, when dropped into a cup of cold water, will form a recognizable soft ball that will flatten on your fingers when removed from water.

At 244°F. to 248°F., a bit of mixture dropped into cold water will hold a definite ball shape that will flatten with slight finger pressure when removed.

At 250°F. to 266°F., a bit of mixture dropped into cold water will form a firm ball shape that will be pliable but resistant to finger pressure when removed from water.

At 350°F., a bit of mixture dropped into cold water will form hard, brittle threads.

Candied Grapefruit, Orange, or Lemon Rind

To use as a garnish, an ingredient, or a confection.

> *3 large, thick-skinned grapefruits, 4 large navel oranges,*
> *or 5 lemons with unblemished skin*
> *Water*
> *2 1/2 cups granulated sugar*
> *2 cups more granulated sugar*

Peel grapefruits, oranges, or lemons, leaving pith attached to skin. Cut peel into julienne strips about 1/4 inch long. Squeeze juice from 1/2 grapefruit, 1 orange, or 1 lemon, and set aside. Reserve remaining fruit for other use. Place peel in a large saucepan and add sufficient water to cover. Place over high heat and bring to a boil. Reduce heat to low; simmer for about 10 minutes. Drain, and repeat three times.

Place juice in a 2-cup measure; add sufficient water to make 1 1/2 cups. Pour into a saucepan and add 2 1/2 cups sugar. Place over low heat and cook, stirring, until sugar dissolves; pour over peel in bowl. Cover bowl and let mixture stand for 8 to 12 hours or overnight. Transfer to a saucepan and cook, stirring, over medium heat until mixture comes to a full boil. Reduce heat to low; simmer for about 1 hour or until peel has absorbed almost all of syrup. Remove from heat, and drain through a colander. Cover a long, flat baking sheet with waxed paper or foil. Spread drained fruit evenly on paper. Spread about 2 cups of sugar in a long, shallow dish. Roll strips of peel in sugar and transfer to racks. Let stand until dry, 3 to 4 hours, at room temperature, stirring occasionally with a fork. Store peel in a tightly covered jar. Makes about 2 cups julienne strips of candied peel.

Chocolate Fruit and Nut Log

This very rich mixture of candied fruit, walnuts, and chocolate improves with aging.

> 6 1-oz. squares bittersweet chocolate, chopped
> 4 ozs. mixed candied fruit, diced
> 12 oz. walnuts, chopped
> 2 to 3 Tbs. dark rum
> 1 cup granulated sugar

Place chocolate in a large, heat-proof mixing bowl. Place bowl over, not in, simmering water; stir until chocolate has partially melted. Remove bowl from heat and continue to stir until it is completely melted and smooth. Place fruit and nuts in work bowl of a food processor or blender; process or blend until finely chopped. Add chopped mixture to melted chocolate and stir until well blended.

Knead enough rum into mixture to make it soft and pliable but not too liquid to hold its shape. Divide into two equal parts. Place each, one at a time, on a lightly sugared work surface and shape into a log. Roll to coat with sugar. Wrap each tightly in waxed paper, then in foil or plastic wrap. Let stand in a cool, dry place 1 to 2 days before serving. Cut across into thick slices to serve. Makes about 24 thick slices.

Lemon Zest Fudge

This is the same rich, thick, and creamy-smooth fudge you had as a child, but it has been transformed into an adult dessert confection. It is less sweet and more chocolaty, with a hint of coffee and tart, tangy, lemon zest.

> *Zest from 1 large or 2 small lemons, finely diced (about 3 Tbs.)*
> *4 1-oz. squares unsweetened chocolate, chopped*
> *2 tsp. instant coffee*
> *1 1/2 cups milk*
> *4 cups granulated sugar*
> *Dash of salt*
> *1 tsp. vanilla extract*
> *4 Tbs. butter*
> *1 cup peeled, chopped, and toasted hazelnuts or walnuts (see Note)*

Butter two 8- × 4- × 3-inch or 9- × 5- × 3-inch loaf pans. Cut lemon zest into julienne strips, and then cut strips across into miniature dice. Place in a saucepan; cover with water. Bring to a boil, lower heat, and let simmer for about 30 minutes. Drain through a fine sieve. Dump onto paper towels and spread out to dry. In top half of a double boiler, combine chocolate and milk. Place over simmering water and cook, stirring frequently, until chocolate is almost melted. Remove pan from water and add instant coffee. Stir until chocolate has completely melted and mixture is smooth. Add sugar and salt. Cook, stirring, over medium heat until sugar dissolves and mixture begins to boil. Then cook without stirring until a candy thermometer registers 234°F. Stir in vanilla. Remove pan from heat. Add butter; push it down into chocolate mixture, but do not stir. Cool, without stirring, to lukewarm (110°F.). (This cooling ensures that fudge will be thick and smooth.) Beat with a large, heavy wooden spoon just until mixture begins to thicken and lose its gloss. Stir in nuts and lemon zest. Pour at once into prepared loaf pans. Cool until firm. Cut into large squares. Makes about 2 pounds or 36 pieces.

Note: To prepare hazelnuts, place whole nuts in a large saucepan. Cover with water by about 2 inches. Add about 2 Tbs. baking soda. Bring to a boil and boil for 3 to 4 minutes. Drain through a colander. One at a time, hold each nut under cold, running water and rub off skin. Coarsely chop nuts and place in a single layer on a long, shallow baking sheet in a 350°F. oven for 15 to 20 minutes, or until lightly browned.

Walnut Fudge

Blond and beautifully rich.

> *2 cups light brown sugar, firmly packed*
> *2 cups granulated sugar*
> *1/2 pint heavy (whipping) cream*
> *1/2 tsp. walnut flavoring*
> *1 tsp. maple flavoring*
> *1 1/2 cups chopped walnuts (about 5 ounces)*
> *3 Tbs. butter*

Coat bottom and sides of an 8-inch square pan heavily with softened butter. Refrigerate while preparing fudge. In a large, heavy saucepan, combine two sugars and cream. Place over medium-high heat and cook, stirring constantly, until sugar dissolves, about 5 minutes. Reduce heat to medium and continue to cook, stirring occasionally until a candy thermometer inserted in mixture registers 240°F. Remove pan from heat; spoon butter over surface. Let stand until cooled to luke-warm, 110°F. on candy thermometer. Stir in butter with a wooden spoon, then add maple and walnut flavorings. Beat mixture until creamy; immediately fold in walnuts and spoon into prepared pan. Let stand until cooled to room temperature. Cut into 1-inch squares. Store in an airtight container with waxed paper between layers. Makes about 2 pounds candy.

French Quarter Pralines

2 cups granulated sugar
1 cup heavy (whipping) cream
1/2 cup light corn syrup
1/4 tsp. salt
1 cup sifted confectioners' sugar
1 tsp. finely ground French roast coffee with chicory, or
*   1 tsp. instant espresso*
2 tsp. vanilla extract
2 Tbs. butter, softened
2 cups coarsely chopped pecans

Line two baking sheets with waxed or parchment paper cut to fit. Place a dab of butter on underside of paper at each corner to hold it in place; set aside. Grease inside of a heavy 2-quart saucepan with butter; add granulated sugar, cream, corn syrup, and salt. Cook, stir-ring, over medium heat, until sugar dissolves and mixture comes to a full boil. Continue to boil, stirring occasionally, until 234°F. on candy thermometer. Immediately remove from heat. Stir in confectioners' sugar, coffee, vanilla, and butter. Mix well. Stir in pecans. Quickly drop by tablespoonfuls onto prepared baking sheets. If candy be-comes too stiff, stir in a few drops of hot water. Makes about 36 pralines.

Grenadine Fudge with Candied Fruit

4 cups granulated sugar
2 cups light (half-and-half) cream
2/3 cup grenadine syrup
1/4 tsp. salt
1 cup finely diced mixed candied fruit

Grease an 8-inch square baking pan with soft butter. Refrigerate until ready to use. In a 5- to 6-quart, heavy saucepan, combine sugar, cream, grenadine syrup, and salt; stir over medium heat until sugar is completely dissolved. Bring to a boil and cook, without stirring, until mixture reaches 234°F. on a candy thermometer. Stir in candied fruit. Immediately remove from heat and let stand at room temperature, *without stirring,* until cooled to 110°F. on candy thermometer. When cool, beat fudge until creamy, about 3 minutes, and pour it into prepared pan. Let stand until firm before cutting. Makes 8 to 10 dozen small pieces.

Chocolate-Coated Popcorn

Sticky, messy, and marvelous.

4 to 5 cups freshly popped, unsalted popcorn, prepared
in a hot-air popcorn machine that requires no oil
4 1-oz. squares semisweet chocolate, chopped
2 Tbs. butter, softened

Place popcorn in a large mixing bowl. Place chopped chocolate and butter in top half of a double boiler over very hot water until partially melted. Remove pan from water and stir until chocolate is completely melted and smooth. Let stand, stirring occasionally, until tepid. Pour melted, tepid chocolate slowly over popcorn in a thin, steady stream, while at same time stirring and lifting kernels as it is added. Use two forks to toss quickly so that chocolate is evenly distributed. (Each popped kernel will not be completely coated.) To serve, loosen mixture from sides of bowl and break into small clusters. Serve in one large bowl for a happy, kooky ending to a buffet supper party. Serves 6 to 10.

Seductive Saucery

Sauces that can transform even the simplest dessert into an haute cuisine creation.

Classic and Not-So-Classic Cream Sauces

Crème Anglaise
(English Custard Cream)

This classic sauce can be flavored in many different ways and served with innumerable desserts.

> *1 1/2 cups milk*
> *4 egg yolks*
> *1/2 cup granulated sugar*
> *1/2 cup light cream*
> *1 tsp. vanilla or lemon extract, or other desired flavoring*
> *1 to 2 Tbs. brandy, rum, or liqueur*

Pour milk into a saucepan and place over low heat until scalded. In a large mixing bowl, beat yolks with a whisk or electric hand mixer until frothy. Add sugar and continue to beat until very pale, thick, and about double in volume. Slowly pour in hot milk, beating as added. Pour mixture back into saucepan and cook over medium heat, stirring constantly from bottom and around sides of pan, until mixture coats spoon. Remove from heat and immediately stir in cold cream and desired flavoring. Transfer to a cold storage bowl. Cover custard surface with plastic wrap and refrigerate until chilled or until ready to serve. Makes about 2 cups.

Notes: Stir a generous amount of dark rum into sauce before chilling, and serve over plum pudding or fruit cake—Much more delicious than Grandma's hard sauce! Add brandy, and spoon over your best apple pie. Or add chocolate liqueur and serve over chocolate ice cream.

Creamy Lemon Sauce I

Prepare sauce as directed. Cool to room temperature. Fold in 3 tablespoons fresh lemon juice and 1 teaspoon grated lemon rind.

Creamy Lemon Sauce II

Prepare sauce as directed. Cool to room temperature. Fold in 1/2 cup commercially prepared lemon curd.

Nesselrode Sauce

Prepare sauce as directed. Cool to room temperature. Fold in one 8-ounce jar Nesselrode sauce.

Creamy Rich Custard Sauce

Whip 1/2 cup heavy cream until soft peaks form. Fold into prepared and cooled sauce.

Whipped Cream Rum Sauce

A dessert sauce worth remembering.

> *2 Tbs. cream cheese, softened*
> *1/4 cup confectioners' sugar*
> *1/2 pint heavy (whipping) cream*
> *3 Tbs. dark Jamaican rum*

In a small bowl, beat cream cheese with powdered sugar until light and fluffy. In a chilled bowl with chilled beaters, beat cream until stiff peaks form. Fold in cream cheese mixture. Add rum and blend well. Refrigerate until chilled or until ready to serve. Makes about 2 cups sauce.

Amaretto Cream Sauce

Amaretto liqueur flavors this creamy, smooth sauce.

> *1 egg, separated*
> *1 3/4 cup granulated sugar*
> *4 Tbs. Amaretto liqueur*
> *1/2 cup heavy (whipping) cream*

In top half of a double boiler, combine egg yolk and sugar; beat until blended. Place over simmering water and continue to beat until mixture is about triple in volume. Remove pan from water; fold in liqueur. Cool custard to room temperature, stirring occasionally. In a chilled bowl with chilled beaters, beat cream until stiff peaks form. In a separate bowl, beat egg white until soft peaks form. Fold beaten egg white and cream into cooled custard. Refrigerate until ready to serve. Makes about 2 cups sauce.

Italian Cream Cheese Sauce

Despite the name, this sauce tastes grand over very American spice cake or gingerbread. It is also quite sensational over fresh fruit, fruit tarts, and baked apples.

1 3-oz. package cream cheese, room temperature
1/2 cup ricotta cheese
1/2 cup heavy (whipping) cream
6 Tbs. confectioners' sugar
1 tsp. vanilla or almond extract

In a mixing bowl, beat cream cheese with ricotta cheese until light and fluffy. Fold in cream, confectioners' sugar, and vanilla or almond extract. Refrigerate until ready to use. Makes about 2 cups sauce.

St. Patrick's Sauce

A grand sauce for a grand day.

1 3-oz. package cream cheese, room temperature
3 Tbs. Crème de Menthe liqueur
1/2 pint heavy (whipping) cream
Confectioners' sugar to taste

In a small bowl, beat cream cheese until light and fluffy. Beat in Crème de Menthe. In a second, larger bowl, beat cream until soft peaks form. Fold in cheese mixture. Makes about 2 1/2 cups sauce.

Note: This is superb over chocolate ice cream, Devil's Food cake, or chocolate pudding—the color combination and taste are sensational. On the lighter side, but equally grand, serve it over fresh, ripe strawberries.

Classic Mousseline Sauce

Possibly the most sophisticated and sensational custard sauce ever created. It was always on the dessert cart at Le Pavillon restaurant in New York where it was offered as a topping for what the French waiter called "fruit salade," a beautiful fresh fruit compote.

> *4 egg yolks*
> *1/2 cup granulated sugar*
> *3 Tbs. brandy, rum, or liqueur of your choice*
> *1/2 pint heavy (whipping) cream*

Place yolks in top half of a double boiler or a large, heat-proof bowl; place over, not in, a large pan of simmering water. Add sugar. Using a wire whisk or hand-held electric mixer, beat until very thick, light, and about triple in volume. Remove from water. Beat until mixture has cooled to room temperature. Fold in brandy, rum, or liqueur. In a chilled bowl with chilled beaters, beat cream until stiff peaks form; fold in yolk mixture. Transfer sauce to a storage or serving bowl. Refrigerate until chilled or until ready to serve. Makes about 3 cups sauce.

Notes: This sauce is also wickedly delicious over chocolate mousse, bittersweet chocolate ice cream, or wedges of un-iced chocolate cake. Flavor it with Framboise (raspberry brandy), and spoon into parfait or wine glasses alternately with fresh raspberries. Or spike it with dark Jamaican rum to top baked apples.

Chocolate Foam Sauce

Stir 4 ounces melted bittersweet chocolate into yolk mixture before folding in whipped cream.

Snow Leopard Sauce

Fold in 6 ounces miniature chocolate morsels.

First-Choice Chocolate Sauces

Instant Chocolate Sauce

Made in a matter of minutes, without cooking.

>   *3 1-oz. squares unsweetened chocolate, chopped*
>   *1/2 cup granulated sugar*
>   *3 Tbs. water*
>   *4 Tbs. brandy, rum, or liqueur*

Combine ingredients in work bowl of a food processor or blender; process or blend until smooth. Makes about 3/4 cups sauce.

Gourmet Shop Bittersweet Chocolate Sauce

I don't think you'll find this sauce in any other cookbook, though I know a number of cookbook authors who use it frequently. Perhaps it's because it's almost too simple to call a recipe, but that is why I think you should have it.

>   *6 ozs. bittersweet chocolate, chopped*
>   *1/2 cup water*
>   *1 Tbs. corn syrup*
>   *1 Tbs. butter*

Combine chocolate, water, and corn syrup in top half of a double boiler. Place over simmering water until chocolate is partially melted. Stir in butter. Remove from heat and stir until mixture is smooth. Makes about 3/4 cup.

Bittersweet Chocolate Rum Sauce

Add 2 tablespoons light or dark rum.

Note: This is a thin sauce that lends itself well to a Nouvelle Cuisine-type presentation: Spoon it into shallow glass dessert bowls or plates with deep rims, and top with scoops of ice cream.

Brown Sugar Fudge Sauce

Serve this one hot; it's sensational over ice cream, angel food cake, or pound cake.

> *1/2 cup heavy (whipping) cream*
> *4 Tbs. butter*
> *1/2 cup granulated sugar*
> *1/4 cup dark brown sugar, firmly packed*
> *1/2 cup sifted cocoa*

In a saucepan, combine cream and butter. Stir over medium heat until butter has melted and cream just begins to boil. Add sugars and stir until completely dissolved. Lower heat, add cocoa, and stir constantly until mixture is smooth. Serve immediately or place over a second pan of simmering water until ready to use. Makes about 1 cup.

Note: You can make this sauce ahead and store it in the refrigerator, but it may thicken when chilled. To reheat, place in top half of a double boiler over simmering water, add a few drops of water if necessary, and stir until warm.

Chocolate Sauce Grand Marnier

The ultimate.

>*4 Tbs. butter*
>*1 1-oz. square semisweet chocolate*
>*1/4 cup cocoa*
>*1/2 cup orange marmalade*
>*1/2 cup light cream*
>*1 Tbs. Grand Marnier liqueur*

Combine butter and chocolate in top half of a double boiler over simmering water. Stir until chocolate has partially melted. Remove pan from water, and stir until mixture is smooth. Add cocoa, marmalade, and cream. Stir over medium heat until mixture comes to a boil. Remove from heat. Stir in liqueur. Serve warm. Makes about 2 cups sauce.

Creamy Chocolate Sauce with Brandy

A lovely sauce that can also be served as a dip for fresh strawberries or other fruit.

>*8 1-oz. squares bittersweet chocolate, coarsely chopped*
>*6 Tbs. heavy (whipping) cream*
>*2 Tbs. brandy*

Place chocolate and cream in top half of a double boiler over simmering water. Cook, stirring occasionally, until chocolate has almost melted. Remove from heat and stir until smooth. Stir in brandy. Serve warm or at room temperature. Makes about 1 1/2 cups sauce.

Old-Fashioned Hot Fudge Sauce

A classic that has never gone out of style.

> *1/2 cup cocoa*
> *1 Tbs. all-purpose flour*
> *1 cup granulated sugar*
> *1 cup hot water*
> *1 Tbs. butter, at room temperature*
> *1 tsp. vanilla or almond extract*

Sift cocoa and flour into a saucepan. Stir in sugar. Slowly add hot water, stirring as added. Cook, stirring, over medium heat until mixture is thick and smooth. Remove pan from heat; stir in butter and vanilla or almond extract. Serve hot. Makes about 2 cups sauce.

Chocolate Apricot Sauce

Dark, smooth, and wickedly delicious.

> *2 ozs. German sweet chocolate, chopped*
> *2 1-oz. squares unsweetened chocolate, chopped*
> *1/2 cup light cream*

1/2 cup apricot jam
2 Tbs. Amaretto liqueur
2 Tbs. butter, room temperature

Combine chocolates in top half of a double boiler; add cream. Place over hot water until chocolates have dissolved, stirring occasionally. Stir in apricot jam. Cook, stirring, until jam has melted. Remove from heat. Stir in liqueur and butter. Serve warm or refrigerate until ready to use. When needed, reheat in top half of a double boiler over simmering water. Makes about 1 cup sauce.

Butterscotch Sauces

Classic Butterscotch Sauce

A sauce for total self-indulgence. Beautifully rich and creamy.

1 1/4 cup dark brown sugar, firmly packed
1/2 cup light corn syrup
4 Tbs. butter
2 Tbs. water
1 tsp. vanilla extract
1/2 cup heavy (whipping) cream

In a saucepan, combine brown sugar, corn syrup, butter, and water. Place over medium heat and stir until mixture comes to a full boil. Immediately remove from heat and stir in vanilla; then slowly add cream, stirring as added. Serve warm or cool. Makes about 1 1/2 cups sauce.

Creole Praline Sauce

Cajun rich!

> *1/2 cup light corn syrup*
> *1/2 çup brown sugar, firmly packed*
> *4 Tbs. butter*
> *1/2 cup heavy (whipping) cream*
> *1/4 cup light rum*
> *1 cup chopped pecans*

In a saucepan, combine corn syrup, sugar, and butter. Cook, stirring constantly, over medium heat until sugar has dissolved and mixture is bubbly. Remove from heat; cool slightly. Stir in cream and rum. Add pecans and stir to mix. Refrigerate until chilled. Makes about 1 1/2 cups sauce.

Bourbon Whiskey Sauce

For steamy hot Christmas pudding or fruit cake, but also for baked apples.

> *2 cups water*
> *1 cup granulated sugar*
> *2 Tbs. cornstarch*
> *3 Tbs. butter*
> *3 Tbs. bourbon whiskey*
> *1/2 tsp. vanilla extract*

In a saucepan, bring water to full boil; stir in sugar and cornstarch. Cook, stirring constantly, until sugar has melted and mixture is clear.

Remove from heat; stir in butter, bourbon, and vanilla. Serve warm or chilled. Makes about 2 cups sauce.

Caramel Walnut Sauce

1/4 cup water
3 Tbs. cornstarch
1 cup light corn syrup
1/4 cup brown sugar, firmly packed
3 Tbs. butter
2 Tbs. dark Jamaican rum
1/2 cup chopped walnuts

In a large saucepan, combine water and cornstarch. Stir until smooth. Stir in syrup and brown sugar. Place over medium heat and cook, stirring constantly, until sauce thickens. Add butter, rum, and walnuts; stir until butter melts. Serve warm or at room temperature. Makes about 1 3/4 cups sauce.

Fruit Sauces

Strawberry Sauce

1 10-oz. package frozen strawberries in heavy syrup
1/4 cup Fraise de Bois or strawberry-flavored brandy
2 tsp. cornstarch
1/2 pint fresh strawberries, hulled and thinly sliced

Break frozen block of berries into small chunks. Place in work bowl of a food processor or blender; process or blend until smooth. Transfer to a saucepan. In a small bowl, combine liqueur or brandy and cornstarch; stir until smooth. Add to puréed strawberries. Cook, stirring, until bubbly. Cover and refrigerate until chilled. Just before serving, stir in sliced fresh strawberries. Makes about 2 cups sauce.

Double-Quick Fruit Sauce

When guests are unexpected.

> *1 8-oz. jar jam or preserves*
> *1 Tbs. butter*
> *1/4 cup brandy, rum, kirsch, or any liqueur compatible*
> *with preserves or jam*

In a saucepan, combine jam or preserves and butter. Place over low heat and cook, stirring, until slightly warmed. Add rum, brandy, or liqueur. Cook, stirring, for about 30 seconds. Transfer to a serving bowl. Serve warm, or cover with plastic wrap and refrigerate until ready to serve. Makes about 1 1/2 cups sauce.

Peach Melba Sauce

Truly, one of the best ways to make Melba Sauce.

> *2 10-oz. packages frozen raspberries packed in syrup*
> *1 Tbs. cornstarch*
> *1/4 cup water*

1/2 cup Cassis syrup
2 Tbs. lemon juice
2 large ripe peaches, peeled and sliced

Place frozen raspberries in a colander over a bowl until berries are defrosted and syrup has drained into bowl. In a medium saucepan, combine cornstarch and water; stir until smooth. Stir in juice from raspberries, Cassis, and lemon juice. Place over medium heat and cook, stirring constantly, until mixture comes to full boil. Remove from heat; stir in defrosted raspberries and peach slices. Cover, and refrigerate until chilled or until ready to use. Makes about 2 cups sauce.

Fresh Peach Sauce

Summertime special.

6 large, ripe peaches
2 tsp. lemon juice
1 cup fresh orange juice
3/4 cup granulated sugar
1 tsp. cornstarch
1/4 cup peach brandy

Peel and pit peaches and slice into a large bowl. Add lemon juice; toss to coat slices. Place about half of peach slices in a second bowl; cover and refrigerate until ready to use. Place remaining peaches in work bowl of a food processor or blender; process or blend until smooth. Transfer to a saucepan. Add orange juice and sugar. Cook, stirring, over medium heat until mixture is bubbly. In a small bowl, stir cornstarch into liqueur; add to peach mixture. Stir to a thick sauce. Cool slightly; transfer to storage bowl. Cover and refrigerate until chilled. Stir in chilled peach slices. Makes about 2 cups sauce.

Fresh Raspberry Sauce

Luxurious!

>*1 1/2 pint fresh raspberries*
>*1/4 cup granulated sugar*
>*2 Tbs. Framboise or raspberry brandy*
>*1 tsp. cornstarch*

Place half of berries in work bowl of a food processor or blender; process or blend until smooth. Strain through a fine sieve, discarding seeds. Pour into a saucepan and add sugar. Cook over low heat, stirring, until sugar has dissolved. In a small bowl, combine liqueur or brandy and cornstarch; stir until smooth. Add to raspberries in saucepan and cook, stirring, until sauce thickens. Remove from heat; cool to room temperature. Stir in remaining berries. Refrigerate until chilled or until ready to serve. Makes about 1 cup sauce.

Very-Lemon Lemon Sauce

A clear sauce with a fresh, lemony taste.

>*1 large blemish-free lemon*
>*1/2 cup granulated sugar*
>*1 Tbs. cornstarch*
>*1 1/4 cups water*
>*3 Tbs. butter*

With a small, sharp knife, cut zest from lemon; cut into 1/8- × 1/4-inch strips. Squeeze lemon and set juice aside. Place strips in a small saucepan and cover with water; bring to a full boil over high heat. Lower heat; let simmer for about 2 minutes. Strain through a fine sieve. Cover with water once more, and again bring to a boil. Strain and blot dry. Set aside. Sift sugar with cornstarch onto paper. Set aside. In a saucepan, bring water to a full boil; stir in sugar-cornstarch mixture. Cook, stirring constantly, until mixture is clear. Remove from heat; stir in butter and lemon juice. Serve hot. Makes about 1 1/2 cups sauce.

Rhubarb Sauce

A piquant sauce that adds summertime flavor to ice cream, custard, or cake.

> *1 1/2 cups peeled and diced rhubarb (about 2 ribs*
> *rhubarb)*
> *1 cup granulated sugar*
> *1 cup fresh orange juice*
> *1 Tbs. grated orange peel*

Combine rhubarb, sugar, orange juice, and orange peel in a saucepan. Bring to boil, reduce heat, and let simmer for 20 to 25 minutes or until sauce thickens. Makes about 2 cups sauce.

Apricot Brandy Sauce

Tart, sweet, and delicious.

> *1 8-oz. package dried apricot halves*
> *3 cups water*
> *1/3 cup granulated sugar*
> *1/4 cup apricot brandy*

Soak apricots in warm water for 1 hour. Place in a saucepan and cook over low heat until very soft. Pour off and discard all but 1 cup of water. Transfer to work bowl of a food processor or blender; process and blend until smooth. Add sugar and brandy; process or blend until sugar has dissolved. Pour into storage bowl. Refrigerate until chilled. Makes about 1 1/2 cups sauce.

Applesauce Whipped Cream

1/2 pint heavy (whipping) cream
1 cup unsweetened applesauce
Confectioners' sugar to taste, optional

In a chilled bowl with chilled beaters, whip very cold cream until soft peaks form. Fold in applesauce. If desired, sweeten with confectioners' sugar. Refrigerate until ready to serve. Makes about 2 cups sauce.

Caramel Apple Creamy Sauce

A lovely, chunky mix of apples, cream, and spices.

3 Tbs. butter
4 or 5 tart, crisp apples, peeled, cored, and coarsely
*   chopped*
1 Tbs. lemon juice
2 Tbs. water
6 Tbs. granulated sugar
1/2 pint heavy (whipping) cream
1/4 tsp. cinnamon

1/4 tsp. nutmeg
1/4 tsp. allspice
2 Tbs. dark rum

In a heavy skillet, melt butter over low heat. Add apples, lemon juice, and water. Cover and cook until slightly softened, about 10 minutes. Sprinkle with sugar; cook and stir until sugar is dissolved and liquid is lightly browned. Pour in cream; add spices and rum. Stir until sauce is bubbly. Serve warm or at room temperature over ice cream or cake slices. Makes enough sauce for 6 servings.

Index

Frostings (*cont.*):
chocolate cream cheese, 52
chocolate fudge, 76–77
classic chocolate butter-
cream, 39
coffee whipped cream, 24
cream cheese nut, 57–58
custard cream, 17–18
fluffy pink, 69
golden satin buttercream,
13–14
Mirabelle whipped cream, 50
mocha buttercream, 63
never-fail buttercream, 98–99
orange buttercream, 67
rich chocolate, 101–102
ricotta whipped cream, 58–
59
rocky road, 46–47
rum buttercream, 62
snow leopard cream, 66
sour cream, 43
Southern-style white icin', 44
spreading, 10–11
uncooked buttercream, with
liqueur, 62–63
whipped cream, 247
white satin buttercream, 15
Frozen desserts:
baked Alaska cake, 21–22
black forest cake, 39–40
cheese Italian-style, 222
Irish coffee, 214
meringue cake with Grand
Marnier sauce, 242–243
Mississippi mud pie, 224
pink cloud angel ring, 244–
246
tropical fruit cream, 196–197
unmolding, 154–155
(*See also* Ice cream cakes;
Ice cream pies; Ice
creams; Ices; Sorbets)
Fruit:
Amaretto cream-filled 177–
178

candied, grenadine fudge
with, 273
chocolate and nut log, 269–
270
fresh, ice creams, 207
fresh, in crème Grand Marnier, 179–180
fresh, sparkling compote,
176
midsummer fresh, cake, 31–
32
pizza, glazed, 144–145
poached, 181–182
rind, candied, 268–269
sauce, 94
truffled, 254–255
winter, compote, 180–181
(*See also* Apple; Apricot;
Banana; Berry; Cherry;
Cranberry; Grapefruit;
Green grape; Lemon;
Orange; Peach; Peach
melba; Pineapple; Rasp-
berry; Strawberry; Tropi-
cal fruit; Tropical fruit
creams)
Fruit desserts, 175–197
Amaretto cream-filled fruit,
177–178
berries with crème anglaise
and tipsy whipped
cream, 173
blueberry-lemon parfait,
184
brandied plums, 187–188
butterscotch peaches, 191–
192
carmelized grapefruit cups,
190–191
croute des fruits, 177
Dody's easy bananas foster,
192–193
fresh fruit in crème Grand
Marnier, 179–180
glazed apples with
Armagnac, 182–183